PATHWAYS TO

Poetry

Poetry Fun for Grades 1-3

by
Phylliss J. Adams
and
Ellen L. Kronowitz

FEARON TEACHER AIDS

A Paramount Communications Company

Publisher: Virginia L. Murphy
Editor: Kristin Eclov
Copyeditor: Lisa Schwimmer
Inside Design: Diann Abbott
Cover Design: Teena Remer
Cover, Poster, and Inside Illustration: Tracy LaRue Hall

ISBN: 0-86653-914-X

Printed in the United States of America

1.9 8 7 6 5 4 3 2 1

Contents

Introduction

Purpose

The value of using poetry in the classroom can be tremendous. The task of searching through poetry anthologies for poems on specific topics and then planning a variety of stimulating, creative, and multi-disciplinary activities can seem overwhelming.

Pathways to Poetry: Poetry Fun for Grades 1-3 was written to help classroom teachers use thematically-grouped poems across the curriculum and consequently enhance children's love and enjoyment of poetry, while promoting the children's literacy development. The poetry themes and the teaching plans provided for each poem offer a variety of activities for integrating your curriculum through poetry.

Organization

Pathways to Poetry: Poetry Fun for Grades 1-3 is organized into five themes:

> Chomp and Chew
> Claws and Paws
> Fears and Feelings
> Special Days and Ways
> Schools and Rules

The themes relate closely to curriculum content areas commonly introduced in grades 1 to 3.

Each theme includes five poems. Permission has been granted by the authors and publishers to copy the poems on charts or transparencies for classroom use only. The poems selected for each theme represent the very best in children's poetry—by both contemporary and traditional poets.

The *Suggested Books* section at the end of each theme provides titles of themed poetry books with other related poems. An annotated list of books for read-aloud and independent reading is also included to extend and enrich each theme.

Poem Plan Organization

For each poem, there is:

- a copy of the poem in a format suitable for duplication.
- a thematic web with a quick overview of the activities introduced in the *Beyond Listening and Reading* section of the teaching plan.
- a teaching plan divided into three sections—*Introducing the Poem; Shared Listening and Reading;* and *Beyond Listening and Reading.*

Suggestions offered in the *Introducing the Poem* section are designed to create interest and help children relate their own experiences to the topic of each poem.

The *Shared Listening and Reading* section invites the children to listen and contribute while poems are read aloud. The following suggestions encourage children to read, respond, and enjoy the poems.

General Suggestions for Listening to and Reading the Poems:

- Read or say the poem in unison.
- Identify specific lines. Have the rest of the children say the remaining lines aloud.
- Use different grouping arrangements for various verses or lines, such as duets trios, quartets, quintets, tables, rows, and so on.
- Pantomime the poem.
- Act out the poem with puppets or flannelboard characters.
- Echo reading (teacher reads and the children echo line by line).

The *Beyond Listening and Reading* section includes learning activities related to the theme of the poem. Refer to the thematic web which provides a quick graphic overview of the activities related to each poem. The titles of the activities are indicated in each of the boxes of the web. Within the teaching plan, the activities are identified by graphic organizers providing quick refer-ences to the curriculum areas each activity focuses on.

Graphic Organizers

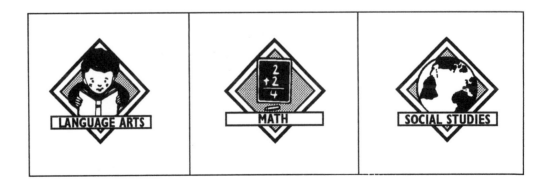

A variety of activities and reproducible pages have been provided to help meet the diverse needs, interests, and achievement levels of the children.

End of Book Material

Poet Bookmarks give bibliographic information about each poet in a bookmark format. The bookmarks can be duplicated for the children or used to share information about each poet while studying his or her poem. *Author Bookmarks* are also provided. The *Credits* section refers to copyright information for each poem introduced in the book. *References* provides a bibliography of comprehensive poetry anthologies and books that have poems related to different themes, as well as music books referred to in the teaching plans.

Special Features

To provide teachers with maximum flexibility:

- the activities fit into the scope-and-sequence of the curriculum for this age group and are not separate add-on activities.
- activities are designed to be used in any order or in any organizational pattern, such as small group, large group, or independent work.
- activities require a minimal amount of searching for materials.
- instructions for all art, cooking, and physical education activities are included.
- teachers can easily expand upon the theme by utilizing the bibliographic information included in the *Suggested Books* section.

Using *Pathways to Poetry: Poetry Fun for Grades 1-3*

Pathways to Poetry: Poetry Fun for Grades 1-3 is a guide to introducing poetry to children. The individual themes are designed to be flexible. The themes can be used for a week, one day a week over a period of a month, or more. The themes, and the poems within each theme, can be used in any order and in any format—large group, small group, or independent work. Teachers decide how to best use the themes in view of their own teaching styles, the needs and interests of the children, and the curriculum.

Enrich and extend *Pathways to Poetry: Poetry Fun for Grades 1-3* with activities, such as the following:

- Conduct weekly poetry readings featuring the children's work, a particular poet, poetry focused around a theme, or a potpourri of poems.
- Designate a bulletin board for displaying poems.
- Identify a "Poet of the Week" and highlight his or her work.

And Lastly

We sincerely hope you and your children enjoy, learn, and develop a love of poetry, as well as have fun with *Pathways to Poetry: Poetry Fun for Grades 1-3*.

Chomp
and Chew

Snack

Give me a sandwich—
   cheese or ham;
Guess you don't know
   how hungry I am.

Give me a hamburger.
   dill pickle, too;
Mustard on top—
   that will do.

Plate of French fries.
   catsup red;
Yes, I'm hungry—
   that's what I said.

—Lois Lenski

10

Pathways to Poetry: Poetry Fun for Grades 1-3 © 1994 Fearon Teacher Aids

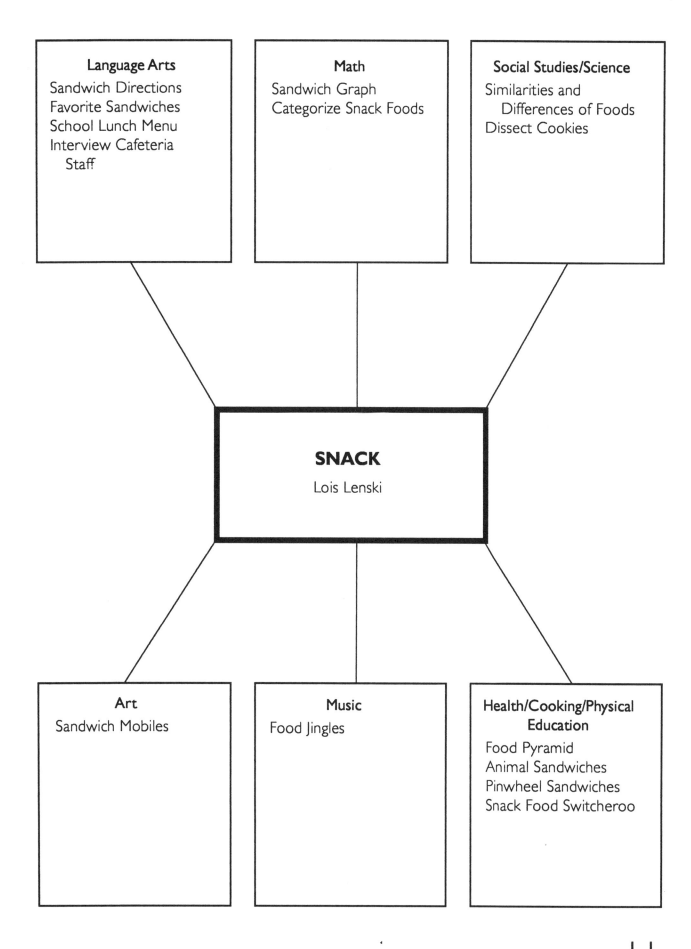

Language Arts

Sandwich Directions
Favorite Sandwiches
School Lunch Menu
Interview Cafeteria
 Staff

Math

Sandwich Graph
Categorize Snack Foods

Social Studies/Science

Similarities and
 Differences of Foods
Dissect Cookies

SNACK

Lois Lenski

Art

Sandwich Mobiles

Music

Food Jingles

**Health/Cooking/Physical
Education**

Food Pyramid
Animal Sandwiches
Pinwheel Sandwiches
Snack Food Switcheroo

Snack

The following suggestions can be used with the poem "Snack." Select the activities that are most appropriate for the needs and age level of the children in the class.

Introducing the Poem

1. Ask each child to complete the sentence "When I'm hungry, I eat ____." Have each child repeat what the children next to him or her said. For example, child 1 says, "When I'm hungry, I eat apples." Then child 2 says, "When I'm hungry, I eat apples and bananas." Continue the activity using each letter of the alphabet.

2. Tell the children the poem, "Snack" is about a very hungry person. Ask the children to suggest similes for hunger, such as hungry as a bear, hungry as a pig, hungry as a horse, hungry as a giant, and so on.

3. Share biographical information about the poet, Lois Lenski. Refer to the Poet Bookmarks section on page 265. The bookmarks can be duplicated for the children or used to share information about each poet while studying his or her poem.

Shared Listening and Reading

1. Read the poem aloud to the children, and encourage comments after the reading. Then display a copy of the poem and have the children read it chorally. Practice reading the poem together. Read the poem several times, selecting ideas from General Suggestions for Listening to and Reading the Poems on page 6.

2. Ask the children if the foods mentioned in the poem are really snack foods. Why would the author name the poem "Snack?" As a class, brainstorm a more descriptive title for the poem. Record the children's ideas on the chalkboard. Have the class vote on their favorite title.

3. Ask the children to think of polite ways to request a snack. Encourage children to share what they would say if they were asking for a snack. Ask the children if saying "Give me," is a polite way to ask for something.

4. Write the poem on the chalkboard or chart paper. Cover the words naming snack foods in the poem with sticky notes. Encourage the

children to name their favorite snack foods. Record the children's ideas on the chalkboard. As a class, choose snack foods from the children's list to substitute in the poem. Write the new words on the sticky notes. Read the new version of the poem together.

Beyond Listening and Reading Activities

Sandwich Directions

Ask each child to write step-by-step directions for making peanut butter and jelly sandwiches. Have on hand the necessary ingredients for making sandwiches—peanut butter, jelly, bread, and so on. Choose a few of the children's recipes. Follow the directions exactly, only doing what the children instruct. This becomes a comical means of underscoring the importance of giving good directions. As a class, write a set of complete directions for making the sandwich.

Favorite Sandwiches

Duplicate the reproducible on page 17 on brown, tan, or white construction paper. Distribute two copies to each child. Encourage the children to write descriptions of their favorite sandwiches on lined paper cut in the same sandwich shape. Have the children make the fillings for their favorite sandwiches out of scraps of colored construction paper. Glue the sandwich fillings to the inside of the two sandwich shapes. Place the sandwich descriptions between the two slices of bread and staple together. Invite the children to share their favorite sandwiches with the class.

School Lunch Menu

Point out that a different, well-balanced lunch is served at school each day. Discuss with the children what kinds of foods need to be included to make up a well-balanced meal. Assign each child a square on a large butcher-paper calendar and have him or her create a lunch menu for that day. You can ask children to either create an "ideal" lunch or one that is actually nutritious. Compare and discuss the actual school lunch menu with the class lunch menu.

Interview Cafeteria Staff

As a class, write a letter of invitation to each cafeteria staff person and specify the date, time, place, and purpose of the interview. Prior to the interview, have the children generate a list of questions to ask the school's cafeteria workers. After the interview, have the children write an appropriate thank-you letter to each staff person.

Sandwich Graph

Make a list of the children's favorite sandwich choices. Create a class graph of the children's responses. Depending upon the ability level of the children, you may want to limit the children's choices to five or six different kinds of sandwiches. Discuss the results of the graph.

Categorize Snack Foods

Before class, combine ingredients for trail mix with other snack foods, such as dried fruits, nuts, M & M's, sunflower seeds, and so on. Divide the class into small groups. Give each group member a paper cup with trail mix. Encourage the children to sort the ingredients by color, shape, taste (salty, sweet, sour, bitter), preference, size, and so on. As a class, discuss how the children categorized the different ingredients.

Similarities and Differences of Foods

Share the books *Bread Bread Bread* by Ann Morris and *Everybody Cooks Rice* by Norah Dooley. Discuss the similarities and differences in the foods eaten by children around the world. If appropriate, locate the countries mentioned in the books on a map or globe.

Dissect Cookies

In preparation for this activity, bake a batch of chocolate chip cookies. Include additional ingredients in the cookies, such as nuts, raisins, M & M's, butterscotch chips, and so on. Give each child a cookie, a paper plate, and a flat toothpick. Have each child dissect his or her cookie to find out what's inside. Encourage the children to list and count the additions in the cookies. Make a chart listing the special additions at the top of the chart. Then write each child's name and number of special treats in his or her cookie. Compare the children's results to discover which special treats are most common in the cookies. Older children can find the average number of nuts per cookie. Provide a second cookie for eating.

Sandwich Mobiles

Have the children make sandwiches out of construction paper. Provide glue, construction paper, scissors, coat hangers, and fishing line. Punch a hole in the top of each sandwich. Tie fishing line to the shapes and then attach them to the coat hanger. Hang the sandwich mobiles from the ceiling.

Food Jingles

Ask the children to list names of food products. Record the children's ideas on the chalkboard. Point out that the songs used in commercials to advertise products are called *jingles*. Encourage the children to recite or sing any jingles they can remember from food or restaurant commercials. Invite older children to choose snack foods and write their own jingles to advertise them. Encourage the children to perform the jingles for the rest of the class.

Food Pyramid

Duplicate and distribute the reproducible on page 18 as a reference. Explain to the children the importance of eating well-balanced meals. Show the children how to use the Food Pyramid on page 18 as a tool to eating healthy. Ask the children why the breads section is the biggest area on the pyramid. Explain that eating breads, grains, vegetables, and fruits is the foundation of a healthy diet. Ask the children what food groups were included in today's school lunch. Have the children create a pyramid on butcher paper featuring magazine pictures of their favorite foods. Discuss the various food pictures the children found and ask which group on the food pyramid each food belongs to.

15

Animal Sandwiches

Provide an assortment of animal cookie cutters and slices of bread. Invite children to use the animal cookie cutters to cut out three of the same shapes from the bread. Have the children carefully spread the animal shapes with their favorite sandwich fillings. Assemble the triple-decker sandwiches and stand the animals up on a plate for everyone to see. Then eat!

Pinwheel Sandwiches

Have the children work in small groups. Give each child a piece of wax paper and a slice of bread. If possible, provide a rolling pin and a plastic knife for each group. Have the children roll out their slices of bread until they are very flat. Place a tablespoon of sandwich filling, such as peanut butter or tuna salad in the middle of the flattened bread and spread the filling almost to the edges. If necessary, help the children roll the bread into a log shape and cut into slices. Invite the children to eat their pinwheel sandwich creations.

Snack Food Switcheroo

Divide the class into groups of two. Invite each pair to choose a snack food to represent, such as apples, potato chips, bananas, and so on. Choose one child to be the leader in the middle of the circle. Arrange chairs in a large circle. Have the pairs of children sit randomly in the circle. The leader stands in the middle of the circle and calls out the name of a snack food. The two players who have chosen that food must switch places in the circle before the leader sits in a chair. The child without a chair is the leader next time.

Favorite Sandwich

Name _____

Directions: Cut out two sandwich shapes. Follow your teacher's directions.

Food Pyramid

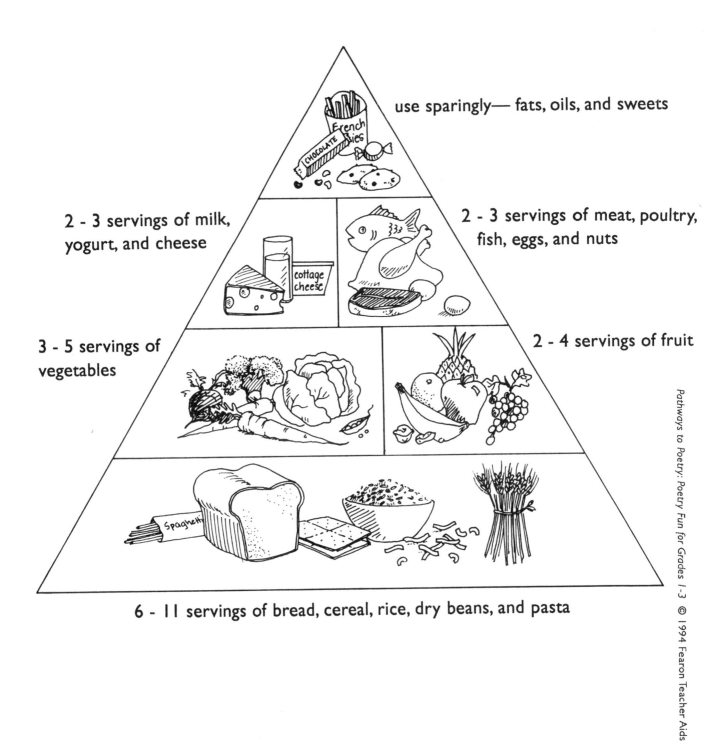

use sparingly— fats, oils, and sweets

2 - 3 servings of milk, yogurt, and cheese

2 - 3 servings of meat, poultry, fish, eggs, and nuts

3 - 5 servings of vegetables

2 - 4 servings of fruit

6 - 11 servings of bread, cereal, rice, dry beans, and pasta

Pathways to Poetry: Poetry Fun for Grades 1-3 © 1994 Fearon Teacher Aids

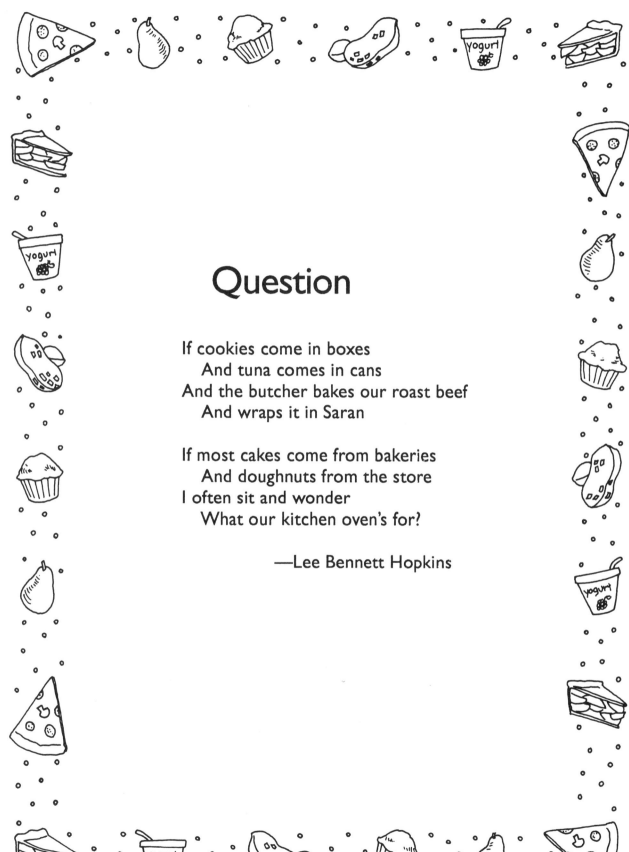

Question

If cookies come in boxes
    And tuna comes in cans
And the butcher bakes our roast beef
    And wraps it in Saran

If most cakes come from bakeries
    And doughnuts from the store
I often sit and wonder
    What our kitchen oven's for?

—Lee Bennett Hopkins

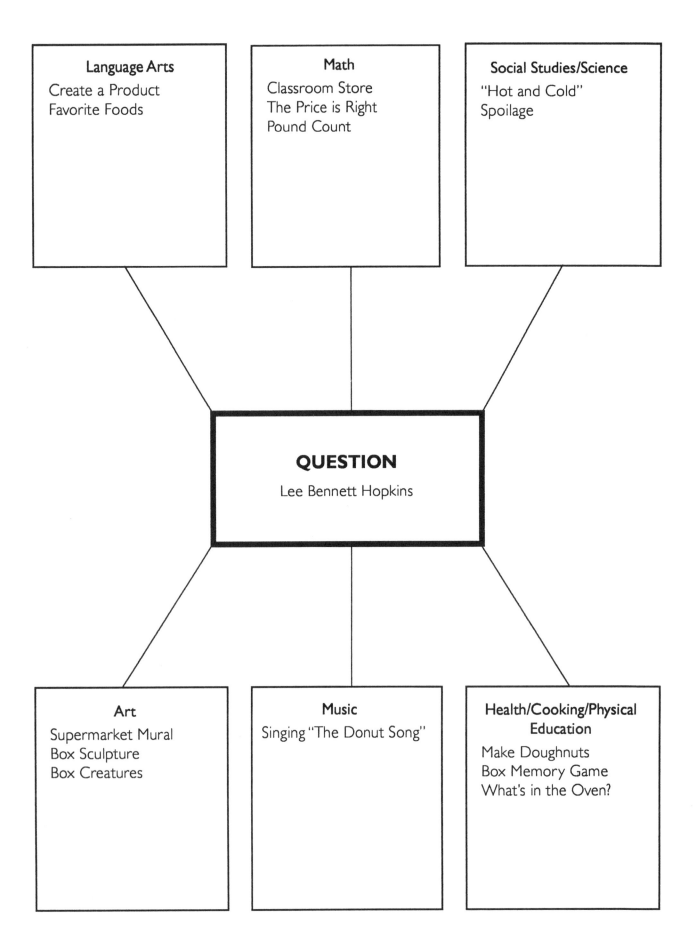

Language Arts
Create a Product
Favorite Foods

Math
Classroom Store
The Price is Right
Pound Count

Social Studies/Science
"Hot and Cold"
Spoilage

QUESTION
Lee Bennett Hopkins

Art
Supermarket Mural
Box Sculpture
Box Creatures

Music
Singing "The Donut Song"

Health/Cooking/Physical Education
Make Doughnuts
Box Memory Game
What's in the Oven?

Question

The following suggestions can be used with the poem "Question." Select the activities that are most appropriate for the needs and age level of the children in the class.

Introducing the Poem

1. Ask children why we use kitchen ovens. Invite the children to think about different kinds of ovens, such as microwave, toaster, and conventional. Ask the children how a microwave is different from a regular kitchen or conventional oven.

2. Ask the children what kinds of foods are cooked in the oven, on top of the stove, or in a microwave. Record the children's responses on the chalkboard.

   Discuss where last night's supper came from—a fast food restaurant, cooked in a microwave, cooked on top of the stove, baked in the oven, grilled on the barbecue, served cold from the refrigerator, served in restaurant, and so on. Record the children's responses on the chalkboard. Encourage the children to draw conclusions about how much of their food is really cooked in the oven.

3. Introduce the term *convenience food.* Explain that convenience foods are foods designed for quick and easy preparation. Ask the children what their favorite fast food is. Encourage the children to name other convenience foods, such as microwave popcorn, frozen pizza, instant oatmeal, and so on. Record the list on the chalkboard.

4. Have the children play the "Choice Game." Explain to the children that you are going to give them some choices to make. Each child must make a choice and move to one side of the room or the other based on their choice. Once the children have made their choices, encourage them to justify their decisions. Ask the class the following questions:

   Which would you rather have, a microwave or an oven? Why?
   Which would you rather have, a refrigerator or an oven? Why?
   Which would you rather have, a television or an oven? Why?
   Which would you rather have, a computer game or an oven? Why?

5. Share biographical information about the poet, Lee Bennett Hopkins. Refer to the Poet Bookmarks section on page 265. The bookmarks can be duplicated for the children or used to share information about each poet while studying his or her poem.

Shared Listening and Reading

1. Read the poem to the children. Discuss whether the poet thinks ovens are necessary—why or why not. Ask the children if they think ovens are necessary.

2. Display a copy of the poem on a chart or transparency. Practice reading the poem together. Read the poem several times, selecting ideas from the General Suggestions for Listening to and Reading the Poems on page 6.

3. Invite volunteers to read the poem several times substituting other food items for the cookies, tuna, roast beef, cakes, and doughnuts mentioned in the poem.

Beyond Listening and Reading Activities

Create a Product

Discuss new product ideas, such as gum that never loses its flavor, cereal that doesn't get soggy in milk, and so on. Record the children's ideas on the chalkboard. Divide the class into small groups. Invite each group to decide on a new product they would like to create. Ask each group to create a product name, design packaging, and posters to advertise their product. Discuss what information is important to include when designing packaging or posters.

Favorite Foods

Divide the class into small groups. Duplicate and distribute the reproducible on page 26, one to each group. Have the children in each group identify their favorite foods that come in boxes, cans, bags, and so on. Encourage younger children to draw pictures of their favorite foods in the boxes. Discuss why products come in different kinds of containers. For example, why doesn't soup come in bags or why most cookies don't come in cans. Ask the children how they would package their favorite foods.

Classroom Store

Have children bring in empty, clean food containers and boxes. Help the children set up a class store. Have the children price their items, make price tags, and buy and sell products in the store. The children can create play money and use adding machines or calculators as cash registers in the class store. For older children, create word problems using the products and play money.

The Price is Right

Collect items from your home or from the class store and display them in front of the classroom. Divide the class into groups of five. Ask each child in the first group to estimate the actual cost of one item. The child closest to the actual price is the winner. The winner is then shown an item, such as a book, and three or four digits that comprise the actual price of the item. The child must arrange the digits in the proper sequence to equal the cost of the item to win the prize. Continue the activity with the remaining groups.

Pound Count

Bring in packages of items that all weigh a pound, such as pinwheel pasta, peppermints, peanuts in the shell, and so on. Divide the class into small groups. Give each group one of the packages weighing a pound. Encourage the children to estimate the number of pieces in the package. Then have each group count the items in the pound. As a class, compare the number of items in each container. Record the results on the chalkboard. Discuss why different amounts of materials can still add up to one pound.

"Hot and Cold"

Discuss how some foods need to be served at certain temperatures, such as popsicles need to be served cold. Have the children list their favorite foods on a class chart. As a class, decide what temperatures each food can be served at and fill out the chart.

	hot	room temperature	cold
Potatoes	+	+	+
Ice Cream	0	0	+
Hamburgers	+	0	0
Pizza	+	+	+

0 = Not Usually
+ = Usually

Spoilage

Divide the class into groups. Give each group four pieces of bread (without preservatives). Have the children lightly rub each slice of bread across their desks. Then, use an eyedropper to sprinkle four drops of water on each slice of bread. Wrap one piece of bread in plastic wrap, one in aluminum foil, place one piece in a sealed container, and leave one slice unwrapped. Ask the groups to observe their pieces of bread every day. Encourage the children to write down or draw pictures of the pieces of bread to keep track of the changes each day. After a period of time, discuss which pieces of bread are moldy and which are not. Discuss with the children the changes in the bread and the nature of mold. Invite the children to find other ways to set up bread mold experiments.

Supermarket Mural

Ask the children to name the different sections and products sold in a supermarket. Record the children's ideas on the chalkboard. Divide the class into small groups. On a large piece of butcher paper, have the children create a supermarket mural. Have each group draw a picture of a different section in a supermarket, such as the bakery, meat, dairy, and so on. Have the children draw or paste pictures of products that belong in each section. Display the mural in the hallway outside the classroom.

Box Sculpture

Collect a variety of sizes of empty food boxes. Give each child a box to decorate and cover with construction paper or paint. As a class, design a class sculpture using each child's box. Encourage small groups of children to rearrange the boxes to create new box sculptures each week.

Box Creatures

To make box creatures:

1. Give each child an empty cereal box to paint.
2. Once the paint is dry, cut through the box with a knife cutting the box in half lengthwise. Cut through the top and down both sides of the box without cutting through the bottom.
3. Encourage the children to add eyes, ears, tongues, and so on, to make box creatures.
4. Have each child place one hand inside the box and try manipulating it like a puppet.

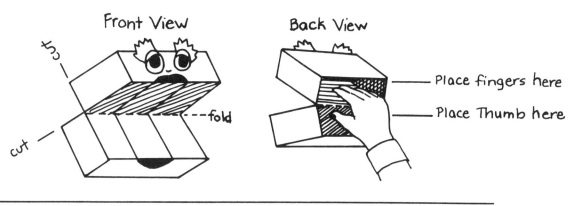

Front View

cut

cut

fold

Back View

— Place fingers here

— Place Thumb here

Singing

Teach children the song "The Donut Song" from *Tom Glazer's Do Your Ears Hang Low?*

Make Doughnuts

This activity requires a hot plate, a kettle of vegetable oil, slotted spoons, long-handled fork, a sandwich bag of powdered sugar, refrigerator biscuits, doughnut cutter, and paper towels. Make sure children wash their hands before this activity. Give each child a refrigerator biscuit. Have children cut a hole in their refrigerator biscuits with a doughnut cutter or small cylinder. Have an adult volunteer gently drop each doughnut and doughnut hole into hot oil with a slotted spoon. Using a long fork or spoon, have an adult volunteer carefully turn the doughnuts so they are browned on both sides. Remove the doughnuts with the slotted spoon and drain on paper towels. Have the children shake the doughnuts and doughnut holes in a small plastic bag of powdered sugar or eat them plain.

Box Memory Game

Collect a variety of empty food boxes. Arrange 5 to 8 boxes in the front of the room. Choose one child to be "It." Send "It" out of the room. Then remove one of the boxes. Have "It" return to the room and guess which box is missing. Choose another child to be "It." Continue playing the game until each child has had an opportunity to play.

What's in the Oven?

Create a play oven out of a cardboard box. Before the activity, place an item of food in the oven. Encourage the children to ask only "yes" or "no" questions to guess what is in the oven. If necessary, give the children examples of "yes" or "no" questions to ask and one or two clues to help children guess the answer. Continue the game as long as the children remain interested.

Favorite Foods

Name _____

Directions: Write or draw pictures of favorite foods that come in boxes, cans, bags, or from the bakery.

OUR FAVORITE FOODS

GROUP MEMBERS	BOX	CAN	BAG	BAKERY
1				
2				
3				
4				
5				

Pathways to Poetry: Poetry Fun for Grades 1-3 © 1994 Fearon Teacher Aids

Alligator Pie

Alligator pie, alligator pie,
If I don't get some I think I'm gonna die.
Give away the green grass, give away the sky,
But don't give away my alligator pie.

Alligator stew, alligator stew,
If I don't get some I don't know what I'll do.
Give away my furry hat, give away my shoe,
But don't give away my alligator stew.

Alligator soup, alligator soup,
If I don't get some I think I'm gonna droop.
Give away my hockey-stick, give away my hoop,
But don't give away my alligator soup.

—Dennis Lee

Pathways to Poetry: Poetry Fun for Grades 1–3 © 1994 Fearon Teacher Aids

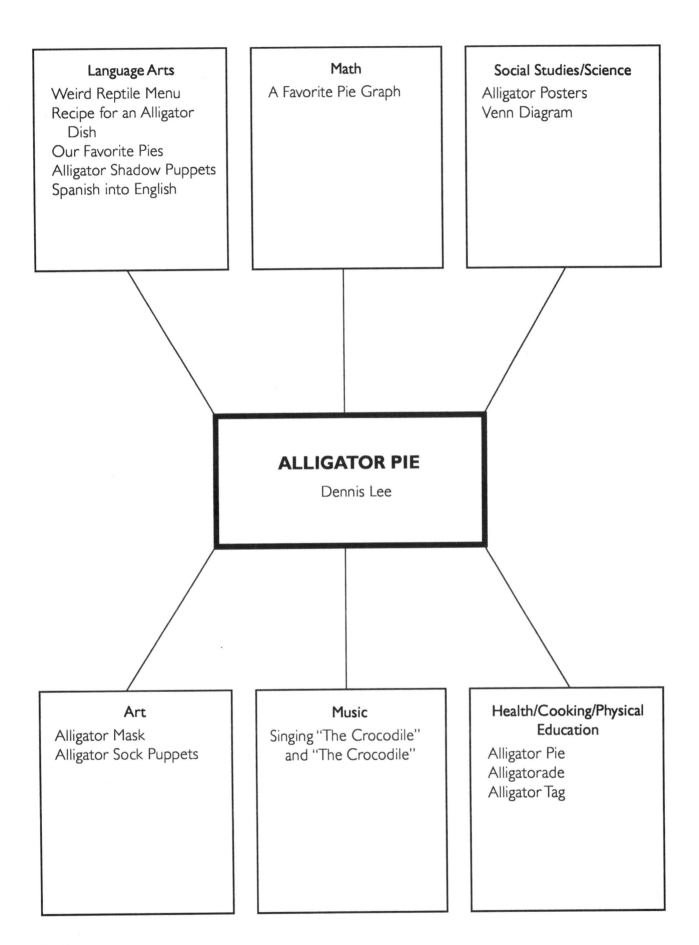

Language Arts

Weird Reptile Menu
Recipe for an Alligator
  Dish
Our Favorite Pies
Alligator Shadow Puppets
Spanish into English

Math

A Favorite Pie Graph

Social Studies/Science

Alligator Posters
Venn Diagram

ALLIGATOR PIE

Dennis Lee

Art

Alligator Mask
Alligator Sock Puppets

Music

Singing "The Crocodile"
  and "The Crocodile"

Health/Cooking/Physical Education

Alligator Pie
Alligatorade
Alligator Tag

Alligator Pie

The following suggestions can be used with the poem "Alligator Pie." Select the activities that are most appropriate for the needs and age level of the children in the class.

Introducing the Poem

1. Initiate a discussion by showing the children a paper plate with pictures of your favorite foods. Give each child a paper plate. Have the children draw their favorite foods on the paper plates. Encourage the children to share their plates with the class.

2. Ask the children how they would feel if they were told they could never again eat their favorite foods.

3. Explain to the class that the poem is about a person with three favorite foods containing the same green main ingredient. Ask the children to guess what the green ingredient might be. Record the children's guesses on the chalkboard.

4. Share biographical information about the poet, Dennis Lee. Refer to the Poet Bookmarks section on page 265. The bookmarks can be duplicated for the children or used to share information about each poet while studying his or her poem.

Shared Listening and Reading

1. Read the poem to the children without saying the title. Ask the children to make up an appropriate title for the poem. Reveal the actual title of the poem. Ask the children which title they like better.

2. Display a copy of the poem on a chart or transparency. Or, display the poster included in this book. Read the poem with the class. Ask volunteers to read the poem substituting their favorite pies, stews, and soups.

3. On a copy of the poem, have the children underline the items in the poem the poet would give away. Have volunteers substitute items they would be willing to give away. Write the children's ideas on sticky notes and cover the underlined words. Read the poem again including the newly substituted words.

4. Display a copy of the poem on a chart or transparency. Practice reading the poem together. Read the poem several times, selecting

ideas from General Suggestions for Listening to and Reading the Poems on page 6.

Beyond Listening and Reading Activities

Weird Reptile Menu

Divide the class into small groups. Encourage each group to think up foods using reptile names, such as chameleon cake. Have the groups design a menu of reptile dishes, including an appetizer, soup, salad, main dish, and dessert. Help each group write out the menu and then illustrate it. Display the reptile menus. Ask the children to select their favorite reptile dish.

Recipe for an Alligator Dish

Have each child create a "Recipe for Alligator." Bind the children's recipes together into the *Alligator Recipe Book.* If necessary, have adults or older students help the children write out the ingredients and the step-by-step directions for each recipe. Encourage the children to include pictures of what the finished alligator dish looks like.

Our Favorite Pies

Discuss the children's favorite pies, soups, and stews. Then ask the class what they would be willing to give up to have their favorite pies. Record the children's ideas on the chalkboard. Duplicate and distribute a copy of the poem "Alligator Pie" on page 27. Have the children substitute his or her favorite pies, soups, and stews for the ones mentioned in the poem. If appropriate, have the children also substitute what they would be willing to give up to have their favorite foods. Give each child a piece of pie-shaped construction paper. Attach the poems to the construction-paper pies and bind into a class book called *Our Favorite Pies.* Display the book in the classroom.

Our Favorite Pies

Alligator Shadow Puppets

Use an overhead filmstrip or slide projector to practice making alligator shadow puppets. Invite several children to read the poem while volunteers make alligator shadow puppets move on the wall or screen.

Spanish into English

The Spaniards were the first Europeans to see alligators. The word alligator comes from the Spanish word el lagarto which means the lizard. Write some Spanish words, for example, mapa, marcha, and león on the chalkboard. Challenge the children to identify the English words for mapa (map), marcha (march), and león (lion). If appropriate, discuss other Spanish words that are part of the English language.

A Favorite Pie Graph

Divide the class into groups of eight children. Cut several paper plates into eighths. Give each child a slice of paper plate pie. Have the children in each group choose a favorite flavor of pie from the following—cherry, blueberry, pumpkin, or lemon. Then they each color the pie slices—cherry-red, blueberry-blue, pumpkin-orange, and lemon-yellow. Have the children in each group arrange their pie slices so all the same colors are next to each other. Glue the slices to a whole paper plate. Have the children in each group count and record on the back of their paper plates, the number of slices of each kind of pie. Discuss how many children in each group liked each kind of pie. Ask the children which pie was the favorite of the class. If appropriate, introduce the term circle graph and explain in more detail.

Alligator Posters

Tell the class that the alligator was an endangered species for several years. Explain what the word endangered means (threatened with extinction). Discuss why people might hunt alligators, such as for food or to use their hides to make shoes, purses, and so on. Brainstorm ideas for how people can help animals that are threatened or endangered. Have the children create "Protect the Alligator" posters. Display the posters in the hallway outside the classroom.

Venn Diagram

Invite the children to read about alligators and crocodiles and then share information they learned with the class. Draw two large overlapping circles on the chalkboard. Label one circle for alligators and the other circle crocodiles. Record the children's responses in the appropriate circles. If a fact is true for both alligators and crocodiles, write that information in the space where the two circles overlap. Looking at the diagram on the chalkboard, discuss the similarities and differences between alligators and crocodiles.

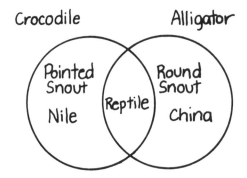

Alligator Mask

Duplicate the reproducible on page 34 on green construction paper. Give a copy to each child. Have the children cut out the eye holes, and then punch a hole on either side of the mask for attaching green yarn. Help each child tie his or her mask. Encourage the children to wear their alligator masks while reading or reciting the poem.

Alligator Sock Puppets

Have each child bring in a white sock. Dye the socks green and let dry. Encourage children to create alligator sock puppets using felt or fabric scraps, buttons, or trim to make teeth, tongues, scales, eyes, and so on. Invite the children to use their puppets to act out the poem.

Singing

Teach the children the song "The Crocodile" from *The Fireside Book of Fun and Game Songs* and a different song called "The Crocodile" from *Tom Glazer's Do Your Ears Hang Low?*

Alligator Pie

Divide the class into groups of eight children. Give each group a chocolate graham cracker ready-made pie crust or make crusts from crushed chocolate cookies and melted margarine. Have each group fill their pies with softened green mint ice cream. Label the pies for each group and freeze overnight. Help the children cut each pie into eight pieces and serve.

Alligatorade

Make individual cups of alligatorade using the following recipe. If you want a darker green color, add a few drops of green food coloring.

1. Have each child squeeze juice from half a lime into a cup.
2. Add 1 cup water and 1/2 teaspoon of honey to each child's cup.
3. Then add two drops of green food coloring and ice. Enjoy the alligatorade.

Alligator Tag

Create a swamp using a large chalk or string circle outside in the grass or on a mat in the classroom. Have all the children kneel inside the circle. Choose one child to be the Alligator in the swamp. Have the other children pretend to be swimming in the swamp. When the Alligator says, "Swim for your life," the Swimmers must move forward on their knees and pretend to swim out of the swamp before being tagged by the Alligator. The first child tagged becomes the next Alligator. If all the Swimmers escape, the same Alligator takes another turn.

Alligator Mask

Name _____

Directions: Cut out the eyes of the alligator mask.

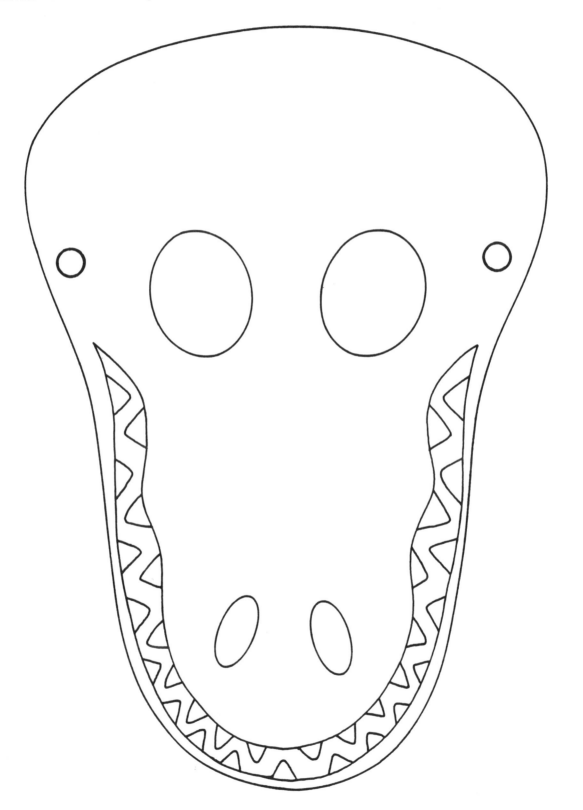

Pathways to Poetry: Poetry Fun for Grades 1-3 © 1994 Fearon Teacher Aids

How do you make a pizza grow?

You pound and you pull and you stretch the dough
And throw in tomatoes and oregano.

Pizza platter for twenty-two,
Pour on the oil and soak it through.

Pizza slices for forty-four,
Chop up onions, make some more.

Pizza pie for sixty-six
With mozzarella cheese that melts and sticks.

Pizza pizza for ninety-nine
With pepperoni sausage ground-up fine.

Pizza pizza stretch the dough,
Pizza pizza make it grow.

—Eve Merriam

Pathways to Poetry: Poetry Fun for Grades 1-3 © 1994 Fearon Teacher Aids

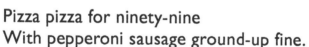

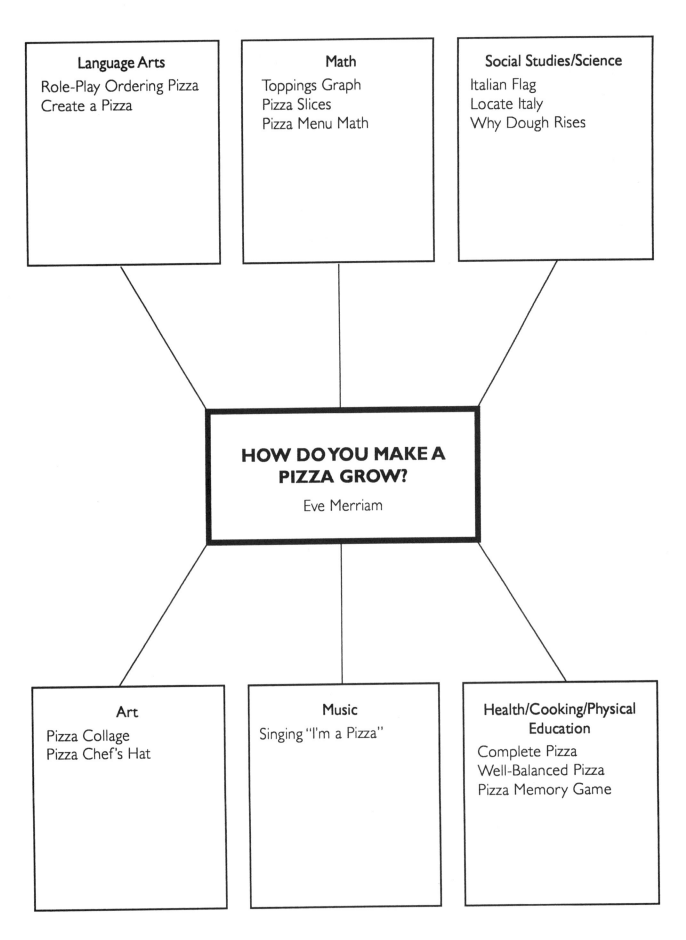

Language Arts

Role-Play Ordering Pizza
Create a Pizza

Math

Toppings Graph
Pizza Slices
Pizza Menu Math

Social Studies/Science

Italian Flag
Locate Italy
Why Dough Rises

HOW DO YOU MAKE A PIZZA GROW?

Eve Merriam

Art

Pizza Collage
Pizza Chef's Hat

Music

Singing "I'm a Pizza"

Health/Cooking/Physical Education

Complete Pizza
Well-Balanced Pizza
Pizza Memory Game

How do you make a pizza grow?

The following suggestions can be used with the poem "How do you make a pizza grow?" Select the activities that are most appropriate for the needs and age level of the children in the class.

Introducing the Poem

1. Ask the children to name things that grow. Record the children's responses on the chalkboard. Briefly discuss the different items on the list.

2. Ask the class if a pizza can grow. Why or why not?

3. Tell the children the title of the poem is "How do you make a pizza grow?" Ask the children how they would make a pizza grow.

4. Share biographical information about the poet, Eve Merriam. Refer to the Poet Bookmarks section on page 265. The bookmarks can be duplicated for the children or used to share information about each poet while studying his or her poem.

Shared Listening and Reading

1. Encourage the children to listen closely as the poem is read aloud. Discuss how you can make a pizza grow.

2. Display a copy of the poem on a chart or transparency. Practice reading the poem together. Read the poem several times, selecting ideas from the General Suggestions for Listening to and Reading the Poems on page 6.

3. Read the poem to the class pausing after each verse. Have the children list the steps for making pizza for ninety-nine. Record the steps on the chalkboard. Ask the children to describe or pantomime how to perform each step, such as chopping onions or stretching the dough.

4. On a copy of the poem, have the children identify and then underline the cooking words in the poem. Discuss what each cooking word means. Encourage the children to list other familiar cooking words.

5. Have the children draw small pictures of ingredients mentioned in the poem. Attach the pictures to tongue depressors. As the poem is read aloud, encourage the children to hold up their picture each time their ingredient is mentioned.

Beyond Listening and Reading Activities

Role-Play Ordering Pizza

Discuss what information is important when ordering or delivering a pizza, such as size, toppings, address for delivery, cost of the pizza, and so on. Record the information on the chalkboard. Using toy telephones, ask volunteers to role-play ordering a pizza. Encourage the children to include all the necessary information when they call. Continue the activity until all children have ordered a pizza or taken an order. Discuss the importance of giving correct information when ordering or answering questions.

Create a Pizza

Give each child a round piece of paper and have him or her create a unique pizza. On the back of their paper circles have the children write a recipe including a list of ingredients and the steps for making their unique pizzas. Have the children share their pizza recipes with the class. Display the pizzas in the classroom.

Toppings Graph

Create a large bar graph on the chalkboard. Ask the children to name their favorite pizza toppings. Record their responses along the bottom of the graph. Give each child a colored square of paper for their favorite pizza topping—peppers-green, pepperoni-red, pineapple-yellow, mushrooms-gray, sausage-brown, and cheese-orange. Help the children tape their squares in the appropriate topping columns on the graph. Encourage the class to stack the squares. Count the number of squares in each column. Point out how the graph shows which pizza topping is the most popular.

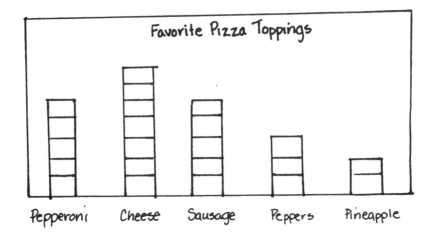

Pizza Slices

Duplicate and distribute the reproducible on page 42. Have the children color and cut out their pizzas. Then ask them to cut their pizzas in half by cutting on the solid line. Compare the parts and explain the fraction $\frac{1}{2}$. Have the children cut the pieces in half again by following the dashed line. Compare and discuss that the pieces are fourths. Have the children show $\frac{1}{4}$, $\frac{2}{4}$, and $\frac{3}{4}$. If appropriate, ask the children to cut these pieces in half to show eighths (cut on the dotted lines). Compare and discuss the fractional parts.

Pizza Menu Math

Write the pizza menu on the chalkboard. As a class, figure out the cost of different pizzas, such as a small pepperoni and mushroom pizza would cost $7.00. Or, create math problems appropriate to the children's ability levels. What is the difference between the cost of a small and a large cheese pizza? How much would it cost to buy two large three-topping pizzas?

Pizza Menu			
	Small	Medium	Large
Cheese	5.00	6.00	8.00
Any one topping	6.00	7.00	10.00
two toppings	7.00	9.00	12.00
three toppings	8.00	10.00	13.00
four or more toppings	9.00	11.00	14.00

Italian Flag

Briefly explain the history of pizza. Identify the colors most often found on pizza—red, green, and white. Discuss how pizza was originally made for Queen Margharita of Italy and included ingredients that were the color of the Italian flag. Have children construct the Italian flag using construction-paper strips.

Locate Italy

On a world map locate the country of Italy. The city of Rome is the capital of Italy. Ask the children to describe the shape of Italy. Point out that Italy is often recognized because it is shaped like a boot.

Share nonfiction books about Italy. Encourage the children to find one fact about Italy and share that information with the class. Record the children's facts on a large chart shaped like Italy.

Why Dough Rises

Explain to the children that pizza crust is made out of dough much like bread dough. The pizza dough is made with yeast which causes the dough to rise or expand. Have each child make his or her own pizza dough. Show the class a package of yeast. Explain that the yeast eats the sugar in the dough mixture and then produces the gas carbon dioxide, which causes the dough to rise and become fluffy.

Divide the class into groups of two. Have each pair follow these step-by-step directions to make their own pizza dough:

1. In a margarine container, sprinkle yeast on 4 tablespoons of warm water.
2. Add $1/2$ teaspoon of cooking oil, $1/4$ teaspoon of honey and 2 tablespoons of flour to the mixture.
3. Take turns kneading the dough on a lightly floured bread board.
4. Cover the dough with plastic wrap and let rise for 20 minutes.
5. Roll the dough out into two 4-inch circles and crimp the edges. Place the pizza crusts on greased cookie sheets and add toppings. Use the pizza crusts for the Complete Pizza activity.

Pizza Collage

Cut out a large circle from red butcher paper. Invite children to cut out pizza toppings from scraps of construction paper, such as brown circles for pepperoni, green strips for peppers, and so on. Arrange and glue the toppings on the pizza collage. Have the children describe the variety of toppings on the pizza collage. Display the collage on a classroom wall.

Pizza Chef's Hat

Chef's hats can be made simply by stapling a white lunch bag to a white headband that can be adjusted for size. Or, use white tissue paper and staple it to a white headband. Encourage the children to wear their chef's hats when making pizza crust in the Why Dough Rises activity or during the Complete Pizza activity. Discuss why pizza chefs wear hats.

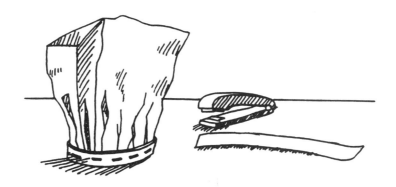

Singing

Teach the children the song "I'm a Pizza" with the hand motions from Peter Allsop's cassette, *For Our Children, Volume II.*

Complete Pizza

Use the pizza crusts made in the Why Dough Rises activity. Or, use English muffin halves for the pizza crusts. Have each child spread 2 tablespoons of tomato sauce on his or her crust. Set out ingredients on paper plates and let children place the designated number of ingredients from each plate—3 olive slices, 2 pepperoni, 2 mushrooms, and 2 mozzarella slices—on their crusts. Encourage the children to skip over any ingredients they don't like. Bake the pizzas at 400° for 8 minutes or until the cheese is melted. Enjoy!

Well-Balanced Pizza

Ask the children to name the ingredients needed to make pizza. Record the children's responses on the chalkboard. Make a pyramid-shaped chart classifying pizza ingredients into the food groups in the Food Guide Pyramid—bread, cereal, rice, pasta, and dry beans; vegetables; fruits; meat, poultry fish, eggs, and nuts; milk yogurt, and cheese; and fats, oils, and sweets. Discuss how pizza can be a well-balanced food.

Pizza Memory Game

Arrange the children in a circle. Choose one child to begin the game by saying "I'm making a pizza and I'm adding [name an ingredient]. The next child must repeat what the first child said and include another ingredient. The game continues around the circle until each child has had an opportunity to add an ingredient.

Pizza Slices

Name: _____

Directions: Follow your teacher's directions.

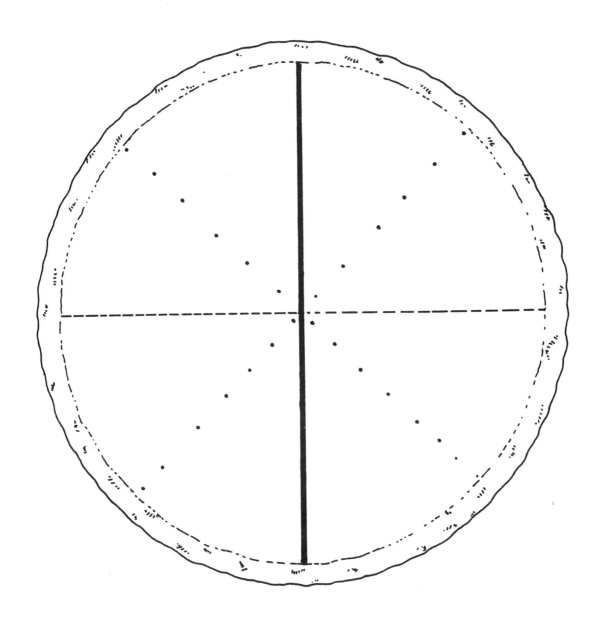

Pathways to Poetry: Poetry Fun for Grades 1–3 © 1994 Fearon Teacher Aids

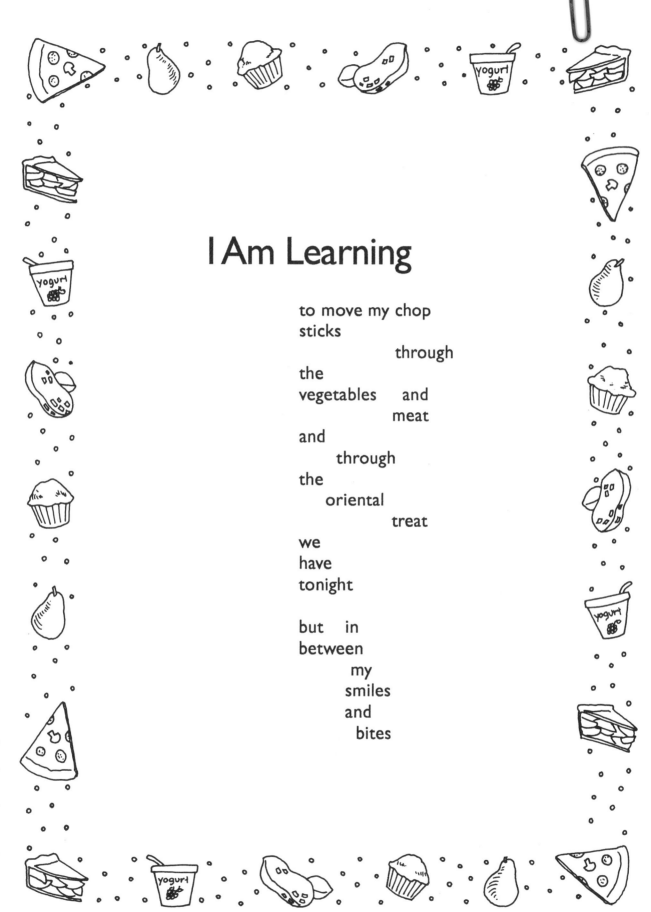

I Am Learning

to move my chop
sticks
                        through
the
vegetables   and
                    meat
and
        through
the
        oriental
                    treat
we
have
tonight

but   in
between
        my
        smiles
        and
            bites

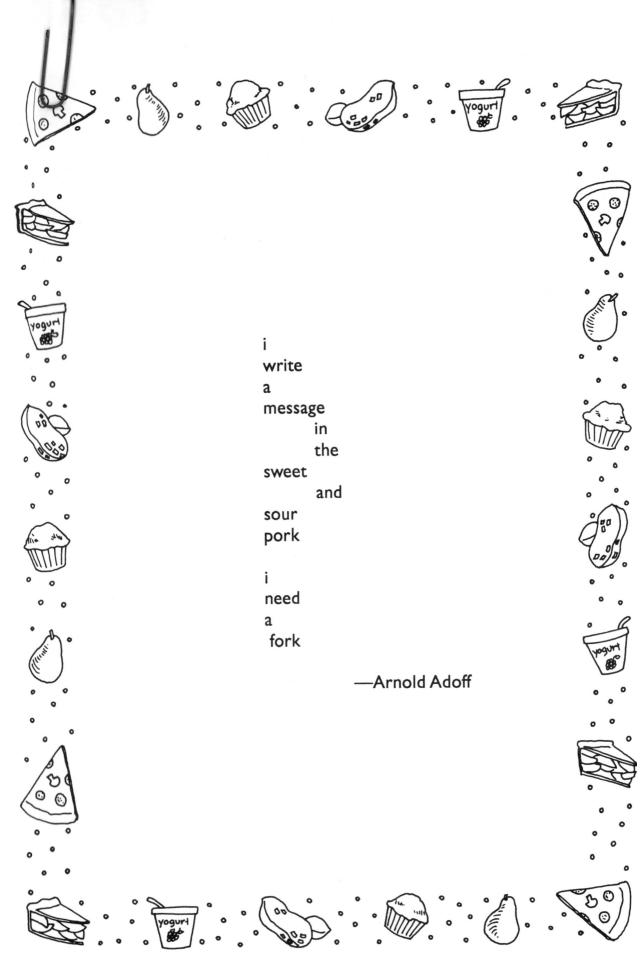

i
write
a
message
        in
          the
sweet
      and

sour
pork

i
need
a
  fork

—Arnold Adoff

Pathways to Poetry: Poetry Fun for Grades 1-3 © 1994 Fearon Teacher Aids

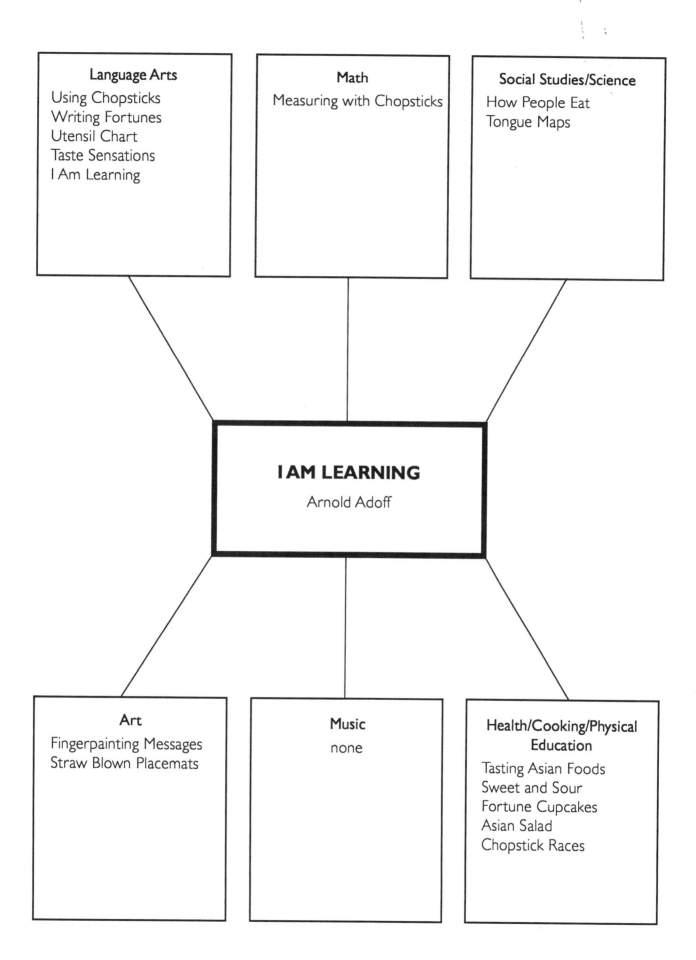

Language Arts
Using Chopsticks
Writing Fortunes
Utensil Chart
Taste Sensations
I Am Learning

Math
Measuring with Chopsticks

Social Studies/Science
How People Eat
Tongue Maps

I AM LEARNING
Arnold Adoff

Art
Fingerpainting Messages
Straw Blown Placemats

Music
none

Health/Cooking/Physical Education
Tasting Asian Foods
Sweet and Sour
Fortune Cupcakes
Asian Salad
Chopstick Races

45

I Am Learning

The following suggestions can be used with the poem "I Am Learning." Select the activities that are most appropriate for the needs and age level of the children in the class.

Introducing the Poem

1. Give each child a fortune cookie. Ask the children if they have ever seen a fortune cookie before. Have the children raise their hands if they have ever eaten Chinese, Vietnamese, Korean, or Japanese food. Then have the children raise their hands if they have ever eaten in a Chinese, Vietnamese, Korean, or Japanese restaurant. Invite the children to name the special foods and customs they observed at the restaurants. Record the responses on the chalkboard. Have the children wait until the end of the poetry lesson to read their fortunes and eat their fortune cookies.

2. Hand out a pair of chopsticks to each child (available at many supermarkets or local restaurants). Invite the children to try experimenting with the chopsticks. Encourage the class to practice picking up objects, such as dried elbow macaroni. Discuss how the children feel about using chopsticks. Point out that people around the world use different eating utensils.

3. Explain that the poem "I Am Learning" is about a person who is having a difficult time eating with chopsticks. Point out that the person in the poem may have some of the same frustrations the children experienced when trying to use chopsticks.

4. Share biographical information about the poet, Arnold Adoff. Refer to the Poet Bookmarks section on page 265. The bookmarks can be duplicated for the children or used to share information about each poet while studying his or her poem.

Shared Listening and Reading

1. Read the poem to the children, pausing before the message is revealed. Ask the children to predict what the message might be. Then read the poem to the children again revealing the message the second time.

2. Display a copy of the poem on a chart or transparency. Have the children look closely at the poem as you read it to them. Discuss how the poem differs from other poems the children have read, such as no capital letters, words scattered around the page, no punctuation, and the poem is skinny and tapered like chopsticks.

3. Ask volunteers to read the poem from the point of view of someone using a fork for the first time. Have the children substitute the word *fork* for the word *chopsticks* and the word *chopsticks* for the word *fork*.

4. Display a copy of the poem on a chart or transparency. Have the children practice reading the poem several times, selecting ideas from the General Suggestions for Listening and Reading the Poems on page 6.

Beyond Listening and Reading Activities

Using Chopsticks

Show the children a pair of chopsticks. Discuss how to use chopsticks. Divide the class into groups of two. Give each pair chopsticks. Encourage the class to practice using chopsticks to pick up rice crackers or elbow macaroni. Ask the children how they would teach someone to use chopsticks. Discuss what hints or tips are helpful to know when using chopsticks.

Writing Fortunes

Give each child a fortune cookie. Invite the children to share their fortunes with the class. Discuss what kinds of messages are found inside fortune cookies. As a class, create some examples of possible fortunes and record them on the chalkboard. Invite the children to write fortunes for their classmates. Give each child small pieces of paper for writing fortunes. Younger children may need to copy examples from the chalkboard. Save the fortunes to use in the Fortune Cupcakes activity.

Utensil Chart

Duplicate and distribute the reproducible on page 52. Have children brainstorm and then add to the chart foods that are eaten using chopsticks, forks, hands, and spoons.

Taste Sensations

Discuss words that describe tastes, such as sweet, sour, salty, and so on. Make a chart on the chalkboard with the following categories—sweet, sour, salty, and bitter. Have children name foods that fit under each category, such as peanuts and popcorn under salty foods. Give each child a paper plate. Help the children divide the plates into four sections. Have the children copy one word in each section—sweet, sour, salty, bitter. Have the children glue magazine pictures or draw foods in the appropriate sections. Encourage the children to share their plates of food with the class.

I Am Learning

Ask the children to think of something they are learning how to do, such as learning how to rollerblade, play baseball, or play the piano. Encourage interested children to share their experiences. Give each child a piece of writing paper. Have the children copy and complete the sentence "I am Learning . . ." Bind the pages into a class book. Throughout the year, encourage each child to write new pages for the class book.

Measuring with Chopsticks

Have each child use a chopstick to measure common objects around the room, such as a book, a desk, and so on. (A math book might be one chopstick long and a desk might be four and a half chopsticks long.) Older children can mark off inches on the chopstick and use it to measure objects more accurately.

How People Eat

Share books about different cultures and their eating habits, such as *How My Parents Learned to Eat* by Ina R. Friedman, *Everybody Cooks Rice* by Norah Dooley, and *Bread, Bread, Bread* by Ann Morris.

Encourage the children to use nonfiction books to find information about eating habits of people in other cultures. Record the children's responses on the chalkboard.

> Many people in Korea, China, Vietnam, and Japan eat with chopsticks.
> In Indonesia, many people use only a spoon to eat.
> In Taiwan, many people consider it rude to eat on the street.
> In Australia, some people eat kangaroo meat.
> In Europe, many people eat with the fork upside down in the left hand.
> In Japan, many people eat sitting on mats on the floor.
> Bedouins living in the Arabian, Syrian, or North African deserts often use bread as an eating utensil.

As a culture or a specific country is identified locate the country or region on a globe or world map. Discuss other interesting information learned about the different cultures.

Tongue Maps

Make sure the class washes their hands before starting this activity. Explain that the tongue is divided into different areas that can taste— sour foods, sweet foods, salty foods, and bitter foods. Have the children draw pictures of their tongues. Give each child a small piece of waxed paper, a sugar cube, lemon drop or sour candy, salty peanuts, and bitter chocolate. Remind the children that there are specific areas of the tongue for each kind of taste. Invite the children to place each food item on various parts of their tongues to identify the different taste zones. Place the uneaten foods on the waxed paper. Help the children draw the different taste areas on their tongue pictures. Invite the children to compare their tongue diagrams. Discuss the children's findings.

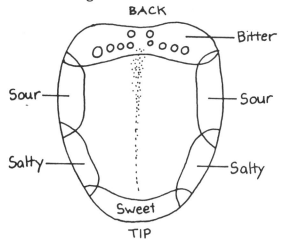

Fingerpainting Messages

Have the children wash their hands before starting this activity. Divide the class into groups of two. Give each child fingerpaint paper and a small amount of sweet and sour sauce. Encourage the partners to use their fingers to write messages to each other in the sauce. Provide paper towels and soapy water for easier clean-up.

Straw Blown Placemats

Give each child a large piece of light-colored construction paper and a large straw. Fill squeeze bottles with tempera paint. Squeeze small droplets of different colored tempera paint on the paper. Use the straw to blow the droplets around the paper. The placemats should be dry before handling them. Laminate the placemats or place between two sheets of clear contact paper.

Tasting Asian Foods

Prior to this activity, send a note home to parents explaining that the children will be asked to bring Asian foods from home on a specific date. Discuss the children's favorite Asian foods. Record the responses on the chalkboard. Then ask the children to bring a variety of Asian foods to school, such as rice noodles, pea pods, bamboo shoots, mung beans, chow mein noodles, tofu, sweet and sour sauce, and so on. Encourage children to try tasting each of the different kinds of foods. Ask the children to identify their favorite food and why. Give each child a fortune cookie to enjoy.

Sweet and Sour

Buy sweet and sour sauce at the grocery. Give each child a small paper plate and one teaspoon of sweet and sour sauce. Encourage the children to taste the sauce. Look at the ingredients on the jar label. Ask the children to try to identify which ingredients make the sauce sweet and which ingredients make it sour. Encourage the class to name other foods that are also sweet and sour at the same time.

Fortune Cupcakes

Give each child small pieces of paper for writing fortunes or use fortunes from the Writing Fortunes activity. Help the children fold the fortunes and carefully wrap them in aluminum foil. Make sure children wash their hands before making cupcakes. Prepare cake batter according to the directions on the package. Pour the batter into paper-lined muffin tins. Have each child stick a fortune down inside each cupcake cup. Bake the cupcakes according to the directions on the package. After the cupcakes have cooled, encourage each child to randomly choose a cupcake and break it open to find the fortune. Be sure to warn the children to watch out for pieces of aluminum foil. Invite the children to eat their cupcakes and share their fortunes.

Asian Salad

Provide a table with a variety of salad ingredients, such as lettuce, mandarin oranges, water chestnuts, chow mein noodles, pineapple, bean sprouts, and so on. Give each child a paper bowl and invite him or her to make a salad. Encourage each child to try eating his or her salad with chopsticks.

PHYSICAL ED.

Chopstick Races

Give each child a container of elbow macaroni and an empty container. The two containers should be placed a distance of six inches apart. Using chopsticks, each child will try to carry as many macaroni as he or she can from one container to another before the allotted time runs out.

Utensil Chart

Directions: List foods eaten with each utensil.

Pathways to Poetry: Poetry Fun for Grades 1-3 © 1994 Fearon Teacher Aids

Suggested Books

Themed Poetry Books

Eats. Arnold Adoff. New York, NY: Lothrop, Lee & Shepard, 1989.

Munching: Poems About Eating. Lee Bennett Hopkins. Boston, MA: Little, Brown and Co., 1985.

Oxford's A Packet of Poems: Poems About Food. Jill Bennett. Oxford, England: Oxford University Press, 1982.

What's on the Menu? Bobbye S. Goldstein. New York, NY: Viking, 1992.

Books for Read-Aloud and Independent Reading

Alligator Arrived with Apples. Crescent Dragonwagon. New York, NY: Macmillan, 1987. The animals and the food they bring to the Great Feast are introduced alphabetically.

The Berenstain Bears and Too Much Junk Food. Stan and Janice Berenstain. New York, NY: Random House, 1985. Mama Bear begins a campaign to convince her family to stop eating junk food by buying healthy foods on a supermarket trip.

Bread Bread Bread. Ann Morris. New York, NY: Lothrop, Lee & Shepard, 1989. A photographic tour of how people around the world enjoy eating bread in many different forms, shapes, and sizes.

Cloudy With a Chance of Meatballs. Judi Barrett. New York, NY: Atheneum, 1980. In the town of Chewandswallow, the weather came three times a day—at breakfast, lunch, and dinner—and it rained soup and juice, snowed mashed potatoes, and stormed hamburgers. The problems can be severe when a town is deluged by food.

Everybody Cooks Rice. Noah Dooley. Minneapolis, MN: Carolrhoda, 1991. A little girl must find her brother before they can eat dinner. As she visits each family in the neighborhood, she samples each family's dinner. She discovers that everybody eats rice, but in different ways.

Frank and Ernest. Alexandra Day. New York, NY: Scholastic Inc., 1988. Animal friends run an old-fashioned diner and translate orders into clever, descriptive idioms. A list of idioms is included at the back of the book.

The Great Jam Sandwich. John Vernon Lord. Boston, MA: Houghton Mifflin, 1972. A wacky explanation for how the residents of a village plagued by wasps solve their problem. The story is written in rhyming verse.

How My Parents Learned to Eat. Ina R. Friedman. Boston, MA: Houghton Mifflin, 1984. A little girl relates the story behind eating at her house using chopsticks some days and eating with knives and forks on other days.

How to Eat Fried Worms. Thomas Rockwell. New York, NY: Dell Publishing Co., Inc., 1977. On a bet, Billy has to eat 15 worms in 15 days. The reader is taken on Billy's humorous adventures to win the bet.

June 29, 1999. David Wiesner. New York, NY: Clarion, 1992. Holly Evans, a third-grade student, has great expectations for her innovative science project. She sent seedlings aloft into the ionosphere. The events of June 29, 1999 are amazing!

No Bean Sprouts, Please! Constance Hiser. New York, NY: Holiday House, 1990. James' mother feeds him health food, but his uncle's gift of a magical lunch box changes the menu in this delightful mystery.

No Fighting, No Biting! Else Holmelund Minarik. New York, NY: HarperCollins, 1958. The adventures of two fighting alligators are humorously told through easy-to-read text and the illustrations of Maurice Sendak.

The Pizza Book. Stephen Krensky. New York, NY: Scholastic, 1992. An informational book full of pizza facts and history including an easy to follow, authentic recipe.

Pizza for Breakfast. Maryann Kovalski. New York, NY: William Morrow, 1990. Frank and Zelda discover that their wish for more customers at their pizza restaurant creates lots of problems.

Stone Soup. Ann McGovern. New York, NY: Scholastic, 1986. A tired and hungry young man tricks a little old lady into making soup from a stone.

Claws and Paws

Mother Doesn't Want a Dog

Mother doesn't want a dog.
Mother says they smell
And never sit when you say sit,
Or even when you yell.
And when you come home late at night
And there is ice and snow,
You have to go back out because
The dumb dog has to go.

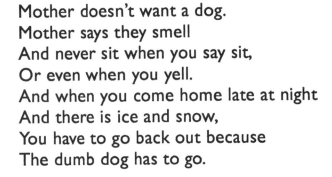

Mother doesn't want a dog.
Mother says they shed
And always let the strangers in
And bark at friends instead
And do disgraceful things on rugs,
And track mud on the floor
And flop upon your bed at night
And snore their doggy snore.

Mother doesn't want a dog.
She's making a mistake.
Because, more than a dog, I think
She will not want this snake.

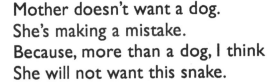

—Judith Viorst

Pathways to Poetry: Poetry Fun for Grades 1-3 © 1994 Fearon Teacher Aids

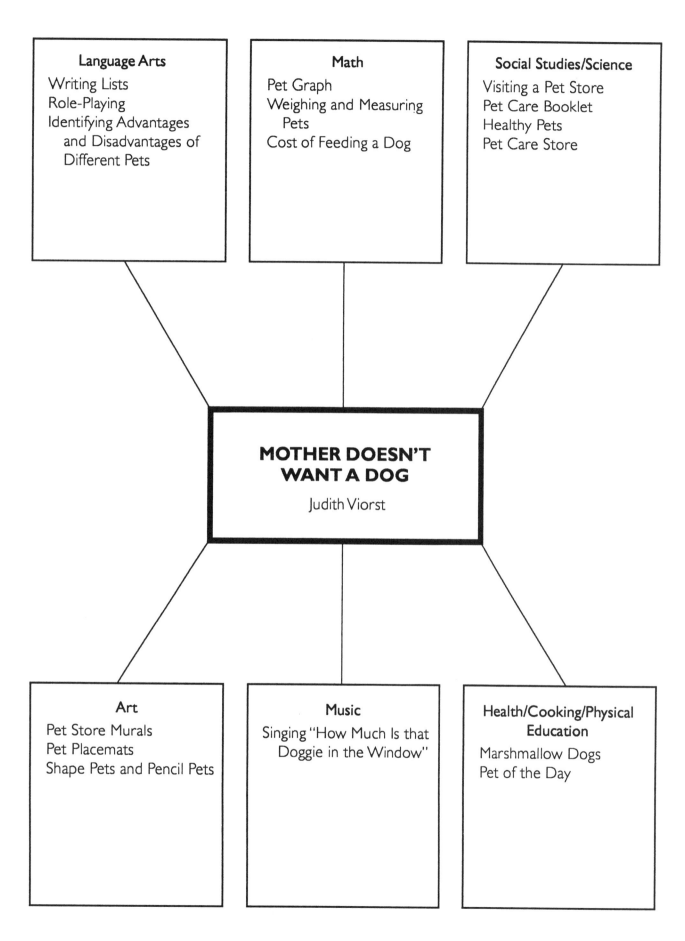

Language Arts

Writing Lists
Role-Playing
Identifying Advantages
    and Disadvantages of
    Different Pets

Math

Pet Graph
Weighing and Measuring
    Pets
Cost of Feeding a Dog

Social Studies/Science

Visiting a Pet Store
Pet Care Booklet
Healthy Pets
Pet Care Store

MOTHER DOESN'T WANT A DOG

Judith Viorst

Art

Pet Store Murals
Pet Placemats
Shape Pets and Pencil Pets

Music

Singing "How Much Is that
Doggie in the Window"

Health/Cooking/Physical Education

Marshmallow Dogs
Pet of the Day

Mother Doesn't Want a Dog

The following suggestions can be used with the poem "Mother Doesn't Want a Dog." Select the activities that are most appropriate for the needs and age level of the children in the class.

Introducing the Poem

1. Ask the children if they have ever wanted to do something their parents didn't want them to do. Invite the children to share their experiences. Discuss how the children were successful or unsuccessful at changing their parents' minds.

2. Ask if any of the children recently received a pet—dog, cat, gerbil, or fish. Discuss whether or not the pet owners' parents were in favor of getting pets. Discuss why some parents may not want pets.

3. Tell the children the title of the poem "Mother Doesn't Want a Dog." Have the children give reasons why a parent wouldn't want a dog. Record the children's ideas on the chalkboard.

4. Share biographical information about the poet, Judith Viorst. Refer to the Poet Bookmarks section on page 265. The bookmarks can be duplicated for the children or used to share information about each poet while studying his or her poem.

Shared Listening and Reading

1. Display a copy of the poem on a chart or transparency. Read the poem aloud. Encourage the children to listen for the reasons mother didn't want a dog. Compare the reasons mentioned in the poem with the children's earlier predictions.

2. Read the poem aloud one or more times, inviting the children to join in reading with you. Clarify, if necessary, the meaning of the words *disgraceful, shed,* and *flop.*

3. Discuss the line from the poem, "She's making a mistake." Encourage the children to share the problems they think a pet snake might cause. Record the children's responses on the chalkboard. Compare the snake ownership problems with the dog ownership problems mentioned in the poem.

4. Display a copy of the poem on a chart or transparency. Have the children read the poem several times, selecting ideas from the General Suggestions for Listening to and Reading the Poems on page 6.

Beyond Listening and Reading Activities

Writing Lists

Divide the class into cooperative work groups. Ask two or three of the groups to create a list of advantages of having a dog for a pet, rather than a snake. Have the remaining groups create a list of advantages of having a snake for a pet, rather than a dog. After a specified time limit, have the groups share their lists. Younger children may need to do this activity as a whole class.

Role-Playing

Discuss how the children would react if they were the mother in the poem. In advance, write the following reasons for not wanting a dog on small pieces of paper. You may wish to add additional ones.

    Dogs smell.
    Dogs don't obey.
    Dogs have to be taken outside to go to the bathroom.
    Dogs shed.
    Dogs bark.
    Dogs make messes on the floor.
    Dogs track in mud.
    Dogs jump on the bed.
    Dogs snore.

Place the slips of paper in a paper bag. Choose one volunteer to play the role of the parent and a second volunteer to play the role of the child. Have the volunteers choose a slip of paper from the bag, and role-play a scene in which the child wants to get a dog and the parent doesn't want a dog based on the reason written on the slip of paper. Continue the activity with different children doing the role-playing.

Identifying Advantages and Disadvantages of Different Pets

Read the book *Can I Keep Him?* by Steven Kellogg. Ask each child to name an animal he or she would most like to have for a pet and tell why. Record the children's responses on the chalkboard. Discuss the advantages and disadvantages of each animal the children identify. As a class, make a chart of the advantages and disadvantages of each animal. Discuss which animals would make the best pets.

Animal	Advantages	Disadvantages
Hamster	doesn't need much space can live in an apartment doesn't cost much to feed	has to stay in cage most of the time may make noise at night
Snake	can go a long time without food	might scare people may not be able to play with a snake

Pet Graph

Take a poll of what kinds of pets are owned by class members. Record the different kinds of pets on the chalkboard. Make a large graph on a chart or chalkboard. At the bottom of the graph, create columns and write the names or display pictures of the different kinds of pets. Leave one space for children who do not own pets. Give the children one square of paper for each pet they own. Have the children draw pictures of their pets in the squares and add to the correct columns on the pictograph. Discuss the results of the poll. Ask the children which is the most popular pet. If few members of the class own pets, conduct the poll by asking children what pet they would choose if they could have a pet. Graph the results.

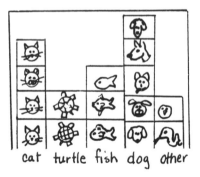

cat   turtle   fish   dog   other

Weighing and Measuring Pets

Prior to this activity, send notes home to parents asking them to help their child with this activity. Explain that the children with pets are going to measure and weigh their pets and share their results with the class. Using a picture, show the class how to measure their dog or cat from nose to tail. Record the measurements. Then explain how they can weigh their own pets. An easy way to weigh a pet is to stand on the scale first and weigh yourself. Then pick up your pet and step on your pet and step on the scale again. The difference between the two weights is the number of pounds the pet weighs.

Record the length and weight of each child's pet on the chalkboard. Compare the children's results. If appropriate, create word problems with the pet information—for example, Andy's dog weighs 16 pounds. Mary's dog weighs 30 pounds. How many more pounds does Mary's dog weigh than Andy's dog?

Cost of Feeding a Dog

Ask children to share information on the types and amounts of food eaten by their dogs. Record the children's responses on the chalkboard. Bring in several newspaper ads that advertise the cost of different brands of dry and canned dog foods. Duplicate and distribute the newspaper ads. Ask the children to compare the prices of the different kinds of dog foods. If appropriate, have the children calculate the cost of feeding a certain size dog for a day or a week.

Visiting a Pet Store

Make arrangements for the class to visit a local pet store. It is important that there are a variety of animals for the children to see and that the animals are healthy. Before the field trip, stress with the children the appropriate ways to handle the animals. Have the children prepare questions ahead of time to ask the pet store personnel, such as where do the animals come from, the kinds of food each animal eats, the cost of purchasing a certain animal, and information regarding care requirements. After returning to the classroom, have the children write thank-you letters to the pet store personnel.

Pet Care Booklet

Have the children make pet care booklets including any information they learned in the Visiting a Pet Store activity. Provide a variety of nonfiction books about pets for the children to read. Invite each child to choose a pet to write about. Have the children include information about the animals' diets, living conditions, need for exercise, and so on. Provide writing paper for the children to record their pet care facts. Have the children draw pictures of their pets on their fact pages, too. Bind all the pages together into a classroom pet care booklet. Encourage the children to select a range of pets to include in the booklet.

Healthy Pets

Discuss the importance of making sure the pet you buy is healthy. Share articles from the newspaper that address the topic of buying healthy pets. Encourage children to bring in other newspaper or magazine articles to share with the class. Suggest children read books that provide additional information on how to identify healthy pets. Invite the children to share their findings with the class.

Pet Care Store

Invite the children to plan and make a Pet Care Store in the classroom. Discuss with the class the type of products they would provide in their store. Record the list on the chalkboard. Use large boxes or bookcases for displays in the store. Involve the class in planning and stocking the store with unopened pet foods brought from home, empty and clean pet food containers, pet toys or pictures of toys, and other items required by pets. Labels, signs, prices, play money, a cash register, advertisements, as well as student-prepared booklets on the care of various types of pets could also be included in the store.

Provide opportunities for small groups of children to engage in dramatic play in the Pet Care Store. Have the children take turns being the owner and the customers. (Be sure to include receipts for the store purchases.)

Pet Store Murals

Make a list of animals that might be seen in a pet store window. Record the list on the chalkboard. Post a long sheet of butcher paper divided into sections on the wall. Have the children work in pairs to create a mural of a pet store window. Encourage the children to select one or two animals to include in their windows. Use construction-paper strips to frame the "pet store windows." Encourage the children to share why they chose certain pets to include in their murals.

Pet Placemats

Each child will need a piece of 12" x 18" heavy paper. On the paper, have each child draw and than color a picture of his or her pet and write its name. If possible, laminate or cover both sides of the placemats with clear contact paper for easy clean-up. Children without pets can design placemats for pets they would like to have or for friends' pets.

Shape Pets and Pencil Pets

Duplicate on different colors of lightweight construction paper the reproducible on page 65. Divide the class into small groups of three or four children. Distribute several copies of each color of the shape reproducible to each group as well as sheets of white construction paper. Have the children cut out the various shapes and arrange them on the white construction paper to create shape pets. Invite the children to add details with crayons.

Pencil pets can also be made by gluing the pet shape to a strip of paper and then gluing the strip to a pencil. Demonstrate how to make a pencil pet using the example as only a guide.

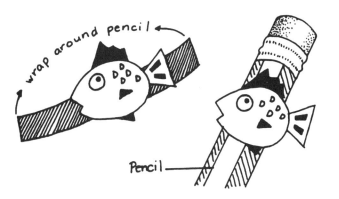

Singing

Teach children the song "How Much is that Doggie in the Window," available in sheet music and on records.

Marshmallow Dogs

To make edible marshmallow dogs, you will need the following ingredients for each child:

    3 regular size marshmallows for the dog's body
    8 miniature marshmallows for the dog's legs
    3 miniature marshmallows for the dog's ears and mouth
    11 toothpicks for attaching the body parts
    icing in a tube to make the eyes

The dog can be constructed as shown in the illustration.

Pet of the Day

Teach the children the game "Pet of the Day." Have the children sit in a large circle. Player 1 passes a stuffed toy dog around the circle to the right, saying to the player seated next to him or her, "This is a dog." Player 2 then takes the dog and says, "A what?" Player 1 responds to Player 2 "This is a dog." Player 2 then passes the dog to the third player, and says "This is a dog." Player 3 asks, "A what?" Player 2 asks Player 1 "A what?" and Player 1 responds again "A dog." The game continues in this fashion, with the question going back each time to Player 1. The dog cannot be passed to the next player until Player 1 has given the response. After Player 1 has started passing the dog around the circle to the right, Player 1 should then start passing a toy snake around the circle in the opposite direction, substituting the word *snake* for the word *dog*. The same procedure is followed for the questions and answers. The first toy to be passed around the circle is named "Pet of the Day."

Shape Pets and Pencil Pets

Name_____

Directions: For shape pets, cut out the shapes. Make shape pets by arranging the shapes on the white construction paper and gluing them in place. For pencil pets, glue the shape pet to a strip of paper and then glue the strip to a pencil.

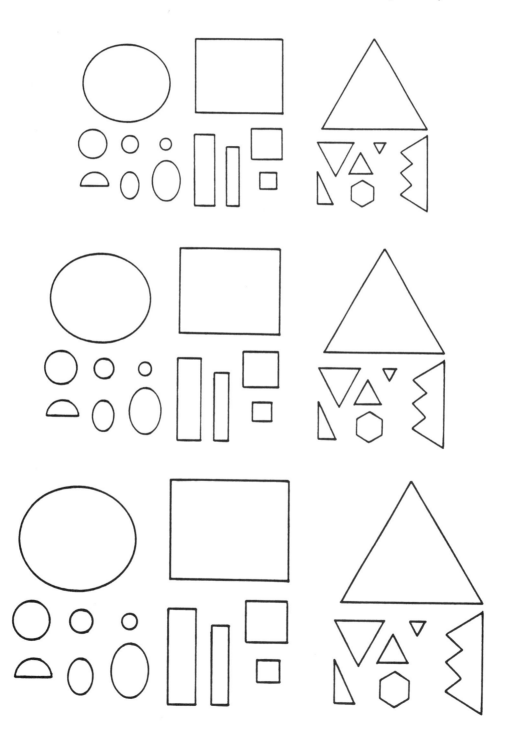

Hot Dog

I have a hot dog for a pet,
The only kind my folks would let
Me get.
He does smell sort of bad
And yet
He absolutely never gets
The sofa wet.
We have a butcher for a vet,
The strangest vet you ever met.
Guess we're the weirdest family yet,
To have a hot dog for a pet.

—Shel Silverstein

Pathways to Poetry: Poetry Fun for Grades 1-3 © 1994 Fearon Teacher Aids

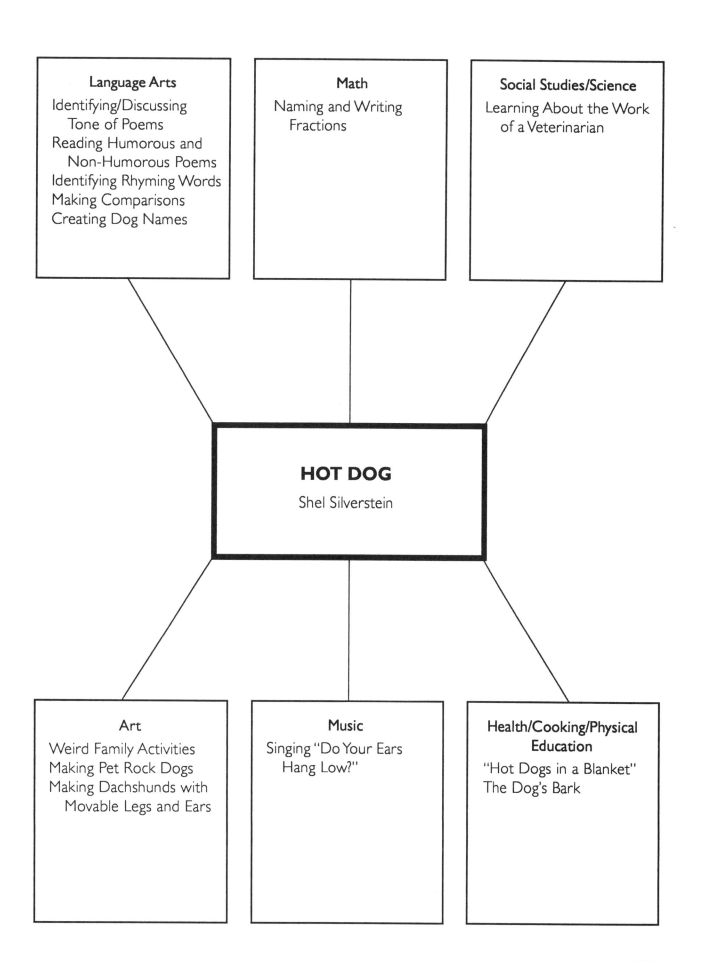

Language Arts

Identifying/Discussing
    Tone of Poems
Reading Humorous and
    Non-Humorous Poems
Identifying Rhyming Words
Making Comparisons
Creating Dog Names

Math

Naming and Writing
Fractions

Social Studies/Science

Learning About the Work
of a Veterinarian

HOT DOG

Shel Silverstein

Art

Weird Family Activities
Making Pet Rock Dogs
Making Dachshunds with
    Movable Legs and Ears

Music

Singing "Do Your Ears
Hang Low?"

**Health/Cooking/Physical
Education**

"Hot Dogs in a Blanket"
The Dog's Bark

Hot Dog

The following suggestions can be used with the poem "Hot Dog." Select the activities that are most appropriate for the needs and age level of the children in the class.

Introducing the Poem

1. Come to class dressed in an unusual way, such as wearing two different shoes, wearing three hats, and so on. Or, come to class showing unusual behavior, such as walking backwards, hiccuping when you speak, and so on. Encourage the class to describe your appearance or behavior. Ask the children if they think your behavior or appearance could be considered unusual or weird. Discuss the meanings of the words *unusual* or *weird*. (The dictionary definition for the word *unusual* is not common or rare. The definition for the word *weird* is odd or fantastic.)

2. Discuss unusual or weird pets, such as pot belly pigs, ferrets, iguanas, llamas, and so on. Encourage children to tell about other pets they would consider weird or unusual.

3. Show children a picture of a dachshund. Ask the children to identify the dog breed. Ask the children if they have ever heard of a dachshund being called by any other name, such as wiener dog or hot dog. Discuss why a dachshund might be called a wiener dog.

4. Share biographical information about the poet, Shel Silverstein. Refer to the Poet Bookmarks section on page 265. The bookmarks can be duplicated for the children or used to share information about each poet while studying his or her poem.

Shared Listening and Reading

1. Show only the title of the poem on a chart or transparency. Have a volunteer read the title aloud. Ask the children what they think the poem is about. Read the poem aloud. Compare the children's predictions with the actual poem.

2. Read the poem aloud several times, inviting the children to join with you. Discuss whether or not someone would really have a hot dog for a pet and a butcher for a vet.

3. Display a copy of the poem on a chart or transparency. Have the children read the poem several times, selecting ideas from the General Suggestions for Listening to and Reading the Poems on page 6.

Beyond Listening and Reading Activities

Identifying/Discussing Tone of Poems

Display a copy of a familiar poem, such as "Mother Doesn't Want a Dog" by Judith Viorst and a copy of the poem "Hot Dog" by Shel Silverstein. Have the children read both poems aloud. Then ask the children how each poem makes them feel. Discuss how poems can make us feel differently even if they are about the same subject.

Reading Humorous and Non-Humorous Poems

Divide the class into cooperative work groups. Provide each group with two or more poetry books, containing examples of humorous and non-humorous poems. (Books by Shel Silverstein and Jack Prelutsky contain numerous examples of humorous poems.) Invite each group to look through the books and select one example of a humorous poem and one example of a non-humorous poem. Ask the children to practice reading their poetry selections in their groups. After a set time period, have each group share their selections with the whole class.

Record the titles of the poems read aloud on the chalkboard. Have the class vote for the two poems they enjoyed the most. Discuss why these two poems were chosen as favorites.

Identifying Rhyming Words

Display a copy of the poem "Hot Dog" on a chart or transparency. Have a volunteer read the poem aloud. Encourage the other children to listen carefully for the rhyming words. Have volunteers underline the rhyming words in the first three lines, next four lines, and in the last four lines. Have children read all the underlined words aloud, noting that all the lines, except one, end with rhyming words and the letters "et."

Making Comparisons

Read aloud or have the children independently read one or more of Harry Allard's books about the Stupid family. (See Suggested Books for Read-Aloud and Independent Reading). Have children compare the situations presented in the books with the activities they illustrate in the activity called Weird Family activities.

Creating Dog Names

Have the children suggest dog names and list the names on the chalkboard. Discuss how dogs are often given names based on how they look such as, Blackie, Spot, Midnight, Tiny, and so on. Encourage the children to add names to the list that could be related to a dog's features. Duplicate and distribute the reproducible on page 74. Have the children read the description, draw a dog to fit each description, and then create a name for the dog based on the dog's features. Provide an opportunity for the children to share their dog pictures. With younger students, you may wish to guide the children through the activity working as a whole class.

Naming and Writing Fractions

Using "hot dogs" cut from paper, show the class how one hot dog can be cut into two equal parts. Hold up one part and write the fraction $1/2$ on the chalkboard. Continue using paper hot dogs to demonstrate the fractions $1/4$, $2/4$, $3/4$, and $4/4$. Write the specific fractions on the chalkboard and point out the meaning of the words *numerator* and *denominator*. If appropriate, have children take turns demonstrating with the hot dogs a specific fraction and the corresponding written form.

Learning About the Work of a Veterinarian

Invite a local veterinarian to speak to the class about his or her work, emphasizing the proper care for keeping pets healthy. Have children prepare questions ahead of time to ask the veterinarian. Discuss the information learned from the guest speaker's visit. After the visit, have the class write thank-you letters to send to the veterinarian.

Weird Family Activities

Remind the children that the family in the poem "Hot Dog" was described as "the weirdest family yet." Invite children to name some common family activities, such as picnics, family vacations, and so on. Divide the class into small groups. Encourage each group to brainstorm weird activities a family could do together. With younger children, you may wish to do the brainstorming activity as a whole class. After a set time limit, give the children drawing or writing paper. Have each child select the activity that he or she thinks is the weirdest and draw a picture showing that activity. Encourage the children to describe their pictures in writing. Provide an opportunity for the children to share their descriptions and illustrations with the class.

Making Pet Rock Dogs

For this activity, each child will need the following: four small flat rocks that are all approximately the same size for the feet, one oval rock for the head, and one larger rock for the body. If possible, have the children collect the rocks needed for this activity. Provide brown and black construction paper, glue, and a variety of colors of paint.

Have the children follow these step-by-step directions:
- Glue four small rocks (feet) to the large rock (body). Let the glue dry.
- Glue an oval rock (head) to the body. Hold the rock in place for a short time while the glue is drying.
- Once the glue has dried, paint the rock dog. Add features, such as eyes, nose, mouth, toenails, and so on.
- Cut out ears and a tail from construction paper and glue in place.

Making Dachshunds with Movable Legs and Ears

Duplicate and distribute the reproducible on page 75. Have children cut out the dog's body, legs, and ears. Provide brads for attaching the body parts. Help the children attach the ears and legs to the dachshund body. Have the children color their dogs and add dog collars. Give the children writing paper and encourage them to write simple adventure stories about their dachshunds. Display the stories and dachshunds around the classroom.

Singing

Teach children the song "Do Your Ears Hang Low?" from *Tom Glazer's Do Your Ears Hang Low?* Children may also enjoy creating body movements to accompany the song.

"Hot Dogs in a Blanket"

Have the class make "Hot Dogs in a Blanket." Divide the class into groups of four. Each group will need the following ingredients:

    2 hot dogs
    2 ready-to-bake crescent rolls
    2 muffin cups for catsup and mustard

Provide the following instructions to the groups:

    1) Cut each hot dog in half.
    2) Cut each crescent roll in half.
    3) Wrap half of the crescent roll around a hot dog half.
    4) Place hot dogs on cookie sheet.
    5) Bake wrapped hot dogs in oven at 350° for 15 minutes.
    6) Dip hot dogs in catsup or mustard.
    7) Eat.

The Dog's Bark

Play the game "The Dog's Bark." Have the children sit in a circle with approximately 9 to 12 inches between each child. One blindfolded player sits in the middle of the circle, holding a whistle or a bell. Tie a stuffed toy dog to a heavy cord or string. The string should be long enough to reach around the circle. Tie the ends of the string together. The toy dog is passed around the circle to the right as the players move the string. When the child in the middle of the circle blows the whistle, the dog must stop. The player, who has the dog nearest to his or her right hand, becomes the Dog's Bark. This player then sits on the floor inside the circle and barks like a dog until the whistle blows again and another child is caught near the dog. The player who has been barking takes the blindfolded player's place in the middle of the circle. The new Dog's Bark then sits on the floor and barks, until the whistle is blown again. The whistle should be blown frequently and at unexpected times. Soft music may be played as the toy dog is moved around the circle.

Dog Names

Name _____

Directions: Draw a dog to match each description. Write the name of each dog on the line.

A dog with long shaggy hair

1

A white dog with black spots

2

A dog with long floppy ears

3

A dog with red hair

4

Pathways to Poetry: Poetry Fun for Grades 1-3 © 1994 Fearon Teacher Aids

Dachshund with Movable Legs and Ears

Name _____

Directions: Cut out the dog's body, legs, and ears. Use brads to attach the legs and ears to the body. Color the dog.

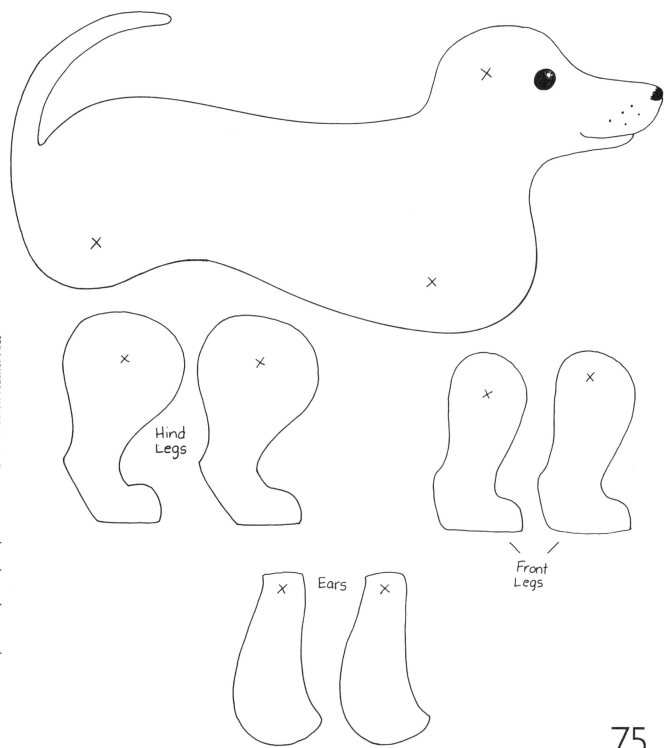

Hind Legs

Front Legs

Ears

Dogs

Dogs big, dogs small
Dogs short, dogs tall
Dogs fat, dogs thin
Dogs that make a dreadful din.

Dogs smooth, dogs hairy
Dogs friendly, dogs scary
Dogs brown, dogs white
Dogs that bark all through the night.

Dogs that run, dogs that walk
Dogs that make you think they'll talk,
Dogs awake, dogs asleep
Dogs for the blind, dogs for the sheep.

The best of all the dogs I know
Goes with me everywhere I go.

—John Kitching

Pathways to Poetry: Poetry Fun for Grades 1-3 © 1994 Fearon Teacher Aids

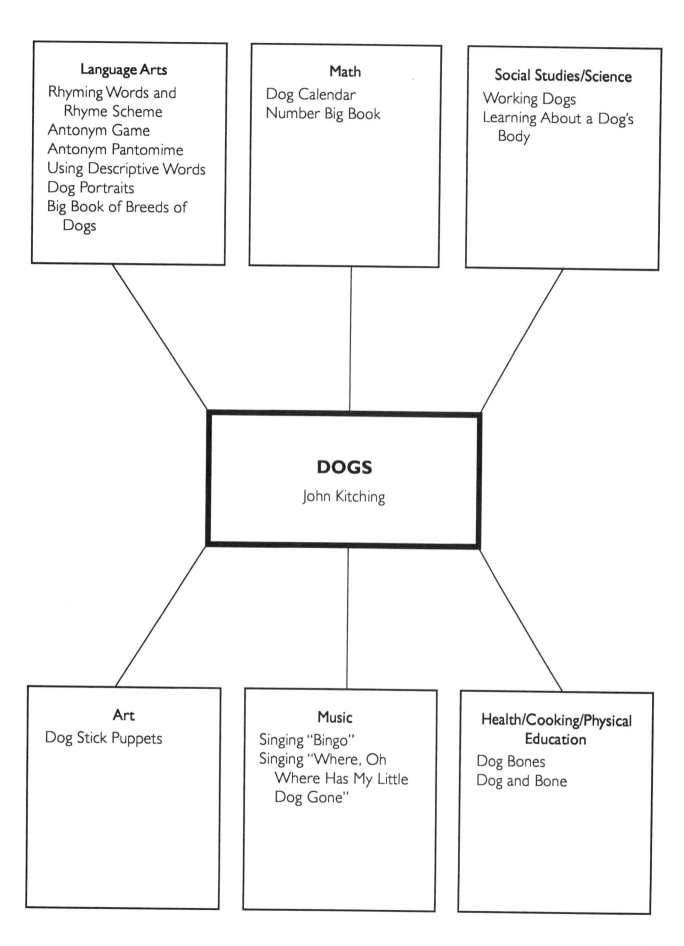

Language Arts

Rhyming Words and
  Rhyme Scheme
Antonym Game
Antonym Pantomime
Using Descriptive Words
Dog Portraits
Big Book of Breeds of
  Dogs

Math

Dog Calendar
Number Big Book

Social Studies/Science

Working Dogs
Learning About a Dog's
  Body

DOGS

John Kitching

Art

Dog Stick Puppets

Music

Singing "Bingo"
Singing "Where, Oh
  Where Has My Little
  Dog Gone"

**Health/Cooking/Physical
Education**

Dog Bones
Dog and Bone

Dogs

The following suggestions can be used with the poem "Dogs." Select the activities that are most appropriate for the needs and age level of the children in the class.

Introducing the Poem

1. Read the book *Clifford, the Big Red Dog* by Norman Bridwell. After reading the book, invite the children to describe Clifford, such as his size, color, and features. Record the descriptions on the chalkboard. Ask the children what they like best about the book.

2. Ask the children to describe their pet dogs. Record the dogs' descriptions on the chalkboard. Encourage the children to compare their dogs' descriptions to the descriptions of Clifford, the dog, from the previous activity. Invite children to share their experiences as dog owners.

3. Share biographical information about the poet, John Kitching. Refer to the Poet Bookmarks section on page 265. The bookmarks can be duplicated for the children or used to share information about each poet while studying his or her poem.

Shared Listening and Reading

1. Read the poem aloud. Ask children to listen carefully for all the different kinds of dogs mentioned in the poem. Provide time for the children to recall the different dogs in the poem. Record the list on the chalkboard. Display a copy of the poem on a chart or transparency. Compare the list of dogs on the chalkboard with the dogs in the poem.

2. Read the first verse. Then invite the children to join in reading the verse. Discuss the verse line by line, encouraging the children to describe the type of dogs they pictured in their minds. Explain the meaning of the phrase *dreadful din*. Have different children pretend to be a dog and make a "dreadful din." Guide the class in reading the other verses of the poem using a procedure similar to the one used for the first verse.

3. Display a copy of the poem on a chart or transparency. Have the children read the poem several times, selecting ideas from the General Suggestions for Listening to and Reading the Poems on page 6.

Beyond Listening and Reading Activities

Rhyming Words and Rhyme Scheme

Display a copy of the poem on the chalkboard or transparency and read the first two lines aloud. Help the children identify the rhyming words by underlining them with a marker. Continue reading each pair of lines, having the children identify and underline the rhyming words. If appropriate, point out the spelling patterns of each pair of rhyming words.

As an extension for older children, divide the class into small cooperative groups. Assign each group one pair of rhyming words. Have the groups list as many other rhyming words as they can within a set time limit. Invite all the groups to share their lists of words.

Antonym Game

Introduce the word *antonym* to the class. Explain that antonyms are words that are opposites, such as big and small, short and tall, and so on. Write the antonyms that appear in the poem on word cards. Add several other antonyms word cards so each child will have one. Distribute the cards to the children. Explain that at a given signal each child should try to find a partner who has the opposite word. After the children find their opposite partners they should stand next to each other until everyone has found their partners. Have each pair read their words aloud. The game may be played one or more times.

Antonym Pantomime

Use the antonym word cards from the Antonym Game activity. Distribute one card to each child. Ask children not to show their cards to anyone. Call on a child to pantomime his or her word. The child who has the opposite word card proceeds then to pantomime his or her word. Class members must guess the two words being pantomimed. After the words are guessed correctly, the activity continues with another pantomime.

Using Descriptive Words

Invite children to bring photographs of their dogs to share with the class. Children who do not own dogs can draw pictures of the dogs they would like to have. Have each child show his or her picture and then place it on the chalk tray or post it on a bulletin board. Ask a volunteer to describe one of the dogs in the pictures. Encourage the other children to identify which dog picture is being described.

Dog Portraits

Show the class several pictures of dogs. Ask the class to brainstorm a list of words to describe each dog including size, color, features, and so on. Record the words on the chalkboard. As a class, identify the words that describe color, size, and features. Write the words under the appropriate headings—Color, Size, and Other Features. Ask a volunteer to choose one word from each column—big, friendly, brown. Point out that by combining words from the three categories you can create a good description of a dog.

Color	Size	Other Features
brown	huge	spotted
black	big	speckled
golden	tiny	friendly
white	large	hairy

Duplicate and distribute the reproducible on page 84. Instruct the class to select three describing words from different columns on the chalkboard to write a sentence about their dog. Then have each child draw his or her dog's portrait inside the frame. Provide an opportunity for children to share their completed portraits and read their sentences aloud.

Big Book of Breeds of Dogs

Discuss how there are different dog breeds, such as poodles, golden retrievers, Chihuahuas, and so on. Provide nonfiction books about dog breeds for the class to read. Encourage the children to choose their favorite dog breeds. Give each child a sheet of 11" x 17" paper. Invite the class to draw or cut out magazine pictures of their favorite dogs. At the bottom of the page, have the children write one or more sentences about the dogs pictured. Write each dog's breed underneath its picture. Bind the pictures into a class big book. Display the book in the class library.

Dog Calendar

Show the children an actual calendar, discuss what calendars are used for and why they are important. Explain how each day in a month is assigned a number and that not every month has the same number of days. Have the class name the days of the week. Write the days in order on the chalkboard.

Duplicate and distribute the reproducible on page 85. If necessary, help children complete the calendar, filling in the days of the week, dates, and so on. After completing the calendar, encourage the children to draw their favorite dog on the top of their calendars. As a class, discuss any special events occurring during the month.

Number Big Book

To develop and reinforce number words and numeral correspondence, have the children make Number Big Books. Explain that each page contains one numeral, one number word, and the appropriate number of dog pictures. Divide the class into small cooperative groups. Ask each group to make big book pages for the numbers zero to ten. When the children are finished, bind each set of eleven pages together into Number Big Books. Encourage the children to share their big books with a kindergarten or preschool class.

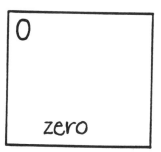

Working Dogs

Ask the children if they have ever heard the term *working dog*. Encourage children to name the two kinds of working dogs mentioned in the poem "Dogs"—Seeing-Eye dog and sheep dog. Ask the children to name other dogs that do useful work or help people, such as hunting dogs, police dogs, and so on. Encourage interested children to do research to find out more information about working dogs and to present the information to the class.

Learning About a Dog's Body

Show the class a photograph of a dog. Ask the children to share facts they know about dogs, such as dogs see in black and white. Record the children's responses on the chalkboard. Ask the class the following questions:

> Why does a dog pant?
> How well can dogs hear? What helps dogs hear?
> Do dogs see as well as people?
> How do dogs communicate?

As a class, discuss the possible answers to the questions. Then read aloud the book *A Dog's Body* by Joanna Cole. Compare information given in the book about dogs to the children's responses. To extend this activity further, have the children make dog-shaped books featuring interesting facts about dogs.

Dog Stick Puppets

Distribute pieces of heavy construction paper (3" x 4" or slightly larger). Have children draw and color a dog's head in the square. Next, have the children cut out the dog heads and glue them to the top of tongue depressors or heavy plastic straws. Encourage children to use their stick puppets to act out the poem as it is read or create new stories about dogs.

Singing

Teach children the song "B-I-N-G-O" from *Singing Bee*. After singing the song through once, the children may enjoy clapping once instead of singing "B," clapping twice instead of singing "B-I," and so on. The children may also enjoy learning the song "Where, Oh Where Has My Little Dog Gone" from *Singing Bee*. Encourage children to create hand movements to go with the song.

Dog Bones

Invite the children to make edible dog bones. The following ingredients are needed to make twelve bones:

> 1 cup peanut butter
> 1 cup powdered milk
> 2 tablespoons honey
> 4 tablespoons crushed graham crackers or vanilla wafers

Mix the peanut butter and powdered milk together. Add the honey and mix well. Divide the dough into twelve pieces, and form each piece in the shape of a dog bone. Roll both sides of the "dog bone" in the crushed graham crackers. Then eat a doggie treat!

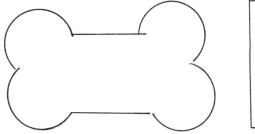
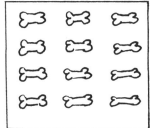

Dog and Bone

Teach children to play the game "Dog and Bone." This is a variation of the game "Hide and Seek." Select a "Safety Area," a spot where children will run to. Choose one child to be the Dog. The Dog closes his or her eyes and counts to a certain number, such as 50. The other children or Bones go and hide. When the Dog finishes counting he or she goes in search of the Bones. When the Dog locates a Bone, the Dog calls out, "I see a Bone, _____" (inserting the child's name). Both the Dog and the Bone race to the safety area. The child, who reaches the safety area last, becomes the Dog for the next game.

Dog Portraits

Name _____

Directions: Write a sentence about your dog. Draw a picture of your dog inside the picture frame.

_____

- -

_____

- -

_____

Pathways to Poetry: Poetry Fun for Grades 1-3 © 1994 Fearon Teacher Aids

Dog Calendar

Name _____

Directions: Write in the month, days of the week, and number the days of the month. Then draw a picture of your favorite kind of dog above the calendar.

Cats

Cats sleep
Anywhere,
Any table,
Any chair.
Top of piano,
Window-ledge,
In the middle,
On the edge,
Open drawer,
Empty shoe,
Anybody's
Lap will do,
Fitted in a
Cardboard box,
In the cupboard
With your frocks—
Anywhere!
They don't care!
Cats sleep
Anywhere.

—Eleanor Farjeon

Pathways to Poetry: Poetry Fun for Grades 1-3 © 1994 Fearon Teacher Aids

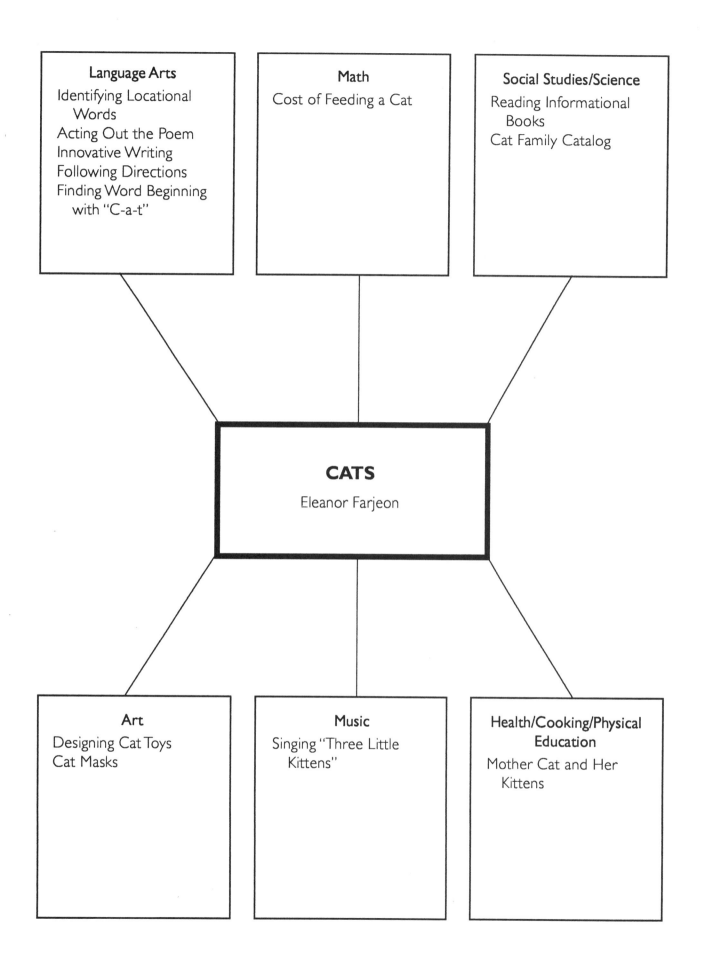

Language Arts

Identifying Locational Words
Acting Out the Poem
Innovative Writing
Following Directions
Finding Word Beginning with "C-a-t"

Math

Cost of Feeding a Cat

Social Studies/Science

Reading Informational Books
Cat Family Catalog

CATS
Eleanor Farjeon

Art

Designing Cat Toys
Cat Masks

Music

Singing "Three Little Kittens"

Health/Cooking/Physical Education

Mother Cat and Her Kittens

Cats

The following suggestions can be used with the poem "Cats." Select the activities that are most appropriate for the needs and age level of the children in the class.

Introducing the Poem

1. Invite children to bring photographs of their cats to school. Have each child show his or her photograph. As the photographs are displayed, identify specific activities the cats are doing, such as playing, sleeping, climbing a tree, and so on. Record the children's ideas on the chalkboard.

2. Encourage the children to brainstorm a list of activities cats like to do. Add the new activities to the list on the chalkboard. Explain how to play the game "Copycat." Ask one volunteer to stand in front of the class and pantomime an activity. The leader challenges the other children to copy his or her actions. The leader chooses the best "Copycat." The Copycat then identifies the pantomimed activity and becomes the next leader. Continue until all the activities have been pantomimed and the words identified.

3. Read the title of the poem to the class. Explain to the children that the poem is actually about a particular activity cats spend a great amount of time doing. Ask the children to predict (or guess) the activity.

4. Share biographical information about the poet, Eleanor Farjeon. Refer to the Poet Bookmarks section on page 265. The bookmarks can be duplicated for the children or used to share information about each poet while studying his or her poem.

Shared Listening and Reading

1. Read the poem aloud as the children listen. Then encourage the children to comment about the poem.

2. Read the poem aloud a second time. Invite the children to close their eyes and recall all the places in the poem where cats were found sleeping. Ask the children if they could see in their minds the places

where the cats were sleeping. Encourage the children to describe the places. If necessary, ask questions to help children with their descriptions, such as "What kind of chair did you see?"

3. List all the places mentioned by the children on the chalkboard. Display a copy of the poem on a chart or transparency. Read the poem aloud a third time, asking the children to join in the reading. As a class, compare the list on the chalkboard with the places mentioned in the poem. Add any additional places to the list on the chalkboard.

4. Display a copy of the poem on a chart or transparency. Have the children read the poem several times, selecting ideas from the General Suggestions for Listening to and Reading the Poems on page 6.

Beyond Listening and Reading Activities

LANGUAGE ARTS

Identifying Locational Words

Display a copy of the poem on a chart or transparency. As a volunteer reads the poem aloud, ask the children to listen for words that show location, such as the words *in, on,* and *top.* Ask several volunteers to underline and read all the locational words in the poem.

Encourage the children to brainstorm other locational words not used in the poem, such as *under, over, beside, near, inside,* and so on. Record the words on the chalkboard. As a class, try substituting the words from the chalkboard for the locational words used in the poem. Discuss how the new words change the poem.

With younger children, give oral directions and have the children "act out" or point to the location, such as sit under a table or stand beside your desk.

Acting Out the Poem

Divide the class into two groups. Identify one group as the readers of the poem and the second group as the "Cats." If appropriate, have the Cats wear the cat masks made in the Cat Mask activity. As the poem is read, encourage the Cats to choose places around the classroom to pretend to sleep. (In advance, eliminate unsafe locations mentioned in the poem, such as the top of piano or window ledge.) After the whole poem has been read, have each Cat tell where he or she is sleeping, using the appropriate locational words, such as *in* the corner or *under* the table. Reverse the roles of the groups and repeat the activity until all children have played both roles.

Innovative Writing

Display a copy of the poem on a chart or chalkboard. Ask the children to identify the words in the poem that name specific places where cats are sleeping, such as table, chair, and so on. Then have volunteers cover the words with sticky notes. As a class, create a new version of the poem by substituting new words for the covered words. Write the new words on the sticky notes. Read the new version of the poem aloud.

Duplicate and distribute copies of the poem "Cats" from page 86. Have children cross out the words that name specific places where cats are sleeping. Then ask the children to create their own versions of the poem by writing new and different places for cats to sleep above the crossed-out words. Invite the children to share their individual poems with the class.

Following Directions

Duplicate and distribute the reproducible on page 93. Ask the children to read the sentences to find out where each cat is sleeping. Have the children cut out the cats from the bottom of the page and glue them in the appropriate locations around the picture. (Note—six cats are pictured but only five cats are used on the page.)

Finding Words Beginning with "C-a-t"

Divide the class into small groups. Within a specified time limit, ask each group to list as many words as they can that begin with the letters c-a-t, such as caterpillar and catalog. Provide dictionaries to help the children locate words beginning with the letters c-a-t. Ask the children to read the dictionary definitions of the words they list. Have each group share their list of words and definitions. Compile an on-going list of c-a-t words on a chart or chalkboard.

Cost of Feeding a Cat

Show the children a can of cat food. Then provide newspaper advertisements for several varieties of canned cat food. Have the children compare the costs of the various brands. Point out that some cats eat one can of food a day and the typical can costs $ .50. Ask the children to figure out how much it would cost to feed a cat for three days, five days, or seven days. Demonstrate how to compute the total cost and the number of cans of cat food eaten over a certain period of time.

Invite older children to make up word problems for classmates to solve. For example: Kevin has one small cat. His cat eats one can of cat food each day. Each can of cat food costs $ .50. How much would it cost to feed Kevin's cat for a week?

Reading Informational Books

Explain to the class that domestic cats are not the only animals that belong in the cat family. Have the children name other "cats," such as lions, tigers, leopards, and so on. Record the children's responses on the chalkboard. Provide nonfictional books about cat family members for the children to read. Ask the children to share information they learned about cats. Record the cat facts on a chart with the following category headings:

Animal	Appearance	Habitat	Diet	Other Features

Cat Family Catalog

Divide the class into pairs or small groups. Suggest each group choose one type of cat to research. Provide a variety of nonfiction books about members of the cat family. As a class, plan the format for each catalog page, such as illustration, name of animal, interesting facts, and so on. Ask each group to provide one or two pages of information and illustrations about their cat to include in a cat catalog. When the groups are finished, bind the catalog pages together to create a booklet called "The Cat Family Catalog."

Designing Cat Toys

Ask children who have cats to identify the toys their cats like best. Display a variety of materials, such as empty spools of thread, plastic rings, cardboard shapes, balls of yarn, and so on. Ask the children how they would use these materials to make cat toys. Divide the class into pairs. Encourage each pair to design and actually make cat toys from the materials provided.

After the cat toys are finished share several advertisements for pet toys with the class. Encourage older children to create advertisements for their cat toys. Share the advertisements with the class.

Cat Masks

Give each child: half a paper plate, seven or more strips of construction paper (approximately 1" x 3" in length), six or more strips of construction paper for whiskers (approximately $1/4$" x 3" in length), glue, crayons, and two pieces of yarn or string. Follow these step-by-step directions:

1. Give each child half a paper plate.
2. Hold paper plate to child's face, and mark where to cut holes for the eyes.
3. Cut out circles for eyes.
4. Again, hold the paper plate to child's face, and mark where the nose should be cut.
5. Cut out a triangle for the nose.
6. Curl each construction-paper strip by rolling it around a pencil.
7. For a furry cat, glue the curled paper strips on the back side of the plate, around the edge.
8. Glue the narrow strips of paper on both sides of the nose to make whiskers.
9. Lastly, poke a hole in both sides of the mask near the ears. Push a piece of yarn through each hole. Adjust the string so the mask will fit the child, and then tie with a knot.
10. Use crayons to decorate the mask.

Singing

Teach the children the song "Three Little Kittens" from *Singing Bee*.

Mother Cat and Her Kittens

Teach children the game "Mother Cat and Her Kittens." To play the game, have the children sit in a wide circle. Select volunteers to be the Mother Cat and the four Kittens. When Mother Cat falls asleep, the Kittens slip away, each hiding in a different place in the classroom. Mother Cat wakes up, and calls for her Kittens by saying, "Meow, meow. Kitten _____ (inserting player's name)." The Kitten responds from the hiding place by calling, "Meow, meow. Here I am." Mother Cat tries to find her Kittens by listening for the source of the meowing sound. Anytime Mother Cat wishes, she can repeat her call and the named Kitten must reply. When all Kittens have been found and returned to the circle, the last Kitten found becomes the Mother Cat. The new Mother Cat selects four new Kittens for the next game.

Cats Sleeping

Name _____

Directions: Read the sentences to find out where each cat is sleeping. Cut out the cats and glue them in the right places.

1. The big fat cat is sleeping on the window ledge.
2. The cat with the long, long tail is in the open cupboard.
3. The cat with spots is on top of the piano.
4. The smallest cat is in the empty shoe.
5. The cat with the longest whiskers is under the table.

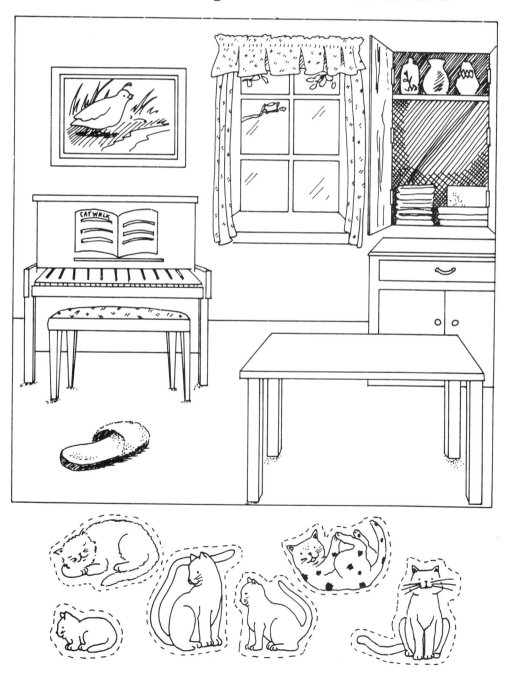

Pathways to Poetry: Poetry Fun for Grades 1-3 © 1994 Fearon Teacher Aids

About Claws and Scratching

Every cat has 4 soft paws

Every paw has 5 sharp claws.

Every claw likes to latch

Onto something it can scratch.

This is how a cat is sure

To get a proper manicure.

—Beatrice Schenk de Regniers

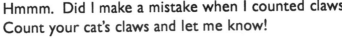

Hmmm. Did I make a mistake when I counted claws?
Count your cat's claws and let me know!

Pathways to Poetry: Poetry Fun for Grades 1–3 © 1994 Fearon Teacher Aids

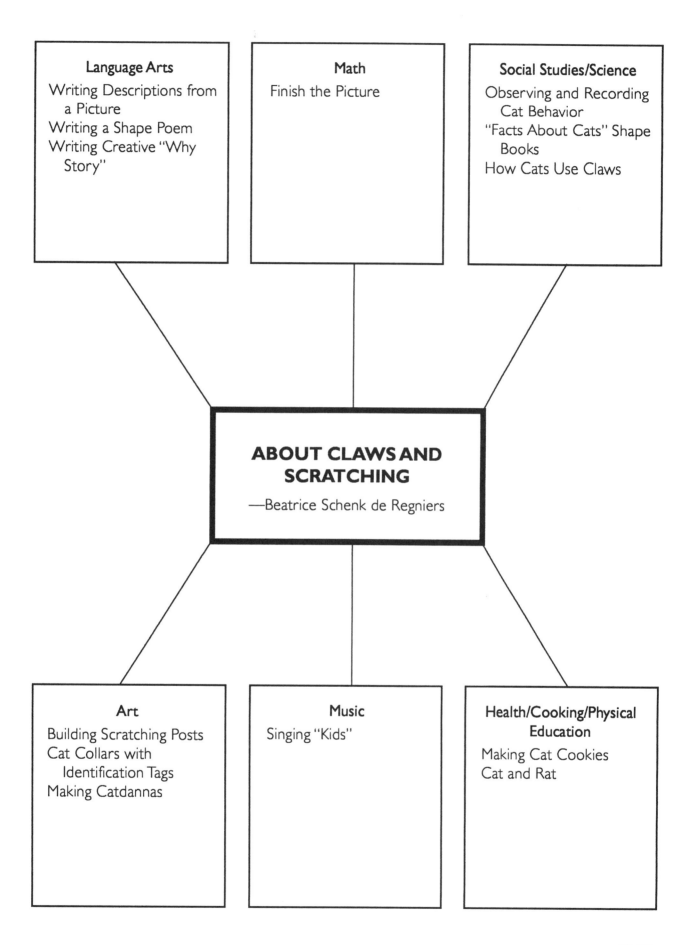

Language Arts

Writing Descriptions from a Picture
Writing a Shape Poem
Writing Creative "Why Story"

Math

Finish the Picture

Social Studies/Science

Observing and Recording Cat Behavior
"Facts About Cats" Shape Books
How Cats Use Claws

ABOUT CLAWS AND SCRATCHING

—Beatrice Schenk de Regniers

Art

Building Scratching Posts
Cat Collars with Identification Tags
Making Catdannas

Music

Singing "Kids"

Health/Cooking/Physical Education

Making Cat Cookies
Cat and Rat

About Claws and Scratching

The following suggestions can be used with the poem "About Claws and Scratching." Select the activities that are most appropriate for the needs and age level of the children in the class.

Introducing the Poem

1. Ask the children if they know any Mother Goose rhymes about animals, especially cats, such as "Pussy Cat, Pussy Cat" or "Hey Diddle, Diddle." Encourage volunteers to recite the rhymes for the class.

2. Read the title of the poem "About Claws and Scratching." Discuss what animal or animals the poem might be about based on the title. Give each child drawing paper. Encourage the children to draw the animal they think the poem is about. Invite the children to share their drawings with the class. List the names of the animals drawn on the chalkboard.

3. Share biographical information about the poet, Beatrice Schenk de Regniers. Refer to the Poet Bookmarks section on page 265. The bookmarks can be duplicated for the children or used to share information about each poet while studying his or her poem.

Shared Listening and Reading

1. Display a copy of the poem on a chart or transparency. Read the poem aloud, asking the children to listen carefully to find out what the poem is about. Give the children an opportunity to make comments. Then, return to the children 's predictions on the chalkboard. Ask the children if there are any other animals on the list that would fit the description of the animal in the poem—4 soft paws, and 5 sharp claws used for scratching.

2. Point out the words *latch, proper,* and *manicure* in the poem and discuss the meaning of each word.

3. Read aloud the question the poet asks at the end of the poem— "Hmmm. Did I make a mistake when I counted claws?" Have the children share their ideas and those who own cats can count and report back to the class. Suggest children also check nonfiction books to find more information about cats. (Note: All cats have five toes,

plus a thumb-like digit called a *dewclaw* on each front foot. Each hind foot has four toes, each equipped with claws.)

4. Display a copy of the poem on a chart or transparency. Have the children read the poem several times, selecting ideas from the General Suggestions for Listening to and Reading the Poems on page 6.

Beyond Listening and Reading Activities

Writing Descriptions from a Picture

Distribute drawing paper and suggest that children who own pet cats draw pictures of their cats. Invite the children who do not have cats to draw pictures of cats they would like to have. Encourage children to be detailed in their drawings. After drawings are completed, randomly distribute them so each child has a cat picture. Have each child write a description of the cat, using only information provided from the drawing. Ask volunteers to read their descriptions aloud, and show the pictures. Discuss how well the written descriptions matched the pictures.

Writing a Shape Poem

Sketch on a poster or on the chalkboard a simple outline of a cat. Then lead the class in composing a free-verse shape poem. First, have children brainstorm words and phrases which come to mind when they hear the word *cat,* such as cuddly, soft, playful, furry, drinking milk, sleeping, purring, and meowing. Record the words on the chalkboard. As a class, select words and phrases from the list on the chalkboard, and then write a poem about cats. Arrange the words around the outline of a cat picture. Encourage children to draw their own pictures of a cat and then write their own shape poems.

Writing Creative "Why" Stories

Read aloud one or more fictional stories which explain certain physical features or behaviors of animals, such as Rudyard Kipling's *How the Camel Got His Hump.* Invite the children to make up fictional "why" stories entitled, "Why Cats Scratch." As a class, brainstorm possible ideas before the children begin writing. For younger children, you may want to develop a group story.

Finish the Picture

Duplicate and distribute the reproducible on page 101. Ask the children to follow the directions on the reproducible and finish the cat picture. You may wish to display a copy of the poem, "About Claws and Scratching."

Observing and Recording Cat Behavior

If possible, make arrangements to have a pet cat in the classroom for a day. Be aware of any pet allergies your class may have. (Or, ask a child's parent to video tape his or her cat.) Display a chart on the chalkboard with headings, such as How the Cat Looks; What the Cat Does; and How the Cat Moves. As a class, discuss the different cat behaviors observed. Record the children's observations on the chart.

"Facts About Cats" Shape Books

As a class, discuss different facts the children know about cats, such as cats purr when they are happy, cats scratch on furniture or scratching posts to sharpen their claws, and so on. Draw handwriting lines on the cat shape on page 102 before reproducing. Give each child a copy of the reproducible. Have children cut out the cat shape. Ask children to write two or more facts about cats on the lines. Bind all the pages together into a booklet. Make a cat-shaped cover out of construction paper. Title the booklet "Facts About Cats." Place the booklet in the classroom library.

How Cats Use Claws

Discuss why cats have claws, such as for catching prey, climbing trees and other objects, defending themselves against other animals or fighting.

Building Scratching Posts

Show the class a picture of a cat's scratching post. Discuss what the scratching post is used for. Have the children who own cats describe some of the different types of scratching posts and the materials they are made from. Divide the class into small groups. Invite the groups to build creative scratching posts using cardboard tubes, boxes, fabric scraps, carpet remnants, and so on. After the scratching posts are finished, encourage each group to create a "catchy name" for their scratching post, and write down at least two of its special features. Provide an opportunity for each group to display their scratching post and read the information they wrote about it.

Cat Collars with Identification Tags

Discuss the fact that pet cats need to wear a collar with an identification tag in case they get lost. Invite the children to make cat collars. Use pinking shears to cut strips of fabric long enough to fit around an average size cat's neck. Cut enough Velcro squares for each child to have two. Help children glue one Velcro square to the underside of one end of the fabric strip and the other square to the right side of the material. Encourage the children to decorate the collars with sequins, glitter, and small buttons. Provide laundry tags for the children to make cat identification tags. Have each child write his or her cat's name on the tag. If there is room, have the children include their home phone numbers on the tags, too. Attach the tags to the collars with yarn.

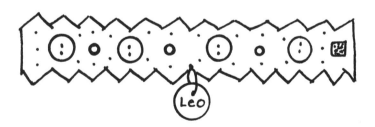

Making Catdannas

Have the children make "catdannas" or bandannas for cats. Provide calico fabric triangles approximately 12 inches at the base and 6 inches from the vertex to the base of the scarf. Fold the long flat edge down three times, approximately 1/2 inch each time. Glue pieces of Velcro to the ends of the "catdannas." Have the children take the "catdannas" home.

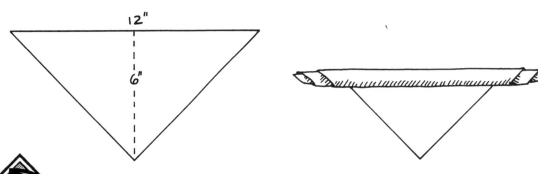

Singing

Teach the children the song "Kids" from *The Sesame Street Book of Songs.*

Making Cat Cookies

Make cat cookies using packaged sugar cookie dough and chocolate and pink tube frosting. Slice the cookie dough into $1/4$-inch slices. Cut several slices into four parts for cat ears. Press two ears on each cookie. Bake cookies on cookie sheets according to the directions on the cookie dough packages. After the baked cookies are cool, invite children to add eyes and whiskers with chocolate frosting. Use the pink frosting for the nose, tongue, and to outline the inner part of the ears.

Cat and Rat

Teach the children the game "Cat and Rat." Choose one player as the Cat and one for the Rat. Have the other children form a circle with clasped hands. The Rat stands inside the circle and the Cat stands outside the circle. The game begins with the Cat saying, "I am the Cat." The Rat says, "I am the Rat." The Cat says, "I will catch you," and the Rat replies, "You can't!" The words *"You can't"* signals the beginning of the chase. The Cat tries to get inside the circle, and the Rat tries to evade the Cat. Both of the children run in and out of the circle, but the other players help the Rat by raising their arms to let the Rat run under. The children in the circle try to stop the Cat's efforts by keeping him or her from breaking through the circle, either in or out. When the Rat is caught, the Rat joins the circle, the Cat then becomes the Rat, and a new Cat is chosen.

Finish the Cat

Name _____

Directions: Follow the directions.

1. Draw the paws on the cat.
2. Draw the toes on the cat.
3. Draw the claws on the cat's toes.
4. Count the claws. How many claws did you draw? _____

Cat Shape

Name _____

Directions: Cut out the cat shape. Write two or more facts about cats on the lines inside the cat.

Pathways to Poetry: Poetry Fun for Grades 1-3 © 1994 Fearon Teacher Aids

Suggested Books

Themed Poetry Books

Cats Are Cats. Nancy Larrick. New York, NY: Philomel, 1988.

Cat Poems. Myra Cohn Livingston. New York, NY: Holiday House, 1987.

Dog Poems. Myra Cohn Livingston. New York, NY: Holiday House, 1990.

A Dog's Life. Lee Bennett Hopkins. San Diego, CA: Harcourt Brace Jovanovich, 1983.

This Big Cat and Other Cat's I've Known. Beatrice Schenk de Regniers. New York, NY: Crown, 1985.

Books for Read-Aloud and Independent Reading

Can I Keep Him? Steven Kellogg. New York, NY: Dial, 1971. A small boy longs for a pet and companionship, and fantasizes bringing home all sorts of pets—dog, cat, deer, tiger, and so on—only to be refused permission by his mom. He finally settles for a two-legged friend, the new boy next door.

Cats. Cynthia Overbeck. Minneapolis, MN: Lerner, 1983. In this Learner Natural Science book, physical characteristics, habits, and behaviors of cats are described.

Clifford, the Big Red Dog. Norma Bridwell. New York, NY: Scholastic, 1988. Emily Elizabeth describes her experiences with her very big, very red dog named Clifford.

A Dog's Body. Joanna Cole. New York, NY: William Morrow, 1986. The physical characteristics of dogs and dog behaviors are described.

The Dog Who Had Kittens. Polly M. Robertus. New York, NY: Holiday House, 1991. A humorous story about Baxter, a basset hound, who becomes a parent for seven kittens.

Emma's Kitten. Nigel Snell. New York, NY: Barron's, 1989. The book describes the care of a kitten, such as proper feeding, bedding, and exercise as well as offering suggestions on handling, grooming, and hygiene.

Henry and Mudge and the Happy Cat. Cynthia Rylant. New York, NY: Bradbury, 1990. In this book (part of the *Henry and Mudge* series), a poor lost shabby cat moves in with Henry and his family and adopts Mudge.

How the Camel Got His Hump. Rudyard Kipling. New York, NY: Peter Bedrick Books, 1985. The tale of how the camel got his big hump is told.

A Pup Grows Up. Sally Foster. New York, NY: Dodd, Mead & Co., 1985. Fifteen different breeds of dogs are described in text and photographs. Information is presented about puppies as well as adult dogs.

Roy's Puppy. Nigel Snell. New York, NY: Barron's, 1989. This book includes how to care for a puppy as well as suggestions for handling, training, and grooming.

Sneakers: Seven Stories About a Cat. Margaret Wise Brown. New York, NY: HarperCollins, 1992. Sneakers, the inky black cat, takes the reader on seven exciting adventures.

The Stupids Die. Harry Allard. Boston, MA: Houghton Mifflin, 1981. In this whimsical book, the Stupid family believes they are dead when the lights go out. Other titles in the *Stupids* series include *The Stupids Step Out,* and *The Stupids Have a Ball.*

The Third-Story Cat. Leslie Baker. Boston, MA: Little, Brown, 1987. Alice, a third-story apartment cat longs to explore the world outside. She escapes one day, and on her tour of the city with a streetwise cat has a frightening experience which sends her rushing home to stay. At least for the time being.

When Cats Dream. Dave Pilkey. New York, NY: Orchard Books, 1991. In the opening pages of this fictional book, cats when they are awake are illustrated in black and white. Vibrant colors are used to illustrate cat's dreams with many unusual cat activities.

Who Says a Dog Goes Bow-Wow? Hank De Zutter. New York, NY: Doubleday, 1993. Animal sounds in different languages are presented in this delightful book.

Fears and
Feelings

Two Wheels

I told you I won't. It's too hard.
I told you I can't. It's too hard.
Didn't I tell you?

My feet, they won't reach.
My hands, they won't steer.
It's too hard.

Watch out—I'm tipping.
Don't let go—I'm falling.
Please: I give up.

Not so fast, not so fast.
I don't like this.
Stop stop stop stop.

Hey, I can't stop.
Hey, I'm riding, I'm riding.
Hey hey hey hey.

Did you see me?
What did I tell you?
It was easy.

—Richard J. Margolis

Pathways to Poetry: Poetry Fun for Grades 1-3 © 1994 Fearon Teacher Aids

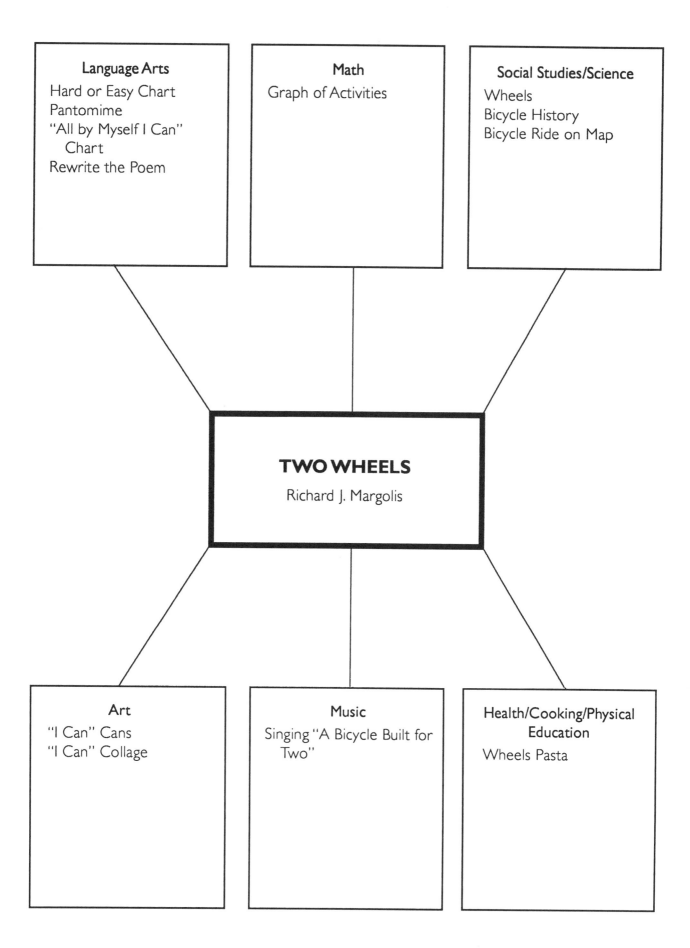

Language Arts

Hard or Easy Chart
Pantomime
"All by Myself I Can"
    Chart
Rewrite the Poem

Math

Graph of Activities

Social Studies/Science

Wheels
Bicycle History
Bicycle Ride on Map

TWO WHEELS

Richard J. Margolis

Art

"I Can" Cans
"I Can" Collage

Music

Singing "A Bicycle Built for Two"

Health/Cooking/Physical Education

Wheels Pasta

107

Two Wheels

The following suggestions can be used with the poem "Two Wheels."
Select the activities that are most appropriate for the needs and age level
of the children in the class.

Introducing the Poem

1. Ask the children how many of them have bicycles or have access to
   bicycles. Encourage the children to discuss what it was like to learn to
   ride a bicycle. Have those children who do not know how to ride a
   bike, describe something else they learned to do that was difficult at
   first.

2. As a class, discuss how it feels to learn to do something new, such as
   riding a bike, playing the piano, and so on. Record the children's
   responses on the chalkboard. Then, discuss how it feels to finally learn
   how to do something. Point out that learning something new is sometimes hard at first but becomes easier and fun with practice.

3. Share biographical information about the poet, Richard J. Margolis.
   Refer to the Poet Bookmarks section on page 265. The bookmarks
   can be duplicated for the children or used to share information about
   each poet while studying his or her poem.

Shared Listening and Reading

1. Read the poem aloud. Then display a copy of the poem on a chart or
   transparency and ask the children to follow along.

2. Read the poem a second time, paragraph by paragraph. Invite the
   children to join in. Read the poem a third time, encouraging the
   children to add expression to their voices as they read.

3. Ask the children to identify whom they think the child in the poem is
   talking to, such as a parent, older brother or sister, and so on. Encourage the children to share who taught them how to ride bikes.

4. Ask the children to identify the word "Hey" as the point in the poem
   when the child starts having fun.

LANGUAGE ARTS

Hard or Easy Chart

Ask the children to think of something they learned to do that used to be hard, but now it's easy, such as reading, swimming, and so on. Have each child write and illustrate the following sentence:

_____ used to be hard, but now it's easy.

Bind all the pages together into a class book.

Pantomime

Have the children name a special skill they have learned. Invite volunteers to come up in front of the room and pantomime one of the activities or skills mentioned, or others not previously named. Encourage the class to guess the activity being pantomimed.

"All by Myself I Can" Chart

Duplicate and distribute the reproducible on page 112. Read the directions with the children. Have the children identify the skills or abilities they can do by themselves, with help, and not yet. Encourage the children to fill out the chart with the help of their parents. After the charts have been returned, discuss the many skills the children can do by themselves.

Rewrite the Poem

Discuss other activities the child in the poem could be learning how to do. Record the children's responses on the chalkboard. Have the children rewrite the poem using other sports or activities in place of bike riding. Point out that the children can leave the first and last stanzas unchanged.

MATH

Graph of Activities

Duplicate and distribute the reproducible on page 113. Take a poll of what kinds of activities the children like to do, such as playing soccer, swimming, reading books, and so on. Record the activities on the chalkboard. Make a large graph on the chalkboard similar to the reproducible on page 113. On the left-hand side of the graph, write five of the children's favorite activities. On the bottom of the graph write in the numerals up to 20. Give each child a sticky note. Ask children to place the sticky note in the row for their favorite activities. Count the number of squares in each column. Encourage the children to use the reproducible to make their own graphs.

Wheels

Share nonfiction books with the class about trucks, cars, motorcycles, and so on. Encourage the children to name vehicles or machines with 1, 2, 3, 4, or 6 wheels. Record the children's ideas on the chalkboard. Ask why vehicles have different numbers of wheels. Make a class chart of vehicles with 1, 2, 3, 4, or 6 wheels. Encourage the children to share any special information about the vehicles with the class.

Bicycle History

Tell the children a little about the history of the bicycle. In 1791, in Paris, the Comte (Count) de Sivrac sat on a wooden hobby horse-like creation and propelled it with his feet(hanging down on the ground) like a scooter. In 1839, a Scot named Kirkpatrick Macmillan made the first bicycle propelled by leg power without the feet touching the ground. If possible, find pictures of the early bicycles in encyclopedias and share them with the children. Provide nonfiction books about the early bicycles for the children to look at. Encourage children to share any information they learn about bicycles with the class.

Bicycle Ride on Map

Duplicate and distribute the reproducible on page 114. Have each child color and then cut out the bicycle at the bottom of the page. Explain to the children that they are going to use the bicycle to follow your directions on the map. Introduce the directional words *north, south, east,* and *west.* Point out the diagram in the corner of the reproducible map with the arrows pointing in the directions of *north, south, east* and *west.* First, ask the children to place their bikes on the word *Start* at the top of the map. Then, instruct the children to move the bikes around the street map using the words *north, south, east,* and *west* as part of the directions. You may want to make a transparency of the reproducible and demonstrate how to move the bicycle using an overhead projector.

"I Can" Cans

Have the children bring in containers with plastic lids, such as potato chip cans, coffee cans, and so on. Paste a strip of paper around each

110

child's can that says "I CAN." Have an adult helper use a knife to cut a slit in the lid for each child. Every time the child masters a skill, he or she can write it on a slip of paper and put the paper in the "I CAN" can. Every few weeks, encourage the children to open their cans to review their accomplishments.

"I Can" Collage

Encourage each child to make a collage of activities or skills he or she can do. Give each child a piece of construction paper. Invite the children to cut out magazine pictures or draw pictures of things they can do. Have the children arrange the pictures into a collage. Display the collages on the classroom wall. Discuss the different activities the children have included in their collages.

Singing

Teach the children the song "A Bicycle Built for Two" from the cassette tape, *Disney Children's Favorites, Vol. 1.*

Wheels Pasta

Show the children uncooked pasta wheels. Cook the pasta wheels and serve with spaghetti sauce.

All By Myself, I Can

Name _____

Directions: Fill in the chart with the help of a parent. Add three more activities you can do by yourself.

ALL BY MYSELF I CAN

	ALWAYS	SOMETIMES	NOT YET/SOON
Dress Myself			
Set the Table			
Make Breakfast			
Clean My Room			
Take out the Garbage			
Make My Bed			
Wash the Dishes			

Pathways to Poetry: Poetry Fun for Grades 1-3 © 1994 Fearon Teacher Aids

Name: _____

Directions: Follow your teacher's directions for making a graph.

Activities

Number of Children: 1 2 3 4 5 6 7 8 9 10 11 12 13 14 15 16 17 18 19 20

Favorite Activities of Our Class

Pathways to Poetry: Poetry Fun for Grades 1-3 © 1994 Fearon Teacher Aids

Bicycle Ride on Map

Name _____

Directions: Cut out the bicycle at the bottom of the page. Use the bicycle to follow your teacher's directions.

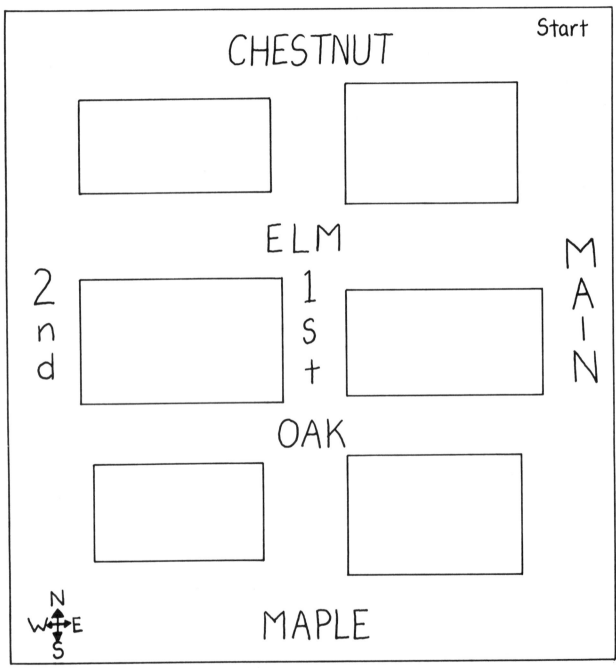

Start

CHESTNUT

ELM

2nd   1st

OAK

MAIN

MAPLE

N W E S

Pathways to Poetry: Poetry Fun for Grades 1–3 © 1994 Fearon Teacher Aids

Nobody Loves Me

Somedays,
nobody loves me
so I go down the names
I know:
    I hate Martha
    I hate James
    I hate Selma
    I hate Jo.
Nobody likes me,
that I know.

Somedays,
everyone loves me
so I go down the names
I know:
    I love Martha
    I love James
    I love Selma
    I love Jo.
Everyone loves me,
I know so!

—Charlotte Zolotow

Pathways to Poetry: Poetry Fun for Grades 1-3 © 1994 Fearon Teacher Aids

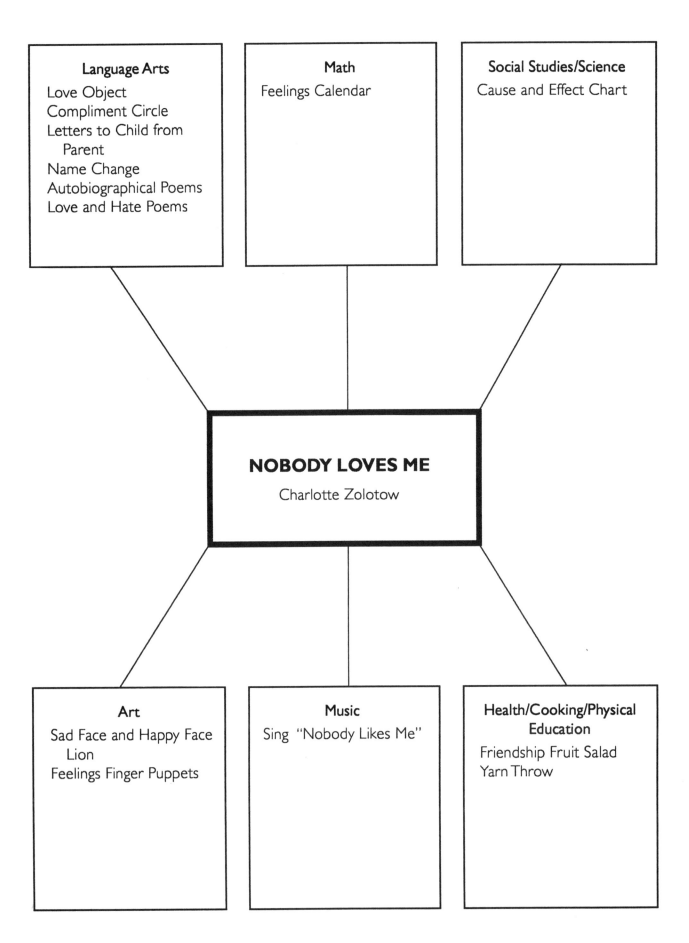

Language Arts

Love Object
Compliment Circle
Letters to Child from
    Parent
Name Change
Autobiographical Poems
Love and Hate Poems

Math

Feelings Calendar

Social Studies/Science

Cause and Effect Chart

NOBODY LOVES ME

Charlotte Zolotow

Art

Sad Face and Happy Face
    Lion
Feelings Finger Puppets

Music

Sing "Nobody Likes Me"

**Health/Cooking/Physical
Education**

Friendship Fruit Salad
Yarn Throw

Nobody Loves Me

The following suggestions can be used with the poem "Nobody Loves Me." Select the activities that are most appropriate for the needs and age level of the children in the class.

Introducing the Poem

1. Ask the children how they feel on good days and bad days. Explain that everybody has good days and bad days. Point out that on good days it is easy to feel good towards others and that we are loved, but on bad days it is easy to feel bad towards others and that nobody loves us. Encourage the children to share their experiences with good or bad days.

2. Ask the children to tell what makes them lovable. Then give each child a strip of paper. Have the children copy and complete the sentence, "I am very lovable because _____." Have the children write the completed sentence on the strip of paper and place it on a chart. Ask volunteers to read the sentences to the class.

3. Read *The Important Book* by Margaret Wise Brown aloud to the class. Discuss what the children think of the book. Emphasize to the children that the most important thing about them is that they are unique and one of a kind.

4. Share biographical information about the poet, Charlotte Zolotow. Refer to the Poet Bookmarks section on page 265. The bookmarks can be duplicated for the children or used to share information about each poet while studying his or her poem.

Shared Listening and Reading

1. Read the poem aloud. Encourage the children to comment on the poem. Display a copy of the poem on a chart or transparency. Read the poem again several times, selecting ideas from the General Suggestions for Listening to and Reading the Poems on page 6.

2. Point to each of the lines with names. Encourage the children to substitute the names of classmates, family members, or friends for the names mentioned in the poem. Ask several volunteers to read their

names mentioned in the poem. Ask several volunteers to read their new versions of the poem.

3. Have the children think of synonyms for the words *love* and *hate*. Explain that the word *synonym* refers to words that have the same or nearly the same meanings. As a class, list words that could be used in place of the words *love* and *hate*. Choose words to substitute in the poem. Then read the new version of the poem aloud. Ask the children if using different words changed the feeling of the poem.

Beyond Listening and Reading Activities

Love Object

Have each child bring to class an object that makes him or her feel loved or special. Tell children to bring their special objects in paper bags. As each child holds up his or her paper bag, have the other children guess the object in the bag. The children can only ask questions that can be answered with "yes" or "no" answers by the owner.

Compliment Circle

Discuss what it means to compliment other people. Explain that a compliment is an expression of respect and kindness. Have the children practice giving compliments to each other. Then give each child a colored square of paper. Have one child begin by complimenting another. The child who is complimented puts his or her colored paper on the floor to indicate that she or he has received a compliment. You need not go in order, but each child must give and receive one compliment. This activity is best conducted in a circle.

Letter to Child from Parent

Duplicate and distribute the reproducible on page 122. Send the reproducible home with each child for his or her parents to complete. Explain to the children that the letters their parents write are special and they will have an opportunity to share them with their classmates.

Name Change

Ask children to create an adopted name that describes their most outstanding quality. Share a name you might adopt for yourself. Point out that this is a common practice among many Native Americans.

Give each child name tags in a star shape to make an adopted name tag to wear for a day. Encourage everyone to call the children by their adopted names.

Autobiographical Poems

Have the children write autobiographical poems using the outline below. Have children share their completed poems with the class.

Name (Elizabeth)
Son/Daughter of (Susan and Len)
Born on (August 22, 1984)
In the state/country of (New Jersey)
Sister/Brother of (Eric and Giles)
Friend of (Samantha)
Likes to (swim)
Is happiest when (skiing)
Wants to be a (zoo keeper)
Is lovable because (she is friendly)

Love and Hate Poems

As a class, help the children write their own poems using the following sentence. I love _____, but I really hate _____. Have the children write the sentence and fill in the blank with their own preferences for each category below:

pets
vegetables
games
desserts
main dishes
hobbies
books
kind of music
sports

Feelings Calendar

Duplicate and distribute the reproducible on page 123. Ask each child to fill in the feelings calendar for a month. Have the children record how they feel at the end of each day with a happy face, a face without a smile or a frown, or a sad face. As a class, discuss what made the day a good day or a bad day. Encourage the children to discuss experiences which affected the outcome of the day for them. At the end of the month, discuss the results from the calendar activity.

Cause and Effect Chart

Discuss with the class how our feelings can affect how we act or react to situations. Create a group cause and effect chart for feelings and actions. On the chalkboard or a large sheet of chart paper, write feelings, such as happy, mad, sad, and silly, down the left-hand side. On the right-hand side for each feeling write possible actions that might occur because of feelings. The chart can be used on an on-going basis by adding additional actions.

Feelings	Actions
Happy	smile at a friend
Mad	scream into my pillow
Sad	hide in my room
Silly	tell a funny story

Sad Face and Happy Face Lion

Give each child a small paper plate, a brad, and a sturdy handle made out of cardboard. Have each child draw a lion face on the paper plate (see illustration) that can be turned one direction to be sad and the opposite direction to be happy. Color the bumpy edge around the paper plate to look like a lion's mane. Attach the handle to the paper plate with the brad. Encourage the children to turn the paper plate to make a sad or happy lion.

Feelings Finger Puppets

To create feelings finger puppets, give each child five self-stick circles of five different colors. Instruct children to draw a face on each circle showing five different emotions, such as happy, sad, silly, scared, mad, and content (showing no emotion). Have the children stick one sticker on each finger. Make up a simple story to tell the children.

Encourage the children to hold up the finger puppet showing how they might feel if they were the character in the story.

happy   sad   content   silly   scared

Singing

Teach the children the song "Nobody Likes Me" from *The Fireside Book of Fun and Game Songs.*

Friendship Fruit Salad

Send a note home to parents asking their child to bring one of the following ingredients for the friendship salad—banana, apple, canned pineapple slices, oranges, and walnuts. Divide the class into small groups. Have each salad-group use butter knives to slice the apples into quarters, cut the bananas into 1/4-inch slices, and chop the pineapple slices into chunks. Have the children divide the oranges into sections, and crack the walnuts into halves. Combine all the ingredients in a big bowl and serve.

Yarn Throw

Use a great big ball of yarn as the children sit in a circle. Explain that as the ball is thrown to each child, he or she should hold on to a piece of yarn before throwing it. Give the ball of yarn to one child and have him or her gently throw it to another child. Continue throwing and unwinding the yarn until each child is woven into the friendship web.

Letter to Child from Parent

Dear Parent(s) or Guardian:

We are reading poems about feelings. One of the poems is called "Nobody Loves Me" by Charlotte Zolotow. It describes a child who sometimes feels that nobody loves him or her and other times he or she feels that everybody loves him or her. Please use this form to write a letter to your child. Seal the letter in an envelope and send it to school. Your child will open and read his or her own letter aloud in class. Thank you for participating in this activity.

	Dear
	I am writing to tell you how much you are loved. The three things I love
	most about you are:
	1.
	2.
	3.
	I am most proud of you when
	Some of the things you do well are:
	1.
	2.
	3.
	I am so happy that you are my child.
	Love,

Pathways to Poetry: Poetry Fun for Grades 1-3 © 1994 Fearon Teacher Aids

Feelings Calendar

Name _____

Directions: Draw a happy face, a face without a smile or frown, or a sad face at the end of each day.

Monday	Tuesday	Wednesday	Thursday	Friday	Saturday	Sunday

Mean

I wonder why
I feel so mean
Was it something I ate?
Maybe a mean bean?

I just yelled at Mom,
Stuck my tongue out at Lee,
I'd pinch the baby
If no one could see.

He's lying there looking
So sweet and so nice,
While I'm full to the top
With sin and vice.

I just stepped on an ant,
I'm looking for more.
And some mud to track in
On Mom's clean floor.

I've been good for days.
At least fifteen;
And it sure feels good
To feel this mean.

—Lois Simmie

Pathways to Poetry: Poetry Fun for Grades 1-3 © © 1994 Fearon Teacher Aids

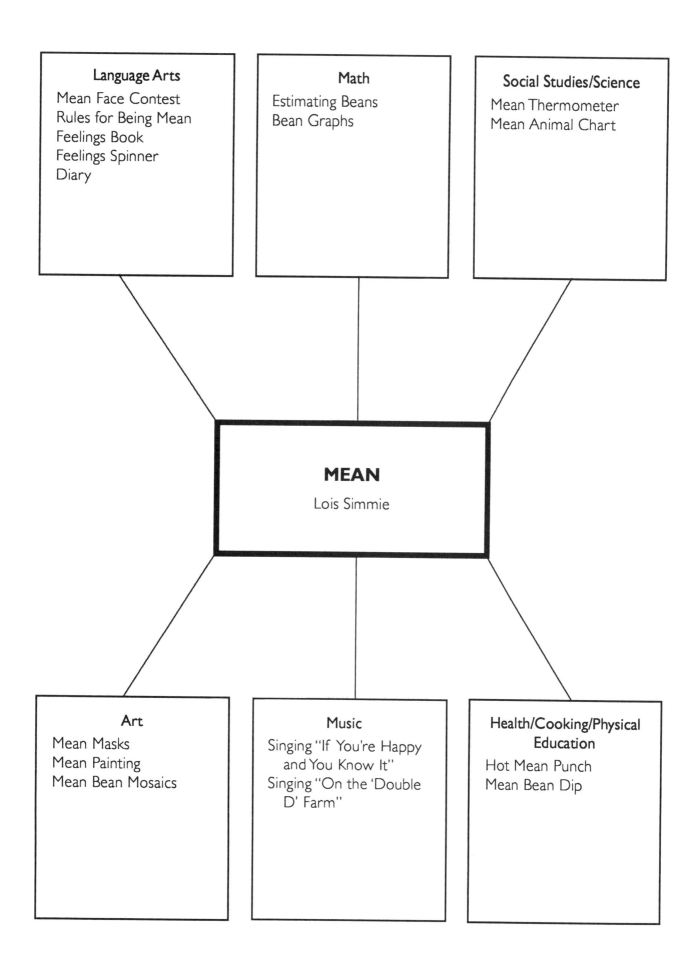

Language Arts

Mean Face Contest
Rules for Being Mean
Feelings Book
Feelings Spinner
Diary

Math

Estimating Beans
Bean Graphs

Social Studies/Science

Mean Thermometer
Mean Animal Chart

MEAN

Lois Simmie

Art

Mean Masks
Mean Painting
Mean Bean Mosaics

Music

Singing "If You're Happy
and You Know It"
Singing "On the 'Double
D' Farm"

**Health/Cooking/Physical
Education**

Hot Mean Punch
Mean Bean Dip

Mean

The following suggestions can be used with the poem "Mean." Select the activities that are most appropriate for the needs and age level of the children in the class.

Introducing the Poem

1. Have the children make the meanest faces they can. Ask the class what the word *mean* means. Have the class name other words that could be used instead of the word *mean*. Record the children's responses on the chalkboard. Introduce the words *sin* and *vice* in the poem's context.

2. Have the children name and describe some behaviors which they consider mean. Encourage children to share the situations under which these mean behaviors took place.

3. Discuss how it feels to act mean. Then ask the children how they feel when someone is mean to them.

4. Share biographical information about the poet, Lois Simmie. Refer to the Poet Bookmarks section on page 265. The bookmarks can be duplicated for the children or used to share information about each poet while studying his or her poem.

Shared Listening and Reading

1. Read the poem to the children. Encourage general comments about the poem.

2. Read the poem again. Ask the children to recall from the poem the mean things the child did. Record the list on the chalkboard. Display a copy of the poem on a chart or transparency. Read the poem together and have the children add to the list any missing items.

3. Have the children read the poem stanza by stanza. Ask the class questions about the poem, such as:

   Is there really something called a mean bean?
   What foods could make a person feel mean?
   What family members are mentioned in verse 2?
   What words in verse 3 describe the baby?
   What mean things are mentioned in verse 4?

4. Using a copy of the poem on a chart or transparency, practice reading the poem several times. Select ideas from the General Suggestions for Listening to and Reading the Poems on page 6.

Beyond Listening and Reading Activities

Mean Face Contest

Hold a mean face contest. Have each child make the meanest face he or she can. Give each child a ballot. Then invite each child to vote for the three meanest faces. Tally the votes. The three children with the highest number of votes win.

Rules for Being Mean

Brainstorm with the children ways in which people are mean to others. Divide the children into groups and give each group paper and crayons. Instruct each group to pick one of the ideas, write the mean rule, and then illustrate it. Have each group show the rest of the class their picture and read the rule. Next, ask groups to use the backside of their papers to change their rules into positive rules and illustrate them. For example, instead of "Make fun of people" the children could write "Say kind words to our friends." Again, have the groups share their rules and illustrations.

Feelings Book

Distribute a piece of paper folded in thirds to each child. Instruct the children to cut out faces from magazines that show different emotions. Ask children to paste the top half of the face on the top third of the paper and the bottom half of the face on the middle third of the paper. On the bottom third, the children should write a sentence stating a situation that the feeling comes from. Bind the pages together by punching holes and using yarn. Cut the book into thirds. The children can flip the pages to create different faces for the same situation, and different situations for the same face.

Feelings Spinner

Use a blank game spinner or make a large spinner. Label the sections on the spinner with feelings, such as angry, tired, sad, lonely, scared, nervous, mean, and so on. Have each child spin the arrow, name the feeling, and describe a situation that would make him or her feel that way.

Diary

Duplicate and distribute the reproducible on page 132. Set aside a regular time each day for the children to record in their diaries one nice thing and one mean or unkind thing they did that day. Have the children keep their diaries for 15 days. Throughout the activity, have children share their entries daily. Younger children may need a new page each day and record for a shorter time period.

Estimating Beans

Place dried beans, such as kidney or garbanzo beans in a glass jar. Have each child estimate the number of beans in the jar and write down his or her guess on a piece of paper. After all the children have made their estimates, count the beans by tens. Add the groups of tens and the leftover beans together to see whose estimate was the closest.

Bean Graphs

Divide the class into groups. Give each group a variety of dried beans in a small plastic bag, graph paper, and glue. Instruct the groups to first, sort the beans into groups by kind of bean. Have the groups glue the beans directly on the graph paper with one bean in each square to make a 3-dimensional bean bar graph. When the children are finished, have the groups share and interpret their graphs.

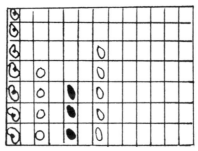

Mean Thermometer

Duplicate and distribute the reproducible on page 133. Have each child cut out and construct his or her own thermometer by following these directions:

1. Cut the slits at the top and the bottom of the thermometer.
2. Color one strip red and the other strip white.
3. Cut out the strips.
4. Glue one end of the white strip to one end of the red strip.
5. Carefully insert the white strip through the bottom slit of the thermometer and then through the top slit.
6. Gently slide the strip up and down to show how you feel.

Explain that a thermometer measures the temperature of the environment around the thermometer. Talk about the measurement of degrees and relate this to the heat measures on the thermometer. When people get angry their body temperatures rise and they get hot. The Mean Thermometer can be used to measure how the children are feeling, such as a cool temperature shows you are happy or a hot temperature shows you are angry, frustrated, or feeling mean. Provide time each day for the children to show on their thermometers how many degrees of <u>mean</u> they feel that day. Have the children share the reasons why.

Mean Animal Chart

Explain that animals, like people, have ways of showing they are angry or upset. Write the following animals on the chalkboard. Ask the children to identify how each animal expresses its anger:

dogs	growl
cats	hiss, scratch
horses	kick, bite
snake	hiss, bite, rattle
birds	peck, dive bomb
skunks	sprays scent

Mean Masks

Collect or have each child bring in a large, paper grocery bag. Encourage the children to decorate the bags with mean faces. Have the children cut out eye, nose and mouth holes. Have the children wear their mean masks for a reading of the poem "Mean."

Mean Painting

Show the class a picture painted only in reds, blacks, purples, and oranges. Discuss how certain colors are often associated with emotions, such as blue represents calm and red represents anger. Provide children with red, black, purple, and orange tempera paint and painting paper. Encourage each child to paint a picture showing a mean feeling.

Mean Bean Mosaics

Divide the class into small groups. Give each group six kinds of dried beans separated into containers, such as margarine tubs. Provide cardboard backing for the mosaics. Have each child draw a mean face on the cardboard. Instruct children to arrange the beans in a mosaic of a mean face. Glue the beans in place. Once the mosaics are dry, display them around the classroom.

Singing

Teach the children the song, "If You're Happy and You Know It." Substitute the word *nasty* for the word *happy* in the song, and make up new verses and actions. The children may also enjoy singing "On the 'Double D' Farm" from *1002 The Complete Children's Song Book.*

Hot Mean Punch

To make hot mean punch, use:

  2 quarts sweet cider
  2 quarts cranberry juice
  4 cinnamon sticks
  2 teaspoons allspice
  2 teaspoons whole cloves

1. Mix all ingredients in a large pot.
2. Bring the mixture to a boil. Keep the children away from the cooking area.
3. Simmer 20 minutes.
4. Remove the spices with a slotted spoon.
5. Then serve (makes 32 cups).

Mean Bean Dip

Follow this recipe to make mean bean dip:

   3 8-oz cans cooked garbanzo beans
   4 cloves minced garlic
   2 teaspoons salt
   juice from 3 lemons
   1 1/2 cups sesame seed paste (tahini)
   1/2 cup parsley
   black pepper
   bunch of celery cut into sticks for dipping

1. Combine all ingredients in a food processor.
2. Add water, if the dip is too thick.
3. Serve on paper plates with celery stick dippers.
   This recipe should make enough dip for an entire class.

Diary

Name _____

Directions: At the end of each day, write one nice thing and one mean thing you did today.

DAY	NICE THING	MEAN THING

Pathways to Poetry: Poetry Fun for Grades 1-3 © 1994 Fearon Teacher Aids

Mean Thermometer

Directions: Cut out the thermometer and the two strips. Follow your teacher's directions.

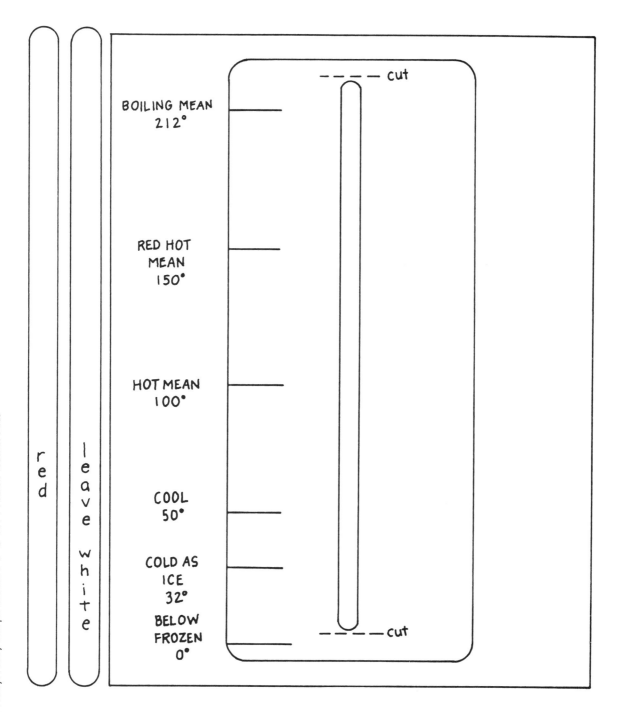

red

leave white

BOILING MEAN
212°

RED HOT
MEAN
150°

HOT MEAN
100°

COOL
50°

COLD AS
ICE
32°

BELOW
FROZEN
0°

- - - - cut

- - - - cut

A Magic Chant

If in the dark you're frightened,
Here's all you have to do.
Say: Igga bigga
Hunka bunka,
Dinka danka doo.

These words give you protection
From ghosts—and witches, too.
Say: Igga bigga
Hunka bunka,
Dinka danka doo.

So if at night a monster
Should whisper "I'll get you,"
Yell: Igga bigga
Hunka bunka
Dinka danka doo.

—Samuel Exler

Pathways to Poetry: Poetry Fun for Grades 1-3 © 1994 Fearon Teacher Aids

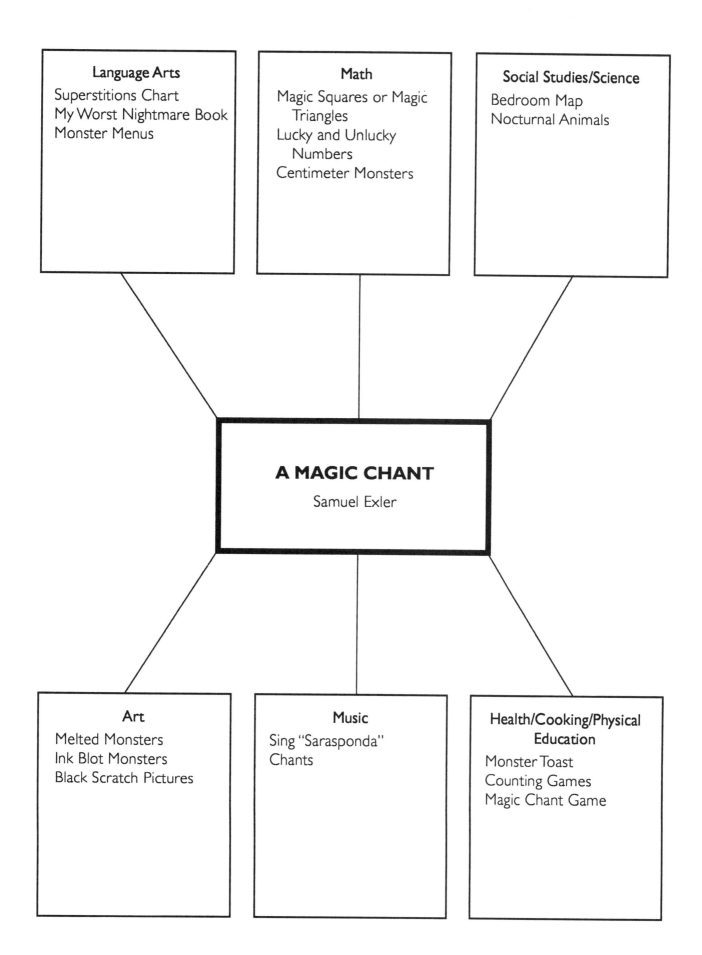

Language Arts
Superstitions Chart
My Worst Nightmare Book
Monster Menus

Math
Magic Squares or Magic Triangles
Lucky and Unlucky Numbers
Centimeter Monsters

Social Studies/Science
Bedroom Map
Nocturnal Animals

A MAGIC CHANT
Samuel Exler

Art
Melted Monsters
Ink Blot Monsters
Black Scratch Pictures

Music
Sing "Sarasponda"
Chants

Health/Cooking/Physical Education
Monster Toast
Counting Games
Magic Chant Game

135

A Magic Chant

The following suggestions can be used with the poem "A Magic Chant." Select the activities that are most appropriate for the needs and age level of the children in the class.

Introducing the Poem

1. Encourage the children to share what frightens them at night. Record the children's responses on the chalkboard. Ask the children if they have ever had a bad dream or nightmare. Invite volunteers to share their experiences.

2. Ask the children to tell where the things that frighten them appear to be, such as under the bed, in the closet, in the basement, and so on.

3. On the opposite side of the chalkboard, list the ways children cope with their fears, such as using a night light, listening to a pleasant bed-time story, having an older sibling or parent look under the bed, and so on.

4. Share biographical information about the poet, Samuel Exler. Refer to the Poet Bookmarks section on page 265. The bookmarks can be duplicated for the children or used to share information about each poet while studying his or her poem.

Shared Listening and Reading

1. Have the children listen as you read the poem aloud to discover something special to do when they are frightened. Encourage comments about the poem.

2. Reread the poem and invite the children to join in saying the chant.

3. Display a copy of the poem on a chart or transparency. Practice reading the poem together. Read the poem several times, selecting ideas from the General Suggestions for Listening to and Reading the Poems on page 6.

4. Discuss the meanings of the words *protection* and *frightened.* Ask the children to think of other words that could be used instead.

5. Ask volunteers to act out monsters while the class orally reads a chant from the poem. Discuss whether the children think saying magic chants would work if they were frightened.

Beyond Listening and Reading Activities

Superstitions Chart

Talk about different superstitions the children are familiar with, such as "step on a crack you'll break your mother's back" or "breaking a mirror means seven years of bad luck." As a class, make a chart of good luck and bad luck superstitions.

Good Luck	Bad Luck
rabbit's foot four leaf clover finding a penny	black cat walking under ladder stepping on a crack

My Worst Nightmare Book

Give each child a piece of cloud shaped paper. Ask children to draw pictures of their worst nightmares. Have each child write sentences about his or her nightmare. Bind the papers together into a class book titled "Our Worst Nightmares."

Monster Menus

Have children name all the possible monsters they can think of. Record the list on the chalkboard. Divide the class into small groups. Ask the groups to make up a list of monster foods by creating one item for each monster, such as King Kong Crunch, Godzilla Gravy, Dracula Donuts, Snake Shake, and Loch Ness Monster Meatballs. Invite each group to share their list with the rest of the class. Encourage older children to work in groups to create recipes for their monster dishes.

Magic Squares or Magic Triangles

Draw two Magic Squares and the Magic Triangle on the chalkboard (see illustration). Challenge the children to figure out what is magic about the squares and the triangle. The answers for the Magic Squares have been provided. Then divide the class into small groups.

Encourage the children to make their own magic squares or magic triangles.

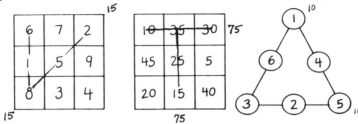

Lucky and Unlucky Numbers

Introduce the lucky numbers 7, 11, 21 and the unlucky number 13. You may want to introduce the term *triskaidekaphobia* (fear of the number 13). Have each child work with a partner to make up as many examples as possible that have the numbers 7, 11, 21, or 13 as the sum, difference, product, or quotient based on the children's abilities. If necessary, provide examples for the children, such as 4 + 3 = 7, 15 - 4 = 11, and so on.

Centimeter Monsters

Make a transparency of the reproducible on page 141. Duplicate and distribute the reproducible on page 141. Show the children how to draw the centimeter monster using the example on the reproducible. Measure the length of each line by counting the number of squares. Then write the number next to the line. Invite the children to create their own centimeter monsters. Encourage the children to share their monsters with the class.

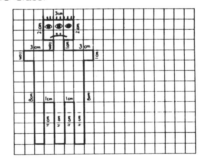

Bedroom Map

Duplicate and distribute the reproducible on page 142. Point out and discuss the example of the bedroom map at the top of the page. Ask each child to take the reproducible home and draw a map of his or her bedroom. Have the children draw an X on the spot in their bedrooms where they think they are most likely to find a monster. Ask the children to bring their maps back to school to share with the class.

Nocturnal Animals

Use a flashlight and a world globe to show the children why it gets dark only on one side of the earth at a time. Explain that the term *nocturnal* means active at night. Have the children make a list of animals that are nocturnal, such as opposums, raccoons, owls, and so on. Encourage older children to do research in nonfiction books about nocturnal animals.

Melted Monsters

Give each child a Styrofoam cup. Have the children use crayons to decorate their entire Styrofoam cups to look like monsters. Instruct the children to outline the key features of their monsters with black ballpoint ink or marker. Place the cups on a cookie sheet and broil in the oven for 3 to 5 seconds.

Ink Blot Monsters

In advance of this activity, put a variety of colors of paint in squeeze bottles. Give each child a piece of heavy drawing paper. Ask the children to fold their papers in half. Have children select paint colors and squeeze blobs of paint on their papers. Fold the papers in half and then unfold to reveal the ink blot monsters. Have children write about the monsters they created. (Younger children can use invented-spelling in their writing.) Invite all children to share their stories and show their monsters.

Black Scratch Pictures

Give each child a piece of drawing paper. Instruct children to first color the entire paper heavily with different colors of crayons (except black). Next, have children color over their entire pictures with black crayon. Lastly, using a paper clip, have the children scratch through the black crayon to make a multi-colored monster.

Singing

Teach the children the song "Sarasponda" from *The Fireside Book of Fun and Game Songs.*

Chants

Have the children as a class make up some chants. Record the chants on chart or chalkboard. Then divide the class into small groups. Have each group select a chant to perform for the entire class. Provide rhythm and percussion instruments for the groups to use in their performances.

Monster Toast

Prepare at least five colors of milk paint by adding several drops of food coloring to each $1/2$ cup of milk. Toast one slice of bread per child and have each child paint a monster face on his or her toast. Enjoy eating the monster toast.

Counting Games

Play traditional counting games that use chants to eliminate children standing in a circle. Note: The slash marks represent the pause as each child is counted one-by-one.

Ibbity/bibbity/sibbitySam
Ibbity/bibbity/steamboat
Up the river/down the river/
Out/goes/you!

My/mother/and/your/mother/live/across/the/way/
One/fifty/-five/North/Broad/way
Every/night/they/have/a/fight/
And/this/ is/what/they/say:
Acka /backa/soda/cracka/
Acka/backa /boo/
If /your /daddy/chews/tobacco/
Out/goes/Y/O/U.

Magic Chant Game

Have the children stand in a circle with one child in the center. The child in the center points to a new person as each word is said in the chant:

Igga bigga.
Hunka bunka.
Dinka danka doo.

Before he or she finishes, the child who is pointed at must call out the name of the person on his or her left. You can have more than one player in the center to speed things up.

Centimeter Monster

Name _____

Directions: Follow your teacher's directions to make the centimeter monster.

Bedroom Map

Name _____

Directions: Draw a map of your bedroom. Place an X where you think a monster might hide.

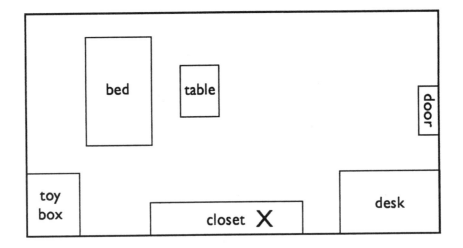

Pathways to Poetry: Poetry Fun for Grades 1-3 © 1994 Fearon Teacher Aids

142

I Am Tired of Being Little

I am tired of being little,
I am sick of being thin,
I wish that I were giant size,
with whiskers on my chin.
No one would dare to tease me,
or to take away my toys,
for I would be much bigger
than the biggest bigger boys.

My folks would pay attention
to everything I said,
they couldn't make me eat my peas
or tell me, "Go to bed!"
I'd never be afraid again
if I were ten-foot-three,
I wish that I were giant size,
instead of small like me.

—Jack Prelutsky

Pathways to Poetry: Poetry Fun for Grades 1-3 © 1994 Fearon Teacher Aids

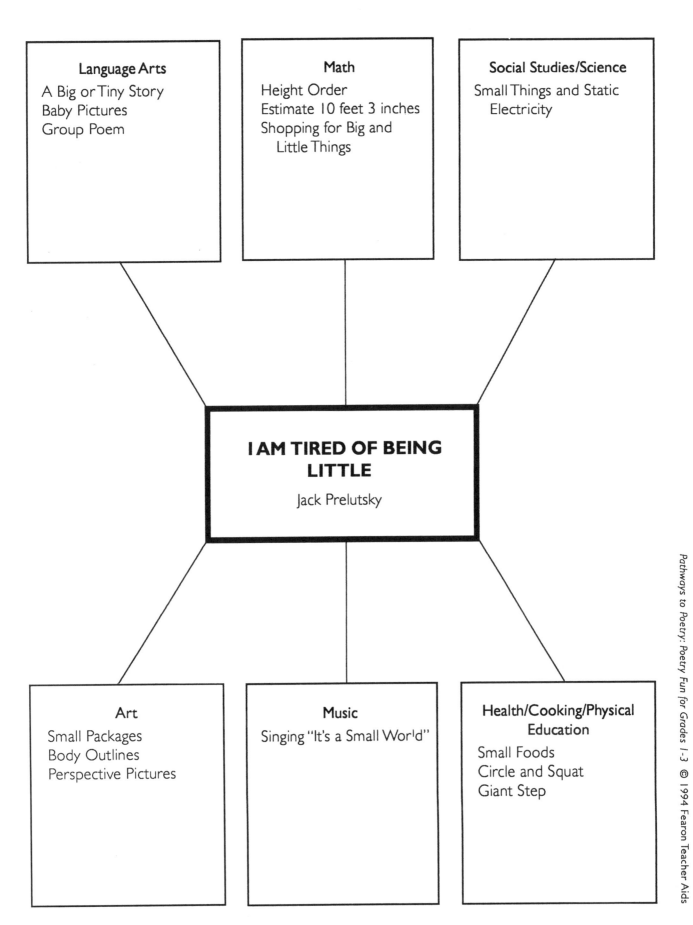

Language Arts

A Big or Tiny Story
Baby Pictures
Group Poem

Math

Height Order
Estimate 10 feet 3 inches
Shopping for Big and
Little Things

Social Studies/Science

Small Things and Static
Electricity

I AM TIRED OF BEING LITTLE

Jack Prelutsky

Art

Small Packages
Body Outlines
Perspective Pictures

Music

Singing "It's a Small World"

Health/Cooking/Physical Education

Small Foods
Circle and Squat
Giant Step

144

I Am Tired of Being Little

The following suggestions can be used with the poem "I Am Tired of Being Little." Select the activities that are most appropriate for the needs and age level of the children in the class.

Introducing the Poem

1. Ask the children to orally complete the sentence "I am tired of _____." Record the children's responses on the chalkboard.

2. Discuss why someone would be tired of being little. List the responses, and contrast the two lists. Ask the children what are the advantages or good things about being little. Then discuss the disadvantages or bad things about being little.

3. Then ask the children the advantages and disadvantages of being a giant. List the children's responses in two columns on the chalkboard. Discuss whether the children would rather be little or be a giant. Have children vote and then compare the results.

4. Share biographical information about the poet, Jack Prelutsky. Refer to the Poet Bookmarks section on page 265. The bookmarks can be duplicated for the children or used to share information about each poet while studying his or her poem.

Shared Listening and Reading

1. As you read the poem aloud, ask the children to listen carefully for the boy's reasons for being tired of being little. Compare the boy's reasons with the children's list recorded earlier.

2. Develop a list of synonyms for the words *little* and *giant*.

3. Ask the children to name other stories that focus on little characters or giants, such as Tom Thumb, Thumbelina, Stuart Little, Paul Bunyan, Jack and the Beanstalk, and so on. Record the children's responses on the chalkboard. Make a chart of characters under the headings of Little People and Giants. Ask the children to help sort the characters by size and write their names under the appropriate categories.

4. Display a copy of the poem on a chart or transparency. Reread the poem several times with each child saying a different line and creating a dramatic gesture to go with the line.

Beyond Listening and Reading Activities

A Big or Tiny Story

Discuss with the children what it would be like to be a giant or very tiny. Encourage the children to write stories about one of their adventures as a giant or a tiny person, and illustrate their stories. Invite volunteers to share their stories and pictures with the rest of the class.

Baby Pictures

Ask the children to bring in baby photos to display on a bulletin board titled, "Good Things Come in Small Packages." Identify the pictures by number only (including your own photo). Give the children time to identify each person in the photographs. After a few days, award a prize to the child who identifies the most babies correctly.

Group Poem

Have each child orally complete the following sentence. "I'd like to be tall as a ___, but really I'm small as a ___." Write each child's sentence on a sheet of tagboard. Ask the children to illustrate their own sentences. Encourage each child to read his or her line of the poem for the class. Display the group poem in the classroom.

Height Order

Ask the children to line up in order according to height from shortest to tallest. Then have the children recite their ordinal places in line, such as first, second, and so on. Attach tape measures to the wall for the children to measure each other's height. Record each child's height beside his or her name on a class height chart. Save the chart until the end of the year. Repeat the activity and compare the changes between the two height charts.

Estimate 10 Feet 3 Inches

Draw a line on the playground with chalk. Have each child estimate the length of 10 feet 3 inches using a chalk line and write his or her name beside the line. After everyone has had a turn, mark off the actual distance of 10 feet 3 inches with a tape measure.

Shopping for Big and Little Things

Duplicate and distribute the reproducible on page 149. Provide magazines and newspaper advertisements. Ask children to cut out two pictures of high priced items, such as cars, boats, and jewels, and two low priced items, such as toothpaste, shampoo, and milk. Have children glue the pictures on the shopping bags and write the appropriate prices which match each picture on the price tags.

Small Things and Static Electricity

Have the children cut out small figures from thin tissue paper and place them in a shallow box or shoebox lid. Cover the box very tightly with plastic wrap. Rub the top of the plastic wrap several times with a piece of wool cloth or a child's pant leg. The figures will dance, demonstrating static electricity.

Small Packages

Duplicate and distribute the reproducible on page 150. Instruct children to cut out the box shape and then decorate it with crayons. Demonstrate how to fold the box on the dotted lines and glue together. Have children select something good that could actually fit in the box, draw it, or cut it out of a magazine and put it inside the box. Ask volunteers to show their boxes to the class. Encourage the class to guess the contents of the box.

Body Outlines

Have each child work with a partner to trace his or her body on butcher paper. Then have the children paint the body outlines with tempera paint and add hair, clothing, and other details. Cut out the body outlines and display them around the room. Encourage the children to write their own names on their body outlines.

Perspective Pictures

Have the children cut skyscraper shapes out of the want ad columns in the newspaper. Children should paste the skyscrapers on pieces of drawing paper. By cutting out pictures of people from magazines and gluing them in front of the buildings, the people appear to be giants.

147

Singing

Teach the children the song, "It's a Small World" from the record *Disney Children's Favorites, Vol. 4* or the official "Its a Small World" album.

Small Foods

Have each child bring in the smallest type of food he or she can find at home, such as sunflower seeds, chocolate chips, and raisins. Give each child a plastic spoon and a paper cup. Have each child take one piece of each kind of food and place it in his or her cup. When all the small foods have been distributed, the children can eat the snack.

Circle and Squat

For this game, limit the playing area for safety reasons. Have each child choose a partner. The child and his or her partner stand behind one another forming a double circle. The inner circle walks to the right and the outer circle walks to the left while the song "It's a Small World" is played. When the music stops, the partners must find each other and squat next to one another. The last pair to find each other is out. The game continues until only one or two sets of partners are left.

Giant Step

Choose a volunteer to be the Giant. The Giant stands at one end of the playing field and the players line up facing the Giant. The Giant instructs one player at a time to either take a baby step or a giant step. Before the player moves, the player must ask, "May I?" The Giant can either say, "Yes, you may," or "No, you may not." The first person to reach and tag the Giant is the next Giant.

Shopping for Big and Little Things

Name _____

Directions: Follow your teacher's directions. Glue pictures on the shopping bags and write the prices on the price tags.

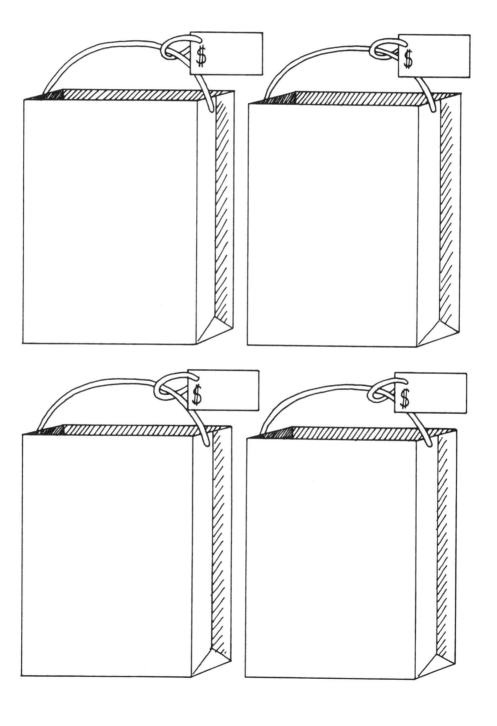

Pathways to Poetry: Poetry Fun for Grades 1-3 © 1994 Fearon Teacher Aids

Small Packages

Name: _____

Directions: Follow your teacher's directions.

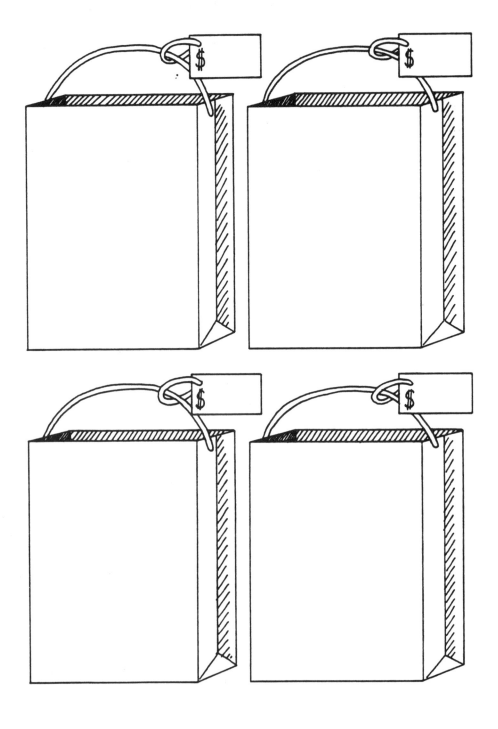

Pathways to Poetry: Poetry Fun for Grades 1-3 © 1994 Fearon Teacher Aids

Suggested Books

Themed Poetry Books

By Myself. Lee Bennett Hopkins. New York, NY: Harper & Row, 1980.

Goosebumps and Butterflies. Yolanda Nave. New York, NY: Orchard Books, 1990.

Something On My Mind. Tom Feelings, with words by Nikki Grimes. New York, NY: Dial, 1978.

The Way I Feel Sometimes. Beatrice Schenk de Regniers. New York, NY: Clarion, 1988.

Books for Read-Aloud and Independent Reading

Alexander and the Terrible, Horrible, No Good, Very Bad Day. Judith Viorst. New York, NY: Atheneum, 1976. Alexander has the worst day ranging from a cereal box without a prize to having to wear his railroad-train pajamas to bed.

Feelings. Aliki. New York, NY: Greenwillow, 1984. A range of emotions—sadness, fear, anger, joy, love, jealousy—are depicted in poems, stories, dialogs, and illustrations.

I Wish I Were a Butterfly. James Howe. San Diego, CA: Harcourt Brace Jovanovich, 1987. A little cricket questions his identity, but a wise old spider helps him to learn he is special in his own way.

The Important Book. Margaret Wise Brown. New York, NY: Harper & Row, 1949. The important things are described about the sun, moon, wind, rain, a bug, other items, and "you" in this classic.

Ira Sleeps Over. Bernard Waber. Boston, MA: Houghton Mifflin, 1972. Ira is faced with a major decision of whether or not to take his teddy bear to sleep over at his friend's house.

The Little Engine That Could. Watty Piper. New York, NY: Platt and Munk, 1954. This is the classic story of the little engine, faced with a tremendous task of getting the toys over the mountain.

Mean Soup. Betsy Everitt. San Diego, CA: Harcourt Brace Jovanovich, 1992. At the end of a bad day, Horace felt very mean. Horace's mother tries to help him by having him make a special soup—mean soup!

On Monday When It Rained. Cherryl Kachenmeister. Boston, MA: Houghton Mifflin, 1989. The thoughts and feelings of a young boy each day of the week are captured in text and photographs.

Revenge of the Small Small. Jean Little. New York, NY: Viking Penguin, 1992. Patty Small is the youngest in the family and her two brothers and sister always tease her. Patty tries to be helpful when they come down with chicken pox, but she is unappreciated. Patty plans her own revenge, and the big kids eventually repent.

There's a Monster Under My Bed. James Howe. New York, NY: Atheneum, 1986. Simon was sure there was a monster under his bed at night—maybe even five monsters! He decided to find out for himself by taking the flashlight and shining the light in the monster's eyes.

There's A Nightmare in My Closet. Mercer Mayer. New York, NY: Dial, 1968. A small boy used to have a nightmare in his closet. He gets rid of the nightmare once and for all, and tucks the monster nightmare in bed with him.

There's Something in My Attic. Mercer Mayer. New York, NY: Dial Books, 1988. A brave girl decides to lasso the big noisy nightmare who lives in the attic over her bed.

Try Again Sally Jane. Mary Diestel-Feddersen. Milwaukee, WI: Gareth Stevens Publishing, 1987. After numerous attempts and encouragement from animal friends, Sally Jane succeeds at roller skating.

Special Days and Ways

Birthday, Birthday, Birthday

Balloons on the ceiling
Balloons on the floor

Hoppy-poppy birthday
Hoppy-pop some more.

Candles on the big cake
Candles on the floor

Huffy-puffy birthday
Huffy-puff some more.

Icing on my fingers
Icing on the floor

Sticky-licky birthday
Sticky-lick some more.

Ice cream on my new shirt
Ice cream on the floor

Slippy-drippy birthday
Slippy-drip some more.

Presents on the table
Presents on the floor

Happy-snappy birthday
Happy-snap some more.

—Nancy White Carlstrom

Pathways to Poetry: Poetry Fun for Grades 1–3 © 1994 Fearon Teacher Aids

Language Arts

"Birthday" Shape Book
Exploring Rhyme and
   Repetitive Patterns
Creating New Verses
The Day I Was Born
Last Year's Birthday/
   Next Year's Birthday
My Birthday Wishes

Math

Months of the Year

Social Studies/Science

Researching Birthday
   Customs
Birthday Customs of
   Varied Cultural or
   Ethnic Groups
Birthday Zodiac Signs

BIRTHDAY, BIRTHDAY, BIRTHDAY

Nancy White Carlstrom

Art

Making Birthday Party
   Hats
Making Piñatas
Making Party
   Noisemakers
Making "I Like You" Cards
   and Envelopes

Music

Singing "Birthday Song"
Singing "Happy Birthday
   to You "

Health/Cooking/Physical Education

Baking a Birthday Cake
Making Ice Cream
Playing "Pin the Tail on the
   Donkey"
A Class Birthday Party

Birthday, Birthday, Birthday

The following suggestions can be used with the poem "Birthday, Birthday, Birthday." Select the activities that are most appropriate for the needs and age level of the children in the class.

Introducing the Poem

1. Initiate a discussion about birthdays by writing the following sentence beginning on the chalkboard. Invite children to complete the sentence orally:

   "On my birthday I like to . . . ."

2. Discuss the fact that birthdays can be celebrated in many different ways, such as having a party, going out to eat, going to an amusement park, and so on. Encourage children to share some of the ways they celebrate birthdays in their families. List the children's responses on the chalkboard and then poll the class to determine which way is most popular.

3. Read the title of the poem aloud. Ask children to predict from the title some of the things that the poem might tell about.

4. Share biographical information about the poet, Nancy White Carlstrom. Refer to the Poet Bookmarks section on page 265. The bookmarks can be duplicated for the children or used to share information about each poet while studying his or her poem.

Shared Listening and Reading

1. Read the poem aloud, asking the children to close their eyes and picture the happenings in their heads. Invite children to share some of the things they pictured, and compare the events in the poem to their previous predictions.

2. Reread the poem one or more times. Then, ask the children questions about what they pictured while listening to the poem, such as:

   How many balloons did you see? What color were the balloons?
   Whom do you think was having a birthday?
   How many candles do you think were on the cake?

What kind of cake did you picture in your head?
What kind of ice cream?
Who did you see joining in the birthday celebration?
What kind of presents did you see?

3. Display a copy of the poem on a chart or transparency. Have the children join with you in reading the words. Reread the poem several times, selecting from among the General Suggestions for Listening to and Reading the Poems on page 6.

4. Invite children to suggest ways that actions and sounds could accompany the reading of some lines of the poem, such as hoppy-pop some more, huffy-puff some more, stickly-lick some more. Divide the class into groups. Assign parts to different groups of children for the actions and sounds, while other children read the lines. Repeat the poem a number of times, changing roles so children have an opportunity to do sounds, actions, and reading.

Beyond Listening and Reading Activities

"Birthday" Shape Book

Have the class make an illustrated book of the poem using paper cut in the shape of a very large cake. Decide in advance who will illustrate which lines, and write the corresponding text. (Several children can work together on an illustration, with one child writing the text.) Bind the completed pages within a cake shape cover made from poster board or heavy construction paper. Place the completed book at the library center for children to enjoy.

Exploring Rhyme and Repetitive Patterns

Display a copy of the poem on a chart or transparency and guide the class in exploring the rhyming and repetitive pattern in the poem. Talk about the poet's selection of the descriptive words hoppy-poppy for the balloons, huffy-puffy for the candles, and so on.

You may also wish to list the rhyming words hoppy-poppy, huffy-puffy, sticky-licky, slippy-drippy, and happy-snappy on the chalkboard and have children underline the root words. If appropriate, help children discover the generalization for doubling the final consonant before adding the suffix y.

Creating New Verses

Invite the children to brainstorm other items that could be found at a birthday party, items not mentioned in the poem. Children might name such items as party hats, noisemakers, punch, paper cups, candy, and so on.

With sticky notes, cover the first word in each line of the poem. Have the children substitute new items and come up with descriptive rhyming words for each item. (You may need to accept non-words for the descriptive rhyming words, or use the same words twice.) After the new verses are created, read the group poem aloud. If you wish, have the class make an illustrated book of the group poem, following a procedure similar to that described in "Birthday" Shape Book activity.

Noisemakers on the ceiling
Noisemakers on the floor

Blowy-showy birthday
Blowy-show some more.

The Day I Was Born

Duplicate and distribute the reproducible on page 166. Ask children to take the page home and have an adult help them complete it. Share the completed pages in class, and then display them on a bulletin board.

Last Year's Birthday/Next Year's Birthday

Divide a wall or large bulletin board into two sections, entitling one "Last Year's Birthday" and the other "Next Year's Birthday." Provide drawing paper for children to draw or paint two scenes, one showing the previous year's birthday and one showing what they would like to do on their next birthday. Provide time for children to orally tell about their pictures.

My Birthday Wishes

Prior to this activity, using cardboard or Styrofoam, make a decorated birthday cake. Punch holes in the top of the Styrofoam for inserting birthday candles. Distribute the reproducible on page 167. Have children write three birthday wishes and draw candles on the cake to show how old they are. Gather the class together, and display the birthday cake and candles. Have each child put as many candles in the holes as he or she is old, count the candles, and read aloud his or her three birthday wishes.

Months of the Year

In advance, write on tagboard cards the names of the months of the year. Distribute the cards to 12 children and have the children line up in sequence, starting with the first month of the year. Distribute the cards a second time asking children to arrange the months in order in a pocket chart.

Then ask all children whose birthdays come in January to stand; have the class count the number of birthdays and have a volunteer record the appropriate numeral on a tag card and place in the pocket chart beside the word *January*. Follow the same procedure for the remaining months. When completed, ask the class comparative questions. "Which month has the greatest number of birthdays?" "Which month has the least number of birthdays?" "How many more children have birthdays in (insert month name) than in (insert month name)?"

Researching Birthday Customs

Guide children in developing a list of questions about the origin of customs related to birthday celebrations. Your list might include some of the following:

How did the custom of lighting candles on birthday cakes start?
Why do we make birthday wishes when we blow out the candles?
How did birthday parties start?
Why do we spank the birthday child?

Provide informational books, such as *Happy Birthday* by Gail Gibbons or *Candles, Cakes, and Donkey Tails* by Lila Perl for older children to find answers to the questions generated. (For more books, refer to the Books for Read-Aloud and Independent Reading section at the end of the theme.) You may wish to organize small groups, asking each group to research a different question. Plan a time when the groups share their findings with each other. With younger children you can read aloud from an informational book and talk about the answers to the questions.

Birthday Customs of Varied Cultural or Ethnic Groups

Invite children of varied cultural or ethnic groups to share their families' special birthday customs. The children may need to gather information from family members at home before reporting to the whole class.

For older children, you may also want to share information about milestone birthdays and coming-of-age ceremonies observed in different countries around the world. *Candles, Cakes, and Donkey Tails* by Lila Perl is a good source of information.

Birthday Zodiac Signs

With older children, share information about the signs of the zodiac. For your information, the ancient Greeks named the signs of the zodiac. The zodiac signs are based on astrology, a non-scientific study of the sun, moon, planets, and stars. Some people think that the position of the stars and planets when a person is born can be used to tell what the person will be like. The year is divided into twelve parts called *signs*. The names, symbols, and dates are as follows:

Name	Symbol	Dates
Aquarius	Water Carrier	January 20 to February 18
Pisces	Fishes	February 19 to March 20
Aries	Ram	March 21 to April 19
Taurus	Bull	April 20 to May 20
Gemini	Twins	May 21 to June 20
Cancer	Crab	June 21 to July 22
Leo	Lion	July 23 to August 22
Virgo	Maiden (Virgin)	August 23 to September 22
Libra	Scales (Balance)	September 23 to October 22
Scorpio	Scorpion	October 23 to November 21
Sagittarius	Archer	November 22 to December 21
Capricorn	Goat	December 22 to January 19

Provide 12 large sheets of construction paper, felt markers, and crayons. Have children who have birthdays falling under the same sign prepare a poster, giving the sign name, an illustration of the symbol for the sign, and the dates. Share with the children a horoscope from a newspaper which predicts the kind of day people born under each of the signs will have. Ask each group to write their own horoscope (prediction for the day) on a piece of writing paper. The horoscopes can be glued to the bottom of the posters. Display the completed posters in sequential order and have each group read aloud the horoscope they created for the day.

Making Birthday Party Hats

Provide colored construction paper, scissors, tape, stapler, and ribbon (or heavy yarn) for children to make birthday party hats. Give the children these directions for making party hats:

1. Decorate the sheet of construction paper with crayons.
2. Roll the sheet into a cone shape. Then tape (or glue) the cone shut.
3. Cut off the bottom edge of the cone to form a circle.
4. If desired, make a tassel for the hat from cut paper strips, pieces of ribbon, or pieces of yarn glued on top of the hat.
5. Staple (or tape) a piece of ribbon (or yarn) on both sides of the hat to tie under the chin.

Have children wear their hats at the Class Birthday Party activity.

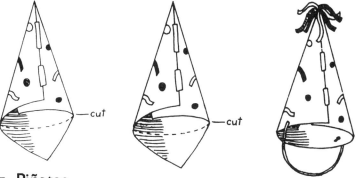

Making Piñatas

Tell the class that a popular blindfold game played at birthday parties comes from Mexico and other Spanish-speaking countries and is called "Breaking the Piñata." The piñata may take many different shapes and forms, such as an animal, bird, or object. The inside of the piñata is hollow and can be filled with candies, small toys, and so on. The piñata is hung overhead in a large room or hung outside from a tree branch. To play the game, each child at the party is blindfolded in turn and given a long stick to hit the piñata and try to break it. Eventually the piñata will break and its contents will come falling out.

Divide the class into three groups to make piñatas. (You may wish to work with each group separately or enlist the aid of older children to assist each group.) Each group will need a large paper grocery bag, newspapers, construction paper, different colors of tissue-paper strips (approximately 3 inches wide), scissors and glue, and ten or more pieces of wrapped candy. Display a chart with directions for the groups to follow:

1. Crinkle newspaper and lightly fill the grocery bag.
2. Put the wrapped candy inside the bag.
3. Close the bag with glue or staples.
4. Fringe the strips of tissue paper and glue around the bag. Start at the bottom or at one side of the bag.
5. Overlap the tissue-paper strips.
6. Add ears, face, legs, tails, or any other features.
7. Let the piñata dry before hanging.

(Note: For older children, you may prefer they make piñatas by using blown-up balloons, covering them with papier-mâché, and adding features to form animals or objects.)

Have children play "Breaking the Piñata" at the Class Birthday Party activity.

Making Party Noisemakers

To make party noisemakers, you will need the following materials for each child: two small paper plates, a popsicle stick (or tongue depressor), and several large buttons (or dried beans). Have the children follow these directions for making the noisemakers:

1. Decorate the back sides of both plates with crayons.
2. Glue (or staple) the popsicle stick to one paper plate.
3. Place the buttons (or beans) on one plate.
4. Staple the two plates together. Make sure the staples are close together so the buttons (or beans) can't fall out.

Children can use the noisemakers at the Class Birthday Party activity.

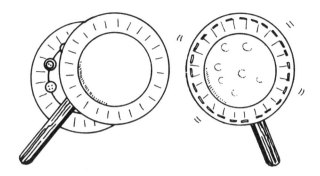

Making "I Like You" Cards and Envelopes

Place the names of all class members in a paper bag. Have each child draw a name from the bag. Provide construction paper for making "I Like You" cards. Each child can make a card for the class member whose name he or she drew. Instruct children to decorate the front of the card, and print the words "(insert child's name), I Like You Because ..." Have the children complete the sentence on the inside of the cards. Have children make envelopes for their cards by folding paper as shown in the illustration. The class members' names can be written on the outside of the envelopes. Have each child open his or her card and read the message aloud during the Class Birthday Party activity.

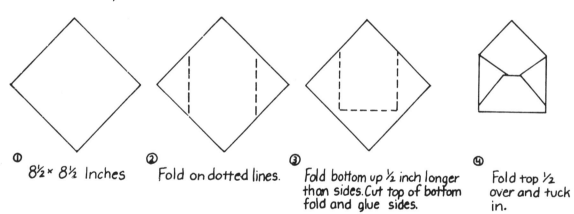

① 8½ × 8½ Inches

② Fold on dotted lines.

③ Fold bottom up ½ inch longer than sides. Cut top of bottom fold and glue sides.

④ Fold top ½ over and tuck in.

Singing

Teach the children the "Birthday Song" from *The Holiday* Songbook. The children might also enjoy singing the song *"Happy Birthday to You"* at the Class Birthday Party activity.

163

Baking a Birthday Cake

Have the class help in baking a birthday cake, by following the directions on the packaged cake mix. Survey the class in advance to find out what kind of cake the children like best. Select the most popular kind of cake to bake. Then, frost the cake, using canned frosting. Decorate the cake with candy sprinkles and write the words *Happy Birthday* with tube frosting. Serve the cake at the Class Birthday Party activity.

Making Ice Cream

Have the class make ice cream. Divide the class into groups of three to five children. Each group will need the following:

    1 three pound coffee can with a lid for holding crushed ice
    1 one pound coffee can with a lid for holding the ingredients
    1 cup of milk
    2 tablespoons sugar
    2 tablespoons canned milk
    1 tablespoon vanilla
    Rock salt
    Crushed ice

Have each group follow these directions:

1. Mix the ingredients in the one pound coffee can. Put on the lid and tape down with masking tape.
2. Put a thin layer of crushed ice on the bottom of the three pound coffee can. Carefully set the one pound can inside the three pound can.
3. Add another layer of ice and rock salt (approximately 4 parts ice to 1 part salt). Continue adding layers of ice and rock salt until reaching the top of the three pound can.
4. Tape down the lid on the three pound can with masking tape.
5. Put newspaper on the floor. Place the can on the newspaper and roll the can back and forth. Take turns rolling the can in your group.
6. After approximately 15 minutes, check to see if the ice cream is frozen. Remove the lid from the three pound can, and pull out the small can. Shake the can up and down. If you do not hear sloshing, the ice cream is ready.

Have labels prepared for each group to place on their cans. Place the cans in a freezer in the lunch room until time to serve at the Class Birthday Party activity.

Playing "Pin the Tail on the Donkey"

Prepare in advance a large poster of a donkey (or other animal, such as a lion, cat, dog, and so on) with the tail missing. Cut tails from construction paper and distribute to each child. Have the children write their names on the tails. Play a cooperation game by having each child find a partner. Blindfold one child, who tries to pin the tail on the donkey following the verbal directions given by his or her partner. After all children have had a turn, provide a prize (or prizes) to the children who pinned the tail closest to where it should be. Play the game at the Class Birthday Party activity.

A Class Birthday Party

Plan as a culmination activity a Class Birthday Party. If you wish, have the children make invitations and invite the school principal, librarian, secretaries, and other school workers.

At the birthday party, children can wear their party hats, play the games "Pin the Tail on the Donkey" and "Breaking the Piñata," sing birthday songs, use their noisemakers, open their "I Like You" cards, and eat cake and ice cream.

Day I Was Born

Dear Parent(s) or Guardian:
We are reading a poem called "Birthday, Birthday, Birthday" by Nancy White Carlstrom.
Please help your child complete this page and have him or her return it to school. We will
share the information in class.

The Day I Was Born

My name is _____ .
                  (first)   (middle)   (last)

I was born on _____ .
             (month)   (day)   (year)

in _____ , _____ .
      (city)   (state)

I weighed about _____ , and was about
               (pounds, ounces)
_____ in length.
    (inches)

I had _____ hair and
        (color)

_____ eyes.
   (color)

My family thought I was _____
_____ .
        (include any information you recall)

In the first few days after I was born _____
_____
_____ .
   (include any information you recall, such as cried, slept, and so on.)

Pathways to Poetry: Poetry Fun for Grades 1-3 © 1994 Fearon Teacher Aids

Birthday Wishes

Name _____

Directions: Write three birthday wishes below, and draw candles on the cake to show how old you are.

I wish _____ .

I wish _____ .

I wish _____ .

Arbor Day: Let's Plant a Tree

It's time to plant a tree, a tree.
What shall it be? What shall it be?

Let's plant a pine — we can't go wrong:
a pine is green the whole year long.

Let's plant a maple — more than one,
to shade us from the summer sun.

Let's plant a cherry — you know why:
there's nothing like a cherry pie!

Let's plant an elm, the tree of grace,
where robins find a nesting place.

Let's plant an apple — not too small,
with flowers in spring and fruit in fall.

Let's plant a fir — so it can be
a lighted outdoor Christmas tree.

Let's plant a birch, an oak, a beech,
there's something extra-nice in each . . .
in winter, summer, spring or fall.
Let's plant a . . .
      why not plant them ALL?

—Aileen Fisher

Pathways to Poetry: Poetry Fun for Grades 1-3 © 1994 Fearon Teacher Aids

Language Arts

Rhyming Words
Crossword Puzzle
ABC Book of Trees
Words That Describe
  Trees

Math

Measuring Size of Tree
Trunks

Social Studies/Science

History of Arbor Day
Luther Burbank and
  John Chapman
Why We Need Trees
Visiting a Tree Farm or
  Nursery
Planting a Tree

ARBOR DAY: LET'S PLANT A TREE

Aileen Fisher

Art

Tree Rubbings
Leaf Prints
Leaf People
My New Tree

Music

Singing "Deep in the
  Woods"
Singing "Arbor Day Song"
Singing "The Green Grass
  Grows All Around"
Singing "I'm a Nut"

Health/Cooking/Physical Education

Tree Salad
Cherry Tarts
Tree Tag

Arbor Day: Let's Plant a Tree

The following suggestions can be used with the poem "Arbor Day: Let's Plant a Tree." Select the activities that are most appropriate for the needs and age level of the children in the class.

Introducing the Poem

1. Ask children in advance of introducing the poem to look around their neighborhood at the various kinds of trees.

2. Ask the children to describe some of the trees they saw. If children mention the name of a particular kind of tree, record the name on the chalkboard. Talk briefly about the beauty of trees and their importance to our environment.

3. Tell children that the word *arbor* is another word for the shelter created by trees, shrubs, and vines. There is a special holiday called *Arbor Day* celebrated each year. People celebrate Arbor Day by planting trees. Share the date for celebrating Arbor Day in your state, mentioning that the date varies from state to state dependent upon the climate.

4. Tell children the title of the poem. Share biographical information about the poet, Aileen Fisher. Refer to the Poet Bookmarks section on page 265. The bookmarks can be duplicated for the children or used to share information about each poet while studying his or her poem.

Shared Listening and Reading

1. Read the poem aloud, asking the children to listen for the kinds of trees mentioned. Invite children to comment about the poem. After reading the poem a second time, ask children to recall all the names of trees the poet talked about. Add the tree names to the list on the chalkboard.

2. Display a copy of the poem on a chart or transparency. Invite children to join in reading the poem. Read the poem together several times, selecting ideas from the General Suggestions for Listening to and Reading the Poems on page 6.

3. Read the poem again, stopping after each couplet to discuss the particular kind of tree mentioned. Encourage children to share any other information about the specific kinds of trees. Since some children may be unfamiliar with the appearance of some of the trees, you may wish to have pictures of the different trees available. If appropriate, discuss the use of the dash and ellipsis mark, and model with your reading what these marks tell you to do.

4. The structure of the poem is ideal for choral reading. Have the whole group read the first two lines, one small group read the repetitive words "Let's plant a (tree name)" and a second small group read the remainder of the couplets. Reverse group roles and repeat.

Beyond Listening and Reading Activities

LANGUAGE ARTS

Rhyming Words

Display the poem on a chart or transparency. Have children identify and underline the rhyming words in the poem. Then make a chart of the rhyming words. Invite children to suggest additional rhyming words for each pair found in the poem. After completing the lists, you may wish to call attention to variant spelling patterns for the same sounds.

Words That Rhyme						
tree	wrong	one	why	grace	small	beech
be	long	sun	pie	place	fall	each
					all	
see	song	fun	sky	face	ball	reach
me	belong	run	my	space	call	teach
he		gun	try	race	hall	

Crossword Puzzle

Duplicate and distribute the reproducible on page 178. Have children individually or with a partner complete the crossword puzzle. Keep a copy of the poem posted for children to refer to if necessary while completing the puzzle.

ABC Book of Trees

Show children several alphabet books, including ones which are organized around a specific topic, such as *Eating the Alphabet* by Lois Ehlert and *City Seen From A to Z* by Rachel Isadora. Suggest that the class make an alphabet book of trees. Begin by listing each letter of the alphabet on the chalkboard or on a chart. Have children name trees that begin with each letter. You may need to provide tree names for some of the letters. Have pictures of unfamiliar trees available to show the children.

Guide the class in deciding what will be included on each page of their alphabet book. For example, younger children may only write the alphabet letter in lowercase and capital letters, draw or cut out pictures of the tree from magazines or plant catalogues, and write the name of the tree.

Older children might write the letter in lowercase and capital letters, draw a picture of the tree, and write a sentence, such as "A is for the apple tree with big red apples to pick." After determining the format of the book, assign each child a page. (Two children may need to work on some pages.) Older children may need to consult nonfiction books to find out information about some of the unfamiliar trees. Bind the completed pages into a book for children to enjoy reading. A list of possible trees for each letter of the alphabet has been provided below. (Suggest the letters X, Y, and Z be used together for a conclusion page.)

A apple, ash, aspen	O oak, orange, olive
B birch, beech, balsa	P pecan, palm, pine, poplar, pear, peach, plum, persimmon
C cherry, cedar, crabapple, cocoa tree	
D Douglas fir, date palm	Q quince
E elm, eucalyptus	R redwood, rubber
F fir, fig	S spruce, sycamore
G ginko	T tamarack, tea tree
H hickory, hemlock	U umbrella tree
I incense cedar	V varnish tree
J juniper	W walnut, willow
K kapok	X
L linden, lime, lemon, larch	Y yew
M maple, mulberry	Z
N nutmeg tree	

Words That Describe Trees

Take the class for a walk around the neighborhood to observe trees. Discuss the types of trees, the differences in sizes, variations in types of leaves, and bark. After returning to the classroom, outline a tree in the center of a piece of poster paper. Label branches with categories, such as size, shape, color, and texture. Invite the class to brainstorm words which describe trees for each of the categories. Some words could be grouped under more than one category. Encourage children to add other words over the next few days.

Measuring Size of Tree Trunks

Organize the class into small groups. Then take the class for a walk around the school community where various sizes of trees can be seen. Using a measuring tape, have each group measure a tree trunk and record its size on a piece of paper. After returning to the classroom, record all the measurements on a chart. Ask comparative questions regarding the size of the tree trunks. For example: How much larger was the trunk Group 1 measured than the trunk measured by Group 4? If you wish, have children make a bar graph depicting the measurements.

SOCIAL STUDIES

History of Arbor Day

Provide nonfiction books, such as *Arbor Day* by Aileen Fisher to use to research the following questions:

Who first had the idea of a special day to plant trees?
Why did this person think planting trees was important?
In what state and year was Arbor Day first celebrated?

Plan a sharing time for children to report their findings. For your information, J. Sterling Morton first had the idea of a tree-planting day. Morton grew up in New York and in Michigan where there were many trees. After college, he moved to Nebraska where there were vast prairies, but few trees. He thought that trees were beautiful as well as essential. Without trees, the wind blew ferociously, rain eroded the soil, and there was no shade. After talking to many people as well as the government, Mr. Morton achieved his goal. In 1872 Nebraska established a special day for planting trees called *Arbor Day*. Morton later went on to become Secretary of Agriculture and talked with people throughout the country about the importance of trees. Today each state in the United States celebrates *Arbor Day* on a date that is good for tree planting in its climate.

Luther Burbank and John Chapman

Provide informational books for children to learn about Luther Burbank and John Chapman, who is better known as "Johnny Appleseed." Both individuals are associated with Arbor Day. For your information, California celebrates Arbor Day on March 7, Luther Burbank's birthday. Burbank's contribution to agriculture is very important because of his development of new kinds of flowers, fruits, and trees as well as his emphasis upon planting orchards, gardens, and groves. Many states along the Ohio River honor John Chapman on Arbor Day for his planting of apple seeds throughout the region in order that settlers would find orchards when they claimed land for settlement.

Why We Need Trees

Divide the class into cooperative work groups. Give each group a set time limit to list reasons why trees are important. To stimulate the children's thinking, you may wish to suggest they think about foods that come from trees, products made from parts of trees, ways trees help plants and animals, how trees help the environment, and so on. Have the groups share their lists with each other. Combine all the groups' ideas onto a class chart. Encourage the children to add other ideas to the chart.

Visiting a Tree Farm or Nursery

If possible, take the class on a field trip to a tree farm or nursery where several varieties of trees can be observed. Encourage the children to prepare questions ahead of time to ask the tree farm or nursery staff. After returning to the classroom, discuss the information the children learned on the field trip. Write thank-you letters or cards to the tree farm or nursery staff.

Planting a Tree

Make arrangements for the class to plant a tree in the schoolyard. (This might be part of a school-wide Arbor Day celebration.) In succeeding weeks, involve the class in caring for the tree and observing the tree's growth.

Tree Rubbings

Give children thin white paper, preferably onion skin paper, and pieces of wax crayons. Pair children with a partner, and take them outside to make tree rubbings. One child can hold the paper on the tree bark while his or her partner rubs the side of the crayon on the paper. Then the roles can be reversed. Display the completed rubbings on a bulletin board or wall, and encourage each child to talk about what the lines and markings look like.

Leaf Prints

At a learning center, place a variety of tree leaves. Provide white construction paper and shallow pans of tempera paint in a variety of colors, such as red, yellow, orange, brown, and green. Instruct children to dip a leaf, vein side down, in the paint, and then press the leaf, paint side down, onto the paper to make a print. Lift the leaf carefully the leaf carefully from the paper and repeat the procedure using other leaves and colors of paint. After the paint is dry, display the leaf prints on a wall or bulletin board.

Leaf People

In advance, invite the children to collect fallen tree leaves and small twigs to bring to school. Provide construction paper for a background. Have children arrange the leaves and twigs to make people. When the children are satisfied with the arrangement, have them glue the leaves and twigs onto the paper. Other body parts can be added from scraps of colored construction paper, magic markers, and crayons.

My New Tree

Ask children to imagine that they are a horticulturist like Luther Burbank. They can create a new tree—one that has never existed before. Tell the children that the tree can be fanciful, such as a money tree or a candy tree, or it can serve an environmental purpose, such as removing pollution from the air. Give each child a sheet of paper. Have children draw, color, and write about their trees. Encourage the children to name their trees, describe them, and tell what special qualities their trees have.

Singing

Teach children the songs "Deep in The Woods" and "Arbor Day Song" from *The Holiday Song Book*. Children may also enjoy learning "The Green Grass Grows All Around" from *The Fireside Book of Fun and Game Songs* and "I'm a Nut" from *Tom Glazer's Do Your Ears Hang Low?*

Tree Salad

You will need a variety of fresh fruits and nuts grown on trees (oranges, bananas, apples, peaches, plums, walnuts) and fruit juices (apple or orange). Or, ask class members to bring one piece of fruit to school for the "Tree Salad." Using close adult supervision have the class help in cleaning or peeling the fruit and chopping it into bite-size pieces. Place the cut-up fruit in a large mixing bowl, and add the fruit juice. Sprinkle in the nuts and stir. Serve at snack time.

Cherry Tarts

You will need canned refrigerator biscuits and canned cherry pie filling, both available at a grocery store. (Check the packaging for servings per can; for 32 tarts you will probably need 4 cans of biscuits and 2 to 3 cans of cherry pie filling.) In advance, cut aluminum foil into 4-inch squares, one for each child. To make individual cherry tarts; instruct children to:

1. Carefully place one biscuit on the foil square.

2. Make a deep thumbprint in the center of the biscuit.

3. Put 1 heaping teaspoon of cherry pie filling including 2 or 3 cherries in the center of the thumbprint.

4. Print their initials on the lower edge of the foil. Then lift the foil carefully and place on a cookie sheet.

Bake the tarts at 375° to 400° for about 8-10 minutes or until golden brown. Remove tarts from the oven, and cool slightly before eating.

Tree Tag

Divide the class into groups of 10 to 15 children. Have each group play separately but in nearby areas of the playground. Mark the areas for the tag games with chalk.

One player is chosen to be "It." "It" begins to chase the other players, trying to tag someone. When a player is about to be tagged, he or she must call out the name of a tree loudly enough for all players to hear. "It" then tries to tag another player, who again calls out a tree name to avoid getting tagged. Tree names can only be used one time. If a player is tagged before calling the name of a tree or repeats a tree previously named, he or she becomes "It" and the game continues.

After a number of tree names have been called, the item to be called could be changed to fruits that grow on trees, or products made from trees.

Crossword Puzzle

Name _____

Directions: Read the poem. Then find the answers to the crossword puzzle.

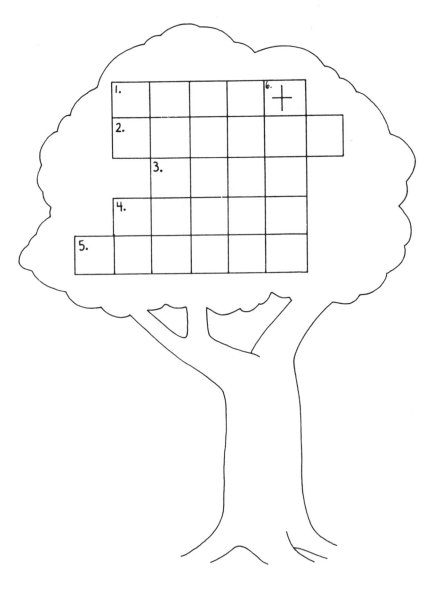

Down

6. planted on Arbor Day

Across

1. to _____ a tree in the ground
2. a kind of fruit pie
3. a tree that is green all year long
4. a tree that gives shade
5. birds that nest in trees

Pathways to Poetry: Poetry Fun for Grades 1-3 © 1994 Fearon Teacher Aids

Ground Hog Day

Ground Hog sleeps
All winter
Snug in his fur,
Dreams
Green dreams of
Grassy shoots,
Of nicely newly nibbly
Roots—
Ah, he starts to
Stir.
With drowsy
Stare
Looks from his burrow
Out on fields of
Snow.
What's there?
Oh no.
His shadow. Oh,
How sad!
Six more
Wintry
Weeks
To go.

—Lilian Moore

Pathways to Poetry: Poetry Fun for Grades 1-3 © 1994 Fearon Teacher Aids

Language Arts

Developing Word
Meaning
Comparing Rhyme
Patterns
Writing a "Why" Story
Finding Out About
Ground Hogs
Tongue Twisters

Math

Word Problems
Weather Calendar
Measuring Length of
Shadows

Social Studies/Science

What is Ground Hog Day?
What Makes a Shadow?
What Made These
Shadows?
Predicting Which Objects
Will Create Shadows

GROUND HOG DAY

Lilian Moore

Art

A Shadow Play
Ground Hog Pop-Up
Puppet

Music

Singing "Ground Hog"
Singing "Woodchuck Song"

Health/Cooking/Physical Education

Ground Hog Sandwiches
Ground Hog Garden Salad
Shadow Tag

Ground Hog Day

The following suggestions can be used with the poem "Ground Hog Day."
Select the activities that are most appropriate for the needs and age level
of the children in the class.

Introducing the Poem

1. Begin a discussion about ground hogs by displaying a picture of one.
   Invite children to describe the ground hog in the picture, and tell other
   information they may know about the animal. Record facts the chil-
   dren mention on a strip of butcher paper under the heading "Things
   We Know." Leave the remaining two columns to be completed in the
   Finding Out About Ground Hogs activity.

   Things We Know   What We Want to Know   What We Learned

2. Explain that there is a special day called "Ground Hog Day" which
   comes each year on February 2. Ask children who know what happens on that day to raise their hands.

3. Tell children the title of the poem. Point out that the poem tells what
   the ground hog does on Ground Hog Day.

4. Share biographical information about the poet, Lilian Moore. Refer to
   the Poet Bookmarks section on page 265. The bookmarks can be
   duplicated for the children or used to share information about each
   poet while studying his or her poem.

Shared Listening and Reading

1. Read the poem aloud, asking the children to listen carefully to find out
   what happens on Ground Hog Day. Encourage the children to comment freely.

2. Read the poem to the children one or more times. Discuss the
   following questions:

   Do you think the ground hog gets cold in the winter? Why or
   why not?

   What does the poem say the ground hog dreams of?

Why do you think the ground hog dreams of things to eat?

When an animal sleeps through the winter, the animal hibernates. How do you think the ground hog feels after hibernating all winter?

In what month do you think the ground hog went to sleep?

According to the poem, what happens if the ground hog sees his shadow? What do you think the ground hog will do?

If the ground hog doesn't see his shadow, what kind of weather is there supposed to be?

Do you think the ground hog can really predict the weather? Why or why not?

3. Display a copy of the poem on a chart or transparency. Discuss the lining of the poem, and if appropriate, the punctuation marks. Show how to interpret with your voice the various punctuation marks. Then have the class read the poem aloud with you two or more times.

4. You may wish to point out the use of alliteration in the poem by having children identify the repeated consonant sounds in the phrase "nicely newly nibbly." Other examples include "green" and "grassy," "stir" and "stare," and "wintry weeks."

5. Divide the class into two groups. Have one group be "ground hogs" and pantomime the actions, while the second group reads the poem. Reverse roles and repeat the reading and pantomiming.

Beyond Listening and Reading Activities

LANGUAGE ARTS

Developing Word Meaning

Read the poem aloud. Then display a copy of the poem on a chart or transparency. List the following words from the poem in a column on the chalkboard: *snug, shoots, stir, drowsy, stare,* and *burrow*. Have the children underline the words one at a time in the poem. Invite children to tell what they think each word means, suggest other words with similar meanings, and use the words in oral sentences. Discuss other meanings for the words *shoots* and *stir.*

Comparing Rhyme Patterns

On a copy of the poem, point out that the rhyme pattern in this poem is different from many other poems the children have read. Read aloud the first three lines. Ask children to find the line in the poem that rhymes with the word *fur.* (The rhyming word can be found in line 10—Stir). Underline the words *fur* and *stir* with a colored marker. Have children find the other rhyming words in the poem, underlining each set with a different colored marker. For each set of rhyming words, point out the spelling patterns to help the children learn that the same sound is often represented with different letters.

Writing a "Why" Story

Ask the children to imagine that they are ground hogs peeking out of their burrows on Ground Hog Day. The sun is shining and they see their shadows. Why are the ground hogs afraid? What do they think? What do they do? Have the children share some of their ideas. Then with a partner or in cooperative groups, invite the children to write a story titled, "Why the Ground Hog Is Afraid of His Shadow." Have the children draw illustrations for their stories, and plan a time for sharing the completed stories.

Finding Out About Ground Hogs

Display the "Things We Know" chart developed in Introducing the Poem. Have the class reread the "Things We Know" column. Then, guide children in identifying things they would like to know about ground hogs. Record the children's questions in the middle column—"What We Want to Know." If necessary, stimulate the discussion by asking children questions about the ground hog—its size, where it lives, favorite foods, animal relatives, how it prepares for hibernation, and so on.

Provide informational books for partners or cooperative groups to locate answers to their questions. With younger children, you may need to read aloud from the informational books. After children have had an opportunity to gather information, have the class discuss the questions listed on the chart, and complete the "What We Learned" column.

Tongue Twisters

Invite children to recite any tongue twisters they may be familiar with, such as "Sally sells seashells by the sea shore." Then teach children the tongue twister, "How much wood would a woodchuck chuck if a woodchuck would chuck wood?" Point out that woodchuck is another name for a ground hog. Repeat the tongue twister several times as rapidly as possible. Point out that the tongue twister uses lots of words that begin with the same consonant sound. Using your name or the name of an animal, help the class develop a tongue twister. Write the tongue twister on the chalkboard. Have a volunteer underline each word that begins with the same consonant sound.

teer underline each word that begins with the same consonant sound.

Have each child select a partner. Working together, ask each pair to create one or more tongue twisters and illustrate each one. For younger children, you may need to suggest categories and examples, such as "The turtle tried to talk on the telephone." Plan a time for the children to share their tongue twisters, and lead the class in saying them.

Word Problems

Review the number of days in a week. Divide the class into small cooperative groups. Give each group the following word problem to solve: The ground hog saw his shadow and there will be six more weeks of winter. How many more days of winter will there be? Encourage children to share how they found the answer, such as multiplying, adding, and so on.

Give children one or more word problem examples using weeks and days. Include multiple step problems, if appropriate, for the age level. For example: Twenty-eight days have passed since the ground hog saw his shadow. How many more days of winter remain?

Invite each group to create a word problem based on weeks and days. Have each group present their word problem for the other groups to solve.

Weather Calendar

Duplicate and distribute the reproducible on page 188. Each child will need two calendars. As a class, write in the month, days of the week, and dates beginning with Ground Hog Day on February 2 and continuing for six weeks. Discuss symbols that will represent the weather (sun, cloud, umbrella, kite, and snowperson). Have the children predict the weather for each day of the next six weeks by drawing in the appropriate symbol in the left-hand triangle. Each day have the children draw, in the right-hand triangle, the symbol showing the actual weather. Compare the predictions to the actual weather.

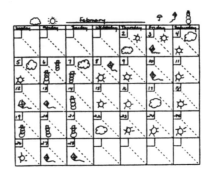

Measuring Length of Shadows

For this activity, you will need two colors of chalk, a chart listing each child's name, and a measuring tape. On a sunny day, take the class outside to the playground. Divide the class into pairs and line up across the playground—each pair standing together. Then, have the children use chalk to draw each other's shadow, labeling the shadow with their names. Using a measuring tape, have children measure and record the length of their shadows on the chart beside their names. Later in the day, return to the playground. Have the children stand in the same places, and draw their shadows again using different colored chalk. Measure the second shadows and record the measurements. After returning to the classroom, compare the lengths of each child's two shadows. Discuss why the shadows varied in length from the first time to the second time.

Lengths of Shadows		
Name	1st Shadow	2nd Shadow

What is Ground Hog Day?

Share information with the class about the orgin of Ground Hog Day. Refer to the Suggested Books for Read Aloud and Independent Reading section at the end of this theme.

What Makes a Shadow?

Read-aloud books, such as *My Shadow* by Robert Louis Stevenson and illustrated by Ted Rand, *Shadow Magic* by Seymour Simon, or *Nothing Sticks Like a Shadow* by Ann Tompert. After reading the books, discuss that shadows are formed when light cannot go through an object. Then take the children outside to look for shadows made by buildings, telephone poles, fences, plants, and so on.

What Made These Shadows?

Duplicate and distribute the reproducible on page 189. For each shadow, ask children to identify what they think made the shadow. Compare the children's written answers.

Predicting Which Objects Will Create Shadows

Collect a variety of objects that will permit light to go through, such as a drinking glass, sunglasses, and so on, and other objects that block the light, such as a book, pencil, or eraser. Have children predict whether or not the object will create a shadow. Using a light source, such as a strong flashlight, overhead projector, or lamp, have the children experiment to determine whether their shadow predictions were correct.

You may wish to place the objects at a learning center and let children experiment with shadows on their own. Encourage the children to try moving the object different distances from the light source to discover that the size of an object's shadow is related to the distance from the light source. Discuss the children's results.

A Shadow Play

Use familiar fairy tales with animal characters, such as "The Three Little Pigs," "The Three Bears," and "Henny Penny," to create shadow plays. Divide the class into small groups. Have each group select a story. Have the children draw and then cut out story characters from black construction paper. Glue heavy tagboard handles to the back of each character. Suspend a white sheet between two chairs. Then direct a lamp or flashlight at the sheet from behind. Invite each group to stand or kneel behind the sheet to perform their shadow play.

Ground Hog Pop-Up Puppet

Give each child a paper cup, a Styrofoam ball that is small enough to fit inside the cup, and a popsicle stick or straw. (If Styrofoam balls are not available, wad paper into a ball and cover it with brown tissue paper. Secure the tissue paper with a rubberband.)

To make the ground hog pop-up puppet, instruct children to:

1. Push the popsicle stick into the Styrofoam ball. (If the stick is loose inside the ball, squirt a drop of glue in the slit, and then re-insert the stick.)
2. Add facial features to the ground hog using markers, crayons, and scraps of construction paper.
3. Poke a slit in the bottom of the cup.
4. Holding the cup upright, slide the popsicle stick through the slit.

Encourage children to practice making the ground hog pop out of his hole, and then go back inside. Invite children to use their puppets while saying the poem.

186

Singing

Teach the children the song "Ground Hog" from *The Fireside Song Book of Birds and Beasts*. The children may also enjoy singing the "Woodchuck Song" from *1002 The Complete Children's Song Book*.

Ground Hog Sandwiches

Help the children prepare ground hog sandwiches. You will need the following ingredients for eight sandwiches:

1 1/2 cups grated cheese
1 cup alfalfa sprouts
mayonnaise
16 slices bread

Mix together grated cheese and alfalfa sprouts. Add enough mayonnaise to moisten. Spread mixture on bread and serve with "Ground Hog Garden Salad."

Ground Hog Garden Salad

Bring in a variety of garden vegetables, such as lettuce, peppers, tomatoes, carrots, onions, and so on. Have the children help clean the vegetables, tear the lettuce into bite-size pieces, chop the peppers and tomatoes using butter knives, and prepare the other vegetables. Toss the vegetables with salad dressing and serve.

Shadow Tag

If the day is sunny, take the children to the playground for a game of "Shadow Tag." Select one player to be "It." When the signal is given, "It" tries to tag a player by stepping on his or her shadow and shouting the name of the tagged player. The tagged player then becomes the next "It."

Weather Calendar

Name _____

Directions: Draw a weather symbol to show what you think the weather is going to be like each day for the next 6 weeks. Then draw a weather symbol to show what the weather each day is actually like.

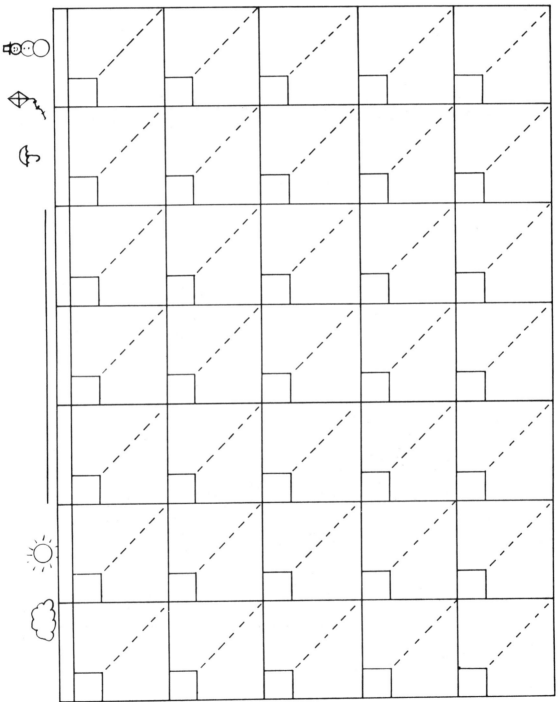

Pathways to Poetry: Poetry Fun for Grades 1-3 © 1994 Fearon Teacher Aids

What Made These Shadows?

Name _____

Directions: For each shadow, write a phrase telling what you think made the shadow.

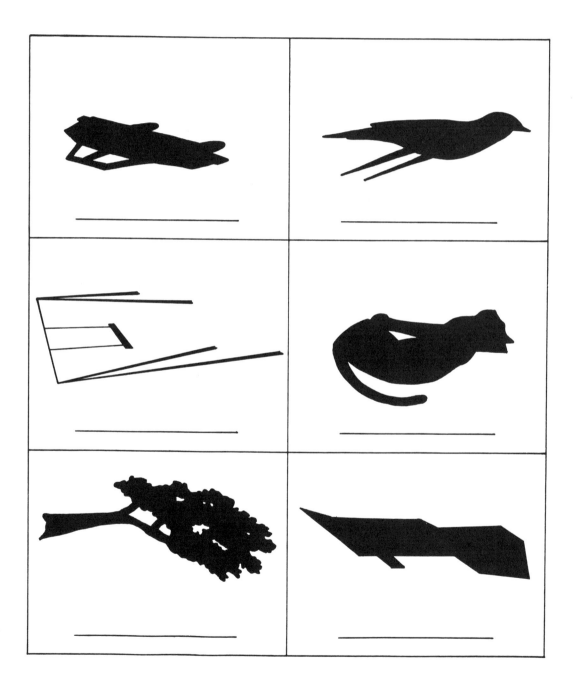

October Fun

Who has a big and smiling mouth,
a tooth up north and two down south?

Beneath his mouth who has a chin
that's rather round and curvy-in?

Who has three corners to his eyes—
the strangest shape, the strangest size?

Who has a nose, three-cornered, too,
where orange light comes shining through?

—Aileen Fisher

Pathways to Poetry: Poetry Fun for Grades 1-3 © 1994 Fearon Teacher Aids

190

Language Arts

Descriptive Words
Illustrating from a
   Description
Pop-Up Riddle Books
Writing Directions for
   Carving a Pumpkin

Math

Shape Search
Jack-O'-Lantern Math
Bingo
Estimating Weight

Social Studies/Science

Visiting a Pumpkin Patch
Growing Pumpkin Seeds

OCTOBER FUN

Aileen Fisher

Art

Shining Jack-O'-Lanterns
Making a Pumpkin Patch
Jack-O'-Lantern Accordion
People

Music

Singing "Whippily,
   Whoppily, Whoop"
Singing "Jack-O'-
   Lanterns"
Singing "Ten Little
   Goblins"
Singing "Halloween
   Song"

Health/Cooking/Physical Education

Baking Pumpkin Seeds
Jack-O'-Lantern Cookies
Jack-O'-Lantern Relay

October Fun

The following suggestions can be used with the poem "October Fun."
Select the activities that are most appropriate for the needs and age level
of the children in the class.

Introducing the Poem

1. Ask children what special holiday comes on October 31 each year.
   Then divide the class into groups of four to six children. Within a
   specified time limit, such as 3 to 5 minutes, ask each group to list all
   the things they associate with Halloween, such as ghosts, witches, black
   cats, and jack-o'-lanterns. When the time is up, have each group share
   their list. You may wish to record a combined list on chart paper.
   (With younger children, you may wish to develop the list as a whole
   class.)

2. Tell children the title of the poem. State that the poem is written as a
   riddle. Discuss briefly what a riddle is. Allow time for children to
   speculate as to whether the answer to the riddle may appear in the list
   of things they associated with Halloween.

3. Share biographical information about the poet, Aileen Fisher. Refer to
   the Poet Bookmarks section on page 265. The bookmarks can be
   duplicated for the children or used to share information about each
   poet while studying his or her poem.

Shared Listening and Reading

1. Read the poem aloud. Ask the children to raise their hands when
   they think they know the answer. Invite children to share their answers after the first reading, and briefly discuss which clue or clues in
   the poem helped them come up with their answers.

2. Ask children to close their eyes and picture in their heads what they
   see as the poem is read aloud a second time. Encourage children to
   describe the jack-o'-lantern they pictured in their heads. As necessary,
   discuss the meaning of the terms *a tooth up north* and *two down south,*
   three-cornered, and so on.

3. Display a copy of the poem on a chart or transparency. Invite children to join in reading the poem. Practice reading the poem together. Read the poem several times, selecting ideas from the General Suggestions for Listening to and Reading the Poems on page 6.

4. Point out the question word *who*, and the different sentence structure used in the second verse. Note that each verse ends with a question mark. Invite volunteers to read the verses aloud, making their voices show that a question is being asked.

5. Sketch an outline of a large pumpkin on the chalkboard. As the first verse is read aloud by the class, select a volunteer to draw in the parts of the jack-o'-lantern. Do the same for the remaining three verses, choosing different volunteers. Erase the jack-o'-lantern face from the pumpkin and repeat the activity.

Beyond Listening and Reading Activities

LANGUAGE ARTS

Descriptive Words

Display a copy of the poem on a chart or transparency. Help the children identify and underline the descriptive words in the poem and cover each one with a sticky note. Invite children to suggest other words that could replace the covered words. Write the suggested words on the sticky notes. Discuss how the word substitutions change what they picture in their heads.

Duplicate and distribute copies of the poem "October Fun" from page 190. Ask children to first cross out the words *big, smiling, one, round, three, strangest,* and *three-cornered.* Have children create their own versions of the poem by writing new words above the crossed-out words. On another sheet of paper, ask the children to draw jack-o'-lanterns to match the new description in the poem. Don't have the children share their illustrations until after the Illustrating from a Description activity.

Illustrating from a Description

Have the children exchange poems from the Descriptive Words activity. Invite the children to draw jack-o'-lanterns to match the new description in the poem. Plan a sharing time for the children to show their illustrations.

Pop-Up Riddle Books

Have the children brainstorm symbols associated with Halloween, such as spiders, ghost, witches, masks, goblins, candy, apples, black cat, costumes, and bats. (Note: If you recorded the list children developed in Introducing the Poem, you can merely add to that list.) Select one symbol and write a class riddle of three or four lines. Invite children to secretly select one Halloween symbol and then write their own riddles.

Duplicate the reproducible on page 199 on construction paper. Give each child a copy. Provide paper for children to draw pictures of their riddle answers. Help children follow these step-by-step directions:

1. Fold the reproducible page in half on the center line.
2. Cut along the dotted lines (through both thicknesses) to the squares.
3. Unfold the page with the squares facing down on the table.
4. Lift the pop-up tab towards you and fold the tab along the crease.
5. Glue the answer picture to the riddle on the pop-up tab.
6. Write the answer to the riddle under the pop-up picture.
7. On the front side of the book, paste a handwritten copy of the riddle.

After the pop-up riddle books are finished, provide time for children to read their riddles to the class. Encourage the children to guess the answer before looking inside the riddle book.

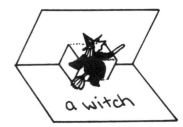

Writing Directions for Carving a Pumpkin

For this activity, you will need as many small pumpkins as you have cooperative groups. In each cooperative group, have children write directions for carving a jack-o'-lantern.

With the whole class observing, have each group read their directions as you carve the jack-o'-lantern. Discuss as the different jack-o'-lanterns are carved whether the directions were complete and how the jack-o'-lanterns differ as a result of the written directions. Save the leftover pumpkin seeds to use in the Baking Pumpkin Seeds activity.

Shape Search

Introduce the geometric term *triangle* for a three-cornered shape, such as the eyes and nose of the jack-o'-lantern, as mentioned in the poem. Ask children to recall the other shape mentioned in the poem—*circle.* Invite the children to search for triangles and circles in the classroom. Then, take the class on a walk around the school building and yard to locate more triangles and circles. Discuss the children's observations upon returning to the classroom. You may wish to have children develop an illustrated poster of objects they found that were shaped like circles and triangles.

Jack-O'-Lantern Math Bingo

Duplicate and distribute the reproducible on page 200. Give each child bingo markers, such as pumpkin seeds, bean seeds, or paper squares. Have children randomly write numerals from 0 to 18 in the squares. Use addition or subtraction flashcards whose answers are within the number series used on the bingo cards. Have children cover the answers to the problems on their bingo cards. The first child to cover four squares down, across, or diagonally is the winner.

Estimating Weight

Bring a large pumpkin to the classroom. Invite each child to pick up the pumpkin, guess its weight, and secretly record his or her estimate on a piece of paper. Before asking children to write down their estimates, invite them to weigh other classroom items to give them a general sense of various weights, such as a 1 pound weight, 5 pound weight, and so on.

After all children have made their estimates, post a class chart for the children to record their names and estimates. Then, as a group, weigh the pumpkin and complete the remaining columns. Older children can compute how many pounds their estimates are over or under the actual weight of the pumpkin.

Weight of the Pumpkin				
Name	Estimated Weight	More Than	Less Than	Actual Weight

Visiting a Pumpkin Patch

Take the class on a field trip to a pumpkin patch. Have children plan in advance questions to be asked and what they expect to see. Upon return, engage in follow-up activities of writing stories about the trip, what they learned, and thank-you letters.

Growing Pumpkin Seeds

Line a glass jar with moistened cotton or paper toweling. Place pumpkin seeds between the cotton and the glass. Keep the cotton damp. In a few days, pumpkin shoots should be seen growing up and roots will begin to grow down. Have children record their observations each day in journals, or keep a class chart of daily observations.

Shining Jack-O'-Lanterns

To make shining jack-o'-lanterns, you will need two sheets of orange construction paper (9" x 12") for each child, yellow cellophane or tissue paper, scissors, tape, and glue. Help children follow the step-by-step directions. (For younger children, you may wish to work in small groups, or enlist the aid of older children or an adult volunteer.)

1. Fold one piece of construction paper in half and draw one eye and half of the nose and mouth.
2. With the paper still folded, cut out the pumpkin, and then the pumpkin's nose and mouth. Unfold and cut out the eyes.
3. Trace the pumpkin and face on a second piece of construction paper to make a second jack-o'-lantern.
4. Glue (or tape) a piece of yellow cellophane (or tissue paper) over one of the jack-o'-lantern faces.
5. Glue the two jack-o'-lanterns together, with the yellow cellophane or tissue paper between them.

Tape the completed jack-o'-lanterns in a window. As the sun strikes them the jack-o'-lanterns will shine.

Making a Pumpkin Patch

In advance, cut strips of orange construction paper in a range of lengths and widths. Each child will need four strips of the same length and width of paper. (The longer or wider the strips, the larger the pumpkin will be.) Have children crisscross the strips (see illustration) and staple (or glue) the center. Next, pull the strips up and glue (or staple) them at the top. Lastly, glue on a stem made from either green construction paper or heavy green yarn.

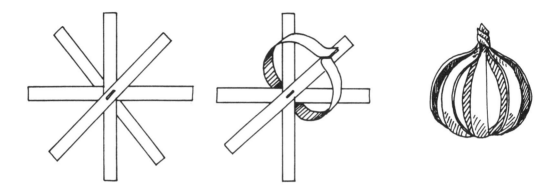

Cover a table with brown construction paper, and display all the pumpkins in the "patch." Encourage children to write creative stories about happenings in the pumpkin patch on Halloween night.

Jack-O'-Lantern Accordion People

Have children draw a pumpkin on orange construction paper. Ask children to cut out the pumpkin. Then have children add facial features with marking pens or crayons. Provide four strips of black construction paper (approximately 1½" wide and 12" long) for each child. Show children how to accordion fold the strips, and glue them to the jack-o'-lantern for arms and legs. Provide scraps of colored construction paper for children to add hands, feet, gloves, shoes, hats, or other features.

197

Singing

Teach the children the songs "Whippily, Whoppily, Whoop," "Jack-O'-Lanterns," and "Ten Little Goblins" from *The Holiday Song Book*. The children may also enjoy learning "Halloween Song" from *An Illustrated Treasury of Songs*.

Baking Pumpkin Seeds

Wash and dry the pumpkin seeds taken from the pumpkins used in the Writing Directions for Carving a Pumpkin activity. Spread the seeds in a shallow pan or on a cookie sheet. Bake seeds in a 350° oven until they are lightly browned or approximately ½ hour. Stir seeds occasionally to assure even browning. Salt lightly and serve!

Jack-O'-Lantern Cookies

Make pumpkin cookies using packaged sugar cookie dough and orange tube frosting, triangle-shaped candy corn, and black licorice rope. Slice the cookie dough into ¼-inch slices. Bake cookies on cookie sheets according to the directions on the cookie dough package. After the baked cookies are cool, invite children to decorate the cookies to look like jack-o'-lanterns. Serve at snack time.

Jack-O'-Lantern Relay

Divide the class into two teams. Have each team line up, and place a jack-o'-lantern, real or paper, on the ground about 12 feet away from the front of the lines. When the signal is given, the first player in each line runs around the jack-o'-lantern, races back to his or her team, tags the next player, and then goes to the end of the line. The tagged players follow the same procedure. The team finishing first is the winner.

Pop-Up Riddle Book

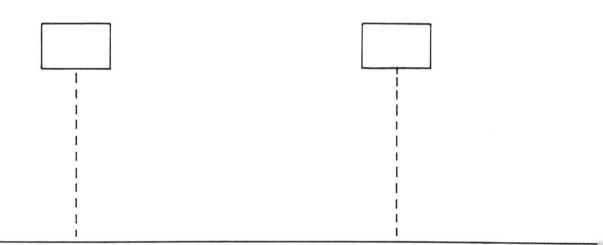

Pathways to Poetry: Poetry Fun for Grades 1-3 © 1994 Fearon Teacher Aids

Jack-O'-Lantern Math Bingo

Directions: Write in numerals from 0 to 18. Follow your teacher's directions.

Pathways to Poetry: Poetry Fun for Grades 1–3 © 1994 Fearon Teacher Aids

Rebus Valentine

You may not 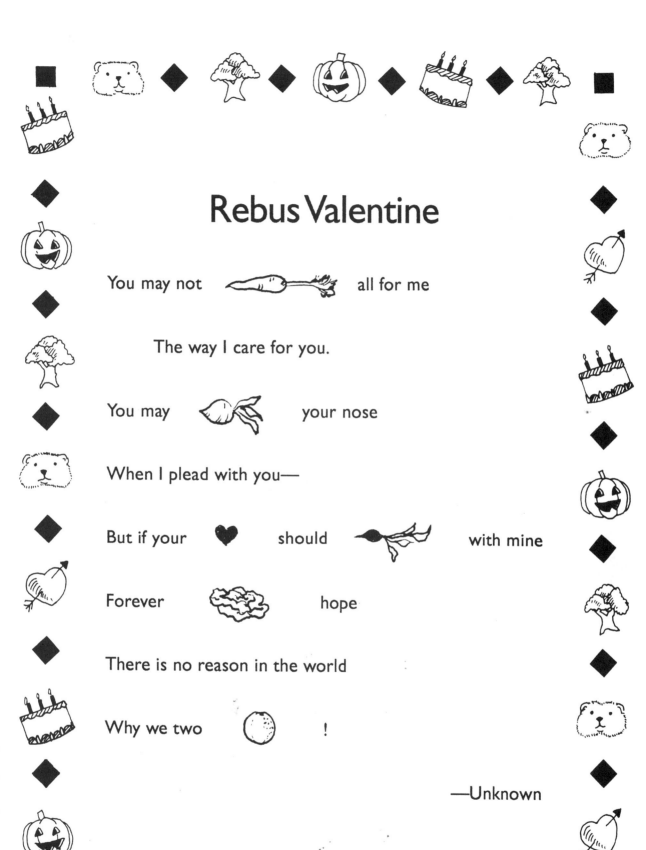 all for me

The way I care for you.

You may [image: leaf] your nose

When I plead with you—

But if your ♥ should [image: leaf] with mine

Forever [image: lettuce] hope

There is no reason in the world

Why we two ◯ !

—Unknown

Pathways to Poetry: Poetry Fun for Grades 1–3 © 1994 Fearon Teacher Aids

Language Arts

Acting Out the Poem with
    Rebuses
Rebus Valentine Messages
Creating Love-O-Grams
Broken Hearts
"Complete the Sentence"
    Hearts

Math

"Toss the Heart" Math
Estimating Hearts

Social Studies/Science

Origin of Valentine's Day

REBUS VALENTINE

Unknown

Art

Heart Puzzle
Making Heart-Shaped
    Butterflies
Queen and King of Hearts
    Paper-Bag Puppets
Making Valentine People

Music

Singing "A Paper of Pins"
Singing "Love Somebody,
    Yes I Do"

Health/Cooking/Physical
Education

Counting Your Heartbeats
Heart Tarts and Valentine
    Punch
"I Have a Valentine" Game

Rebus Valentine

The following suggestions can be used with the poem "Rebus Valentine." Select the activities that are most appropriate for the needs and age level of the children in the class.

Introducing the Poem

1. Display a heart made from a large sheet of red construction paper. Write the words *Valentine's Day* on the heart. Invite children to brainstorm words they think of when someone says, "Valentine's Day." Record the children's responses on the heart.

2. Encourage children to recall some of the messages printed on valentines. Record the messages on the chalkboard. Share the messages from some commercial valentines, too.

3. Write a message, such as "Will you be my valentine?" on a sheet of paper. Have a volunteer read the message to the class. Then replace the words *be* and *valentine* with rebuses.

Have children read the message with the rebuses. Clarify the meaning of the word *rebus* as a picture substituted for a word. If any of the valentine messages printed on the chalkboard contain a word or words which could be represented with rebuses, erase the words and ask volunteers to draw in the rebuses.

4. Tell children the title of the poem. Have children predict if the poem will have some words replaced by rebuses. Mention that the poet who wrote the poem is unknown.

Shared Listening and Reading

1. Display a copy of the poem on a chart or transparency. Before reading the poem aloud, have children identify the name of each rebus. Invite children to join in reading the poem by identifying each rebus at the appropriate time.

2. Read the poem aloud one or more times, encouraging children to read with you. Clarify, if necessary, the meaning of the words *plead* and *elope*. Read the poem several times, selecting ideas from the General Suggestions for Listening to and Reading the Poems on page 6.

3. Ask children to help you identify and write the word each rebus stands for on a sticky note. Then discuss the word or words each rebus sounds like and write these words on the same sticky notes. Invite children to read the poem again using the real words instead of the rebuses.

carrot	turnip	beet
care at	turn up	beat

Beyond Listening and Reading Activities

Acting Out the Poem with Rebuses

Give each child six pieces of heavy construction paper, approximately 4¹/₂" x 9". Have children draw and color the six rebuses used in the poem, one on each piece of paper. Then invite the children to read the poem and hold up the rebus cards at the appropriate times. Repeat the activity several times, having part of the class say the words of the poem and the other part show the rebus cards.

Rebus Valentine Messages

Write the following valentine messages on a chart:

My <u>heart</u> beats for you.
We'd make a great <u>pair</u>.
You have the <u>key</u> to my <u>heart</u>.
My heart <u>pants</u> for you.
I'm <u>nuts</u> about you.
I have my <u>eye</u> on you.
You're the <u>apple</u> of my <u>eye</u>.

As each message is read aloud, discuss what rebus could be used to stand for each underlined word. Invite volunteers to sketch rebuses on sticky notes, and then cover the words. Help younger children draw rebuses.

Encourage children to create other messages using rebuses. Record some of their messages on the chalkboard. Distribute red construction paper, and if necessary, demonstrate how to cut out a heart. Have children make a valentine with a rebus in the message. Post the rebus valentines on a bulletin board or wall.

Creating Love-O-Grams

Explain what a telegram is. Invite children to create a special type of telegram called a Love-O-Gram. Working with a partner, invite children to cut out letters and words from magazines and newspapers to use in their love-o-grams. After arranging the letters and words to create messages, have children glue their messages onto cards or sheets of red construction paper. Some children may wish to combine both words and pictures for their messages. Schedule a sharing time after the messages are completed.

Broken Hearts

Divide the class into cooperative work groups, providing dictionaries for each group, two copies of the reproducible on page 210, and scissors. Encourage the groups to first brainstorm compound words beginning with the word *heart*, such as heartbeat, heartache, and so on. Next, have children write the two parts of the compound word on the heart with one part of the word on each half. Have the children cut out each heart and write a sentence using the compound word on the back side. Lastly, cut each heart into two jagged sections (as in the example on the reproducible) to make a mini-puzzle.

When groups have finished, collect all the heart halves, separating them into two piles—one pile beginning with *heart* and the other pile with the second part of the compound word. Distribute all the heart halves, giving one to each child. Challenge each child to find his or her matching heart half. When all the children have found their partners, have the partners read the compound words and sentences aloud.

"Complete the Sentence" Hearts

For a learning center activity, make a variety of sizes of paper hearts, cutting each one in two jagged pieces. Write sentence beginnings, such as the following on one half of each heart:

Valentines are . . .
On Valentine's Day I . . .
Some valentines are . . .
I like to give valentines to . . .
My favorite valentine says . . .

Have children find the matching heart halves and complete the sentences. After a number of hearts have been completed, plan a sharing time.

"Toss the Heart" Math

Make a large poster size calendar for the month of February. Place the calendar in the center of a table. Divide the class into teams of four or five children. In turn, a member from each team stands about 6 feet from the table and tosses a specified number of candy hearts (four or five hearts usually works well) onto the calendar. The numbers on which the hearts land are added together by the teams. The first team answering correctly receives a point. The team with the highest score is the winner. If a heart lands on a line, the number does not count.

You can vary the game to suit the age and ability level of the children. Younger children can toss the hearts and find the sum of the largest and smallest numbers.

Estimating Hearts

Fill a small clear jar with candy hearts. Give children sticky notes to write their names and the number of hearts they think are in the jar. After all the children are finished have the children read their estimates and place the sticky notes in columns on a large piece of butcher paper. Then have the class count the exact number of hearts in the jar. Using the sticky notes, identify whose estimate is correct. Have younger children arrange the sticky notes from smallest to largest numeral.

Origin of Valentine's Day

Ask children to identify various symbols associated with Valentine's day, such as candy, cards, cupid, flowers, lace, and hearts. Divide the class into small groups. Suggest the groups read informational accounts of the origin of the holiday. (See Books for Read-Aloud and Independent Reading at the end of this theme.) Schedule time for the groups to share their findings. During the sharing time, develop a cooperative chart by listing some of the key information about Valentine's Day within the outline of a large heart.

For younger children, you may need to conduct this activity with the whole class by reading aloud from informational books. A good resource would be *Valentine's Day* by Gail Gibbons which provides an easy, concise account of the holiday's origin.

Heart Puzzle

Duplicate on tag or heavy construction paper the reproducible on page 211. Give each child a copy. Instruct children to first color and decorate the front of the heart and then write a valentine message on the back side. After the children cut out the heart, have them cut it into a number of puzzle pieces. Have each child place his or her puzzle pieces in an envelope. The puzzles can be used at a learning center.

Making Heart-Shaped Butterflies

You will need the following materials: wooden clothespins, black tempera paint, pipe cleaners, 3" x 1¹/₂" red construction-paper squares, and a range of other colored pieces of construction paper, such as pink, violet, yellow, black, and so on. Have each child follow these step-by-step directions. (You may wish to enlist the assistance of other adults and/or older children to help younger children.)

1. Paint the clothespin with black tempera paint for the butterfly body.
2. Cut two hearts from the 3" red squares and two hearts from the 1¹/₂" red squares for wings.
3. Decorate the wings with smaller hearts cut from a variety of colors of construction paper.
4. Glue the four wings onto the clothespin.
5. Glue two pipe cleaners to the top backside of the clothespin. Bend the pipe cleaners to form the antennae.
6. Cut out two small hearts to glue on the end of the antennae.

After the butterflies are thoroughly dry, suspend them with threads or fishing line from the ceiling or from wire hangers bent to form mobiles.

Queen and King of Hearts Paper-Bag Puppets

Teach children the well-known nursery rhyme, "The Queen of Hearts" which appears in numerous nursery rhyme books. Provide small paper bags and colored construction paper, such as red, pink, black, and so on. Instruct children to lay the paper bags flat on their tables with the flap at the top. The puppets can be decorated with construction-paper crowns, and various size hearts. Facial features can be completed with crayons. Encourage children to use their paper-bag puppets, while saying the nursery rhyme "The Queen of Hearts."

Making Valentine People

Provide a variety of different-size squares and colors of construction paper for cutting out hearts to make all the parts of the body. Then have children arrange the hearts into heart people. Then glue the hearts on sheets of white construction paper. Invite children to give their creations names and/or write sentences telling about them.

Singing

Teach children the songs "A Paper of Pins" and "Love Somebody, Yes I Do" from *The Holiday Song Book.*

Counting Your Heartbeats

Show an illustration of the human heart and share appropriate information with the children. Discuss points, such as the human heart is not really heart-shaped, the heart pumps blood through the body, exercise helps to keep the heart healthy, and you can count your heartbeats (pulse). Show children how to count their heartbeats for 15 seconds. Place two fingers on the inside of the wrist and press firmly until you feel a pulse.

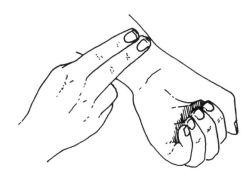

Heart Tarts and Valentine Punch

Using a heart-shaped cookie cutter, have each child cut out two hearts from bread. Have the children spread a red-colored jelly or jam on one of the hearts and top with the second heart.

Prepare Valentine Punch by following the directions on a package of red Kool Aid. Pour the Kool Aid into ice cube trays and freeze. (Use more than one package of Kool Aid, if necessary.) At snack time, place one or two flavored ice cubes in each cup and fill with ginger ale. Serve the Valentine Punch with the Heart Tarts.

"I Have a Valentine" Game

Seat the children in a circle. Choose one child to be "It" and stand in the middle of the circle. Select another child to be the Postal Worker and stand outside the circle. The Postal Worker calls out, "I have a valentine for _____ from _____," naming two children in the circle. "It" tries to tag one of the two children when they try to change places. If "It" is successful, the tagged child becomes the new "It." At frequent intervals, select different children to be the Postal Worker.

Broken Hearts

Directions: Follow your teacher's directions for writing compound words.

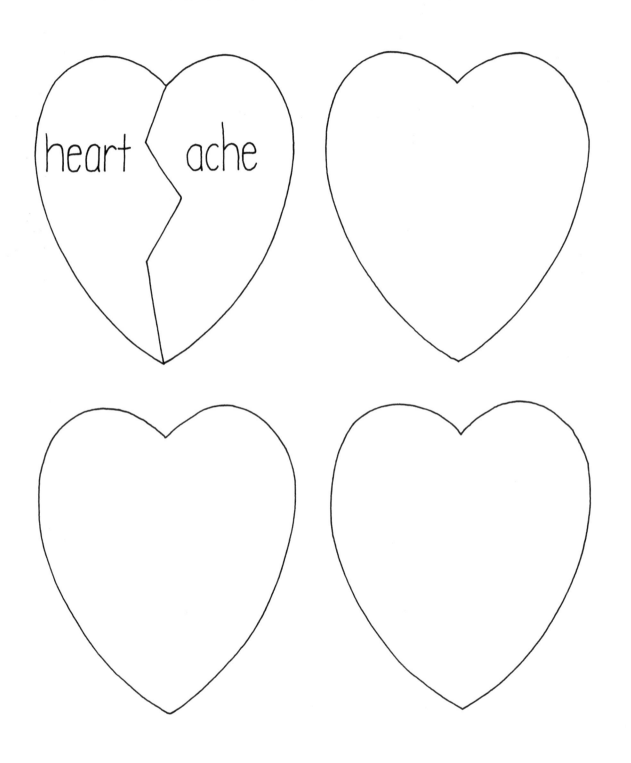

Pathways to Poetry: Poetry Fun for Grades 1-3 © 1994 Fearon Teacher Aids

Heart Puzzle

Directions: Color and decorate the front of the heart. Write a valentine message on the back side. Cut out the heart. Cut the heart into several puzzle pieces.

Suggested Books

Themed Poetry Books

Birthday Poems. Myra Cohn Livingston. New York, NY: Holiday House, 1989.

Birthday Rhymes, Special Times. Bobbye Goldstein. New York, NY: Doubleday, 1993.

Halloween ABC. Eve Merriam. New York, NY: Macmillan, 1987.

Halloween Poems. Myra Cohn Livingston. New York, NY: Holiday House, 1989.

Happy Birthday. Lee Bennett Hopkins. New York, NY: Simon & Schuster, 1991.

Ring Out Wild Bells: Poems About Holidays and Seasons. Lee Bennett Hopkins. San Diego, CA: Harcourt Brace Jovanovich, 1992.

Valentine Poems. Myra Cohn Livingston. New York, NY: Holiday House, 1987.

Books for Read-Aloud and Independent Reading

Arbor Day. Aileen Fisher. New York, NY: Thomas Y. Crowell, 1965. The background on the celebration of Arbor Day is told in this book.

Candles, Cakes, and Donkey Tails. Lila Perl. New York, NY: Clarion, 1984. Birthday traditions including the origin of celebrating birthdays and explanations for things associated with birthdays, such as birthday spanks and lighted candles are explained. Other birthday traditions from around the word are described.

City Seen From A to Z. Rachel Isadora. New York, NY: Greenwillow, 1983. The bustling city serves as the theme for this alphabet book.

Eating the Alphabet: Fruits and Vegetables from A to Z. Lois Ehlert. San Diego, CA: Harcourt, Brace Jovanovich, 1989. In this themed ABC book, readers are introduced to a wide variety of fruits and vegetables.

The Great Kapok Tree. Lynne Cherry. San Diego, CA: Harcourt Brace Jovanovich, 1990. Set in the Amazon rain forest, a man with an ax begins to chop down a huge kapok tree. Many different animals, who make the tree their home try to convince the man to not destroy their home.

The Half-Birthday Party. Charlotte Pomerantz. New York, NY: Clarion, 1984. Daniel stages a half-birthday party for his six-month-old sister, and all the guests bring half a present.

Halloween. Gail Gibbons. New York, NY: Holiday House, 1984. Many traditions followed on Halloween are presented, including carving jack-o'-lanterns, dressing up in costume, and displaying decorations.

Halloween. Joyce K. Kessel. Minneapolis, MN: Carolrhoda Books, 1980. Answers to questions, such as where jack-o'-lanterns come from, why black cats are associated with Halloween, why people once thought that witches come out on Halloween night, and other strange and interesting facts are presented.

Halloween Stories and Poems. Caroline Feller Baur. New York, NY: Lippincott, 1989. This book contains a collection of Halloween stories and poems drawn from varied authors and poets.

Happy Birthday. Gail Gibbons. New York, NY: Holiday House, 1986. The origins of birthday celebrations and customs are described, along with explanations of astrological signs.

It's Groundhog Day! Steven Kroll. New York, NY: Holiday House, 1987. Rolan Raccoon takes drastic steps to prevent Godfrey Groundhog from looking for his shadow on Groundhog Day!

Johnny Appleseed. Reeve Lindberg. Boston, MA: Little Brown, 1990. Rhymed text and illustrations relate the life of John Chapman.

Johnny Appleseed. Steven Kellogg. New York, NY: William Morrow, 1989. Marvelous illustrations and text recount tales about John Chapman and his life.

My Shadow. Robert Louis Stevenson. Illustrated by Ted Rand. New York, NY: G. P. Putnam, 1990. Joyous illustrations showing children all over the world with their shadows.

Nothing Sticks Like a Shadow. Ann Tompert. Boston, MA: Houghton Mifflin, 1984. Rabbit and Woodchuck engage in an argument when Rabbit says he can escape his own shadow if he wants to. After making a bet, Rabbit tries desperately to get rid of his shadow. The surprise ending proves them both to be correct.

On The Day You Were Born. Debra Frasier. San Diego, CA: Harcourt, Brace Jovanovich, 1991. The natural miracles of the Earth—gravity, tides, migration, and so on—are described in simple words and radiant collages.

The Seven Sleepers. Phyllis S. Busch. New York, NY: Macmillan, 1985. In this book, the author describes how various animals survive the winter season by hibernation, including an informative account of the ground hog.

Shadow Magic. Seymour Simon. New York, NY: Lothrop, Lee and Shepard, 1985. Simple explanations are provided for what shadows are, how they are formed, and how to make different shadow animals with hands.

Someday a Tree. Eve Bunting. New York, NY: Clarion Books, 1993. The big old oak tree on Alice's family's farm—the tree she loves dearly—has been poisoned by pollution. After realizing that the tree cannot be saved, Alice plants some acorns, hoping that someday there will be another tree.

A Tree Is Nice. Janice May Udry. New York, NY: HarperCollins, 1984. The 1957 Caldecott Award book describes the delights to be had in, with, and under a tree.

Valentine's Day. Dennis Brindell Fradin. Hillsdie, NJ: Enslow Publishers, 1990. This book describes the history of Valentine's Day and the various ways it is celebrated. It is a part of the Best Holiday Books series.

Valentine's Day. Gail Gibbons. New York, NY: Holiday House, 1986. The origins of Valentine's Day, ways in which it is celebrated, and why it is a special day are described.

Weird: The Complete Book of Halloween Words. Peter R. Limburg. New York, NY: Bradbury Press, 1989. Designed for older boys and girls, this book explores definitions and historical backgrounds for Halloween words, such as *haunt,* and *prank.*

What Happened Today, Freddy Groundhog? Marvin Glass. New York, NY: Crown, 1989. It's Freddy Groundhog's turn to dig his way to Farmer Green's pasture so he can come out and look for his shadow.

School
and Rules

First Day of School

I wonder
if my drawing
will be as good as theirs.

I wonder
if they'll like me
or just be full of stares.

I wonder
if my teacher
will look like Mom or Gram.

I wonder
if my puppy
will wonder
where I am.

—Aileen Fisher

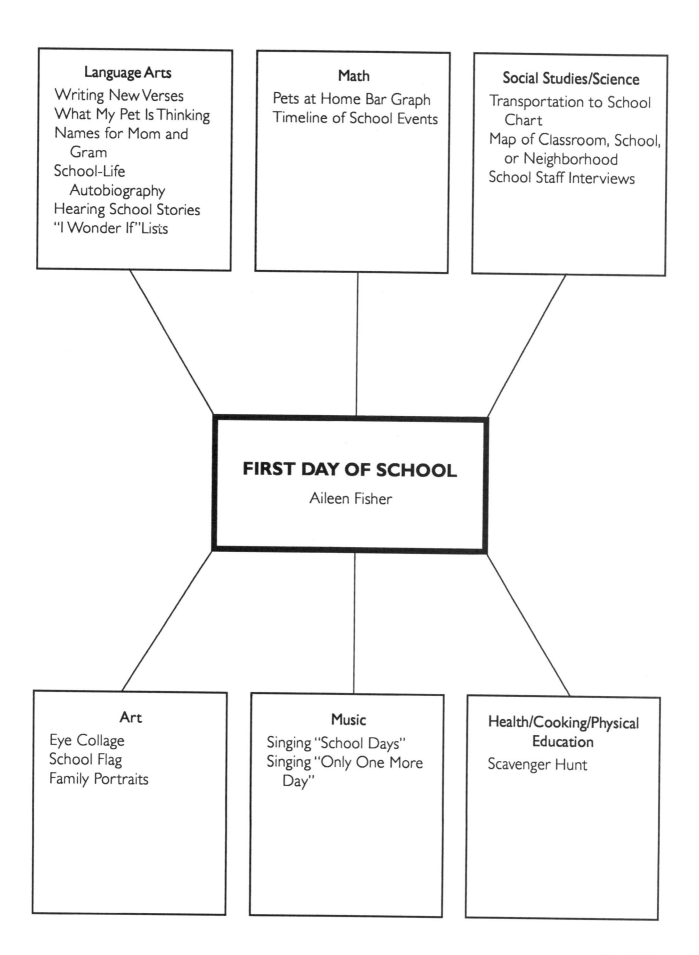

Language Arts

Writing New Verses
What My Pet Is Thinking
Names for Mom and
    Gram
School-Life
    Autobiography
Hearing School Stories
"I Wonder If" Lists

Math

Pets at Home Bar Graph
Timeline of School Events

Social Studies/Science

Transportation to School
    Chart
Map of Classroom, School,
    or Neighborhood
School Staff Interviews

FIRST DAY OF SCHOOL

Aileen Fisher

Art

Eye Collage
School Flag
Family Portraits

Music

Singing "School Days"
Singing "Only One More
    Day"

**Health/Cooking/Physical
Education**

Scavenger Hunt

First Day of School

The following suggestions can be used with the poem "First Day of School." Select the activities that are most appropriate for the needs and age level of the children in the class.

Introducing the Poem

1. Begin a discussion of the first day of school by sharing some of the feelings you had the night before and the things you wondered about. Ask the children to think back to the first day of school. Invite volunteers to tell how they felt the night before school. Ask questions such as "Were you excited?" and "What did you wonder about?"

2. Tell the children that the title of the poem is "First Day of School." Explain that the child in the poem wonders about several things concerning the first day of school. Have the children predict some of the things that the child in the poem might wonder about. Record the children's predictions on the chalkboard.

3. Share biographical information about the poet, Aileen Fisher. Refer to the Poet Bookmarks section on page 265. The bookmarks can be duplicated for the children or used to share information about each poet while studying his or her poem.

Shared Listening and Reading

1. Read the poem aloud to the class. Then have the children compare their predictions to the things the child in the poem wondered about.

2. Display a copy of the poem on a chart or transparency. Read the poem one or more times, encouraging the class to read with you. Point out that all four verses begin with the same words, "I wonder if." Have volunteers frame with their hands these words in each verse. You may also wish to point out that this poem is different from many that they have read because it doesn't rhyme.

3. Invite volunteers to read the verses aloud, using their voices to show that they are wondering about something. Have the class reread the poem several times, selecting from among the General Suggestions for Reading and Listening to the Poem on page 6.

4. Talk about who the word *theirs* refers to in the first verse. Have children suggest words that could replace *theirs,* such as *the other boys and girls.* Write these words on sticky notes and cover the word *theirs* in the first verse. Have the children reread the verse with the new substitutions. Follow a similar procedure for the word *they'll* in verse two.

5. Ask children whether the child in the poem thinks the teacher is a woman or a man, and find the verse that gives a clue. Cover the words *Mom* and *Gram,* and invite volunteers to contribute words that might be used if the teacher were a male. Have the class reread the verse with the new words.

Beyond Listening and Reading Activities

Writing New Verses

Display a copy of the poem. After the poem is reread aloud, invite the children to write new verses for the poem, telling things they wondered about before the first day of school. Suggest that the children begin their verses with the words "I wondered if," rather than "I wonder if," and talk about the tense change. You may wish to have children illustrate their verses and then bind the completed pages into a class book.

What My Pet Is Thinking

Discuss the various kinds of pets the children have and talk about how their pets must feel when they leave them on the first day of school. Duplicate and distribute the reproducible on page 224. Instruct children to draw pictures of their pets and write in the speech balloon what they think their pets are thinking. Children who do not own pets can either draw the puppy from the poem and write his or her thoughts or illustrate and write thoughts for the pets they would like to own.

Names for Mom and Gram

Write the word *Mom* on the chalkboard. Invite children to contribute words they use to refer to their Moms, and list the words on the chalkboard. Be sensitive to children's different family situations. Encourage children who speak languages other than English to share the words for Mom in their languages. Follow a similar procedure for the word *Gram.*

School-Life Autobiography

Introduce the term *autobiography*. Invite the children to write their school-life autobiographies, beginning with kindergarten and continuing to their current grade in school. Discuss some of the events the children could include, such as where they went to school, who their teacher was, something they remember as special about the year, and so on.

Distribute copies of the reproducible on page 225. Have children use one page for each year in school. For younger children, you may wish to write sentence beginnings on the page before duplicating and have children complete the sentences. For example: My teacher's name was _____. I learned _____. One day we _____.

Have children cut out the school pages, and make school covers from colored construction paper using the school shape as a pattern. Children can draw doors and windows on the cover with crayons. Staple the pages inside the covers to make individual books.

Hearing School Stories

Read aloud one or more stories about school, such as *The Teacher from the Black Lagoon* by Mike Thaler or *Never Spit on Your Shoes* by Denys Cazet. Have children compare their own school experiences with the experiences mentioned in the books.

"I Wonder if" Lists

Divide the class into small cooperative groups. Have the groups make "I wonder if" lists about the next grade in which they will be enrolled. Encourage the groups to share their lists with the whole class. If some of the things the class members wonder about can be answered by children in the next grade or a teacher of the succeeding grade, invite them to the class to respond to the children's questions.

Pets at Home Bar Graph

Have children make a class bar graph of their pets at home. First, ask the children to list the kinds of pets they own. As the children make suggestions, write them on the bottom of a large sheet of graph paper. As a class, decide on a color code for each pet, such as blue for cat, red for dog, white for mouse, and so on. Have the children come up, one-by-one, to mark on the graph the pets they have at home. After everyone has had a turn, count the number of pets in each group. Ask the children comparative questions and help them draw conclusions.

Timeline of School Events

Ask children to recount the most important school or class events that have happened since school began. Write each of these events on a separate piece of paper, leaving room for children to illustrate them later. After the children have suggested the events, such as a new child in the classroom, field trip to the zoo, party for Halloween, and so on, ask the children to help you arrange the events in order. Number the events after all the children agree on the sequence. Ask volunteers to illustrate the events and paste them together in numerical order. Older children can identify the month that these events occurred and make a timeline based on the months.

Transportation to School Chart

On a large sheet of paper, make a chart of the various ways children came to school on the first day, such as by foot, car, bicycle, bus, van, and so on. The children can each write his or her own names under the appropriate headings. Discuss the results.

Map of Classroom, School, or Neighborhood

Depending on the developmental level of the children, have the children make a map together of either the classroom, the school, or the immediate neighborhood. This activity can be extended to actually constructing a model of the school using boxes and scrap materials. Or, on an actual neighborhood map, older children can work with directional cues to find various key locations. (For example, "Walk four blocks east of the school on Oak Street, and one block south on Chestnut Street. What will you find there?") Children can also identify their homes on the map, if this is a neighborhood school.

School Staff Interviews

As a class, decide upon five school staff members to interview. Make up interview questions, write letters inviting staff members to an interview, deliver the invitations, and then after the interviews, write thank-you letters. Take a photo of each staff member at the interview and post them on an attractive bulletin board with quotes from the interviews.

Eye Collage

Have each child make a collage of staring eyes cut from magazines. Use black construction paper as the background. Display the collages on the walls. Discuss with the children how they feel when they look at the collages.

School Flag

Divide the class into small groups. Have each group design a school flag which reflects the community, the school name, the school mascot, or the school population. Provide construction paper, paint, scrap paper, glue, and scissors to make the flags. Then display the school flags in the hallway outside the classroom.

Family Portraits

Give each child an oval piece of construction paper. Have each child draw portraits of one of the people or animals he or she left at home on the first day of school. When the children are finished, the pictures can be mounted on a class bulletin board under the heading, "Those at Home Who Wait and Wonder."

Singing

Teach children the songs "School Days" or "Only One More Day" from the book in *The Fireside Book of Fun and Game Songs.*

Scavenger Hunt

Divide the class into groups of three. Have each group go on a scavenger hunt to familiarize themselves with the school and the staff. Give each group a paper bag to collect the items and a list of items to check off. For example, the Principal's signature, rubberband from the secretary, bandadge from the nurse, bookmark from the librarian, computer-paper strip from the computer lab. Before the children begin, establish guidelines for waiting for signatures, how to ask for items, what the time constraints are, and so on. Notify the staff members involved ahead of time. Arrange a welcome to the First Day of School treat for the children when they return to the classroom.

What My Pet Is Thinking

Directions: Draw a picture of your pet. In the balloon, write what your pet might be thinking on the first day of school.

224

Pathways to Poetry: Poetry Fun for Grades 1-3 © 1994 Fearon Teacher Aids

School-Life Autobiography

Directions: Write about each year you have been in school.

Wiggly Giggles

I've got the wiggly-wiggles today,
And I just can't sit still.
My teacher says she'll have to find
A stop-me-wiggle pill.

I've got the giggly-giggles today;
I couldn't tell you why.
But if Mary hiccups one more time
I'll giggle till I cry.

I've got to stamp my wiggles out
And hold my giggles in,
Cause wiggling makes me giggle
And gigglers never win.

—Stacy Jo Crossen and Natalie Anne Covell

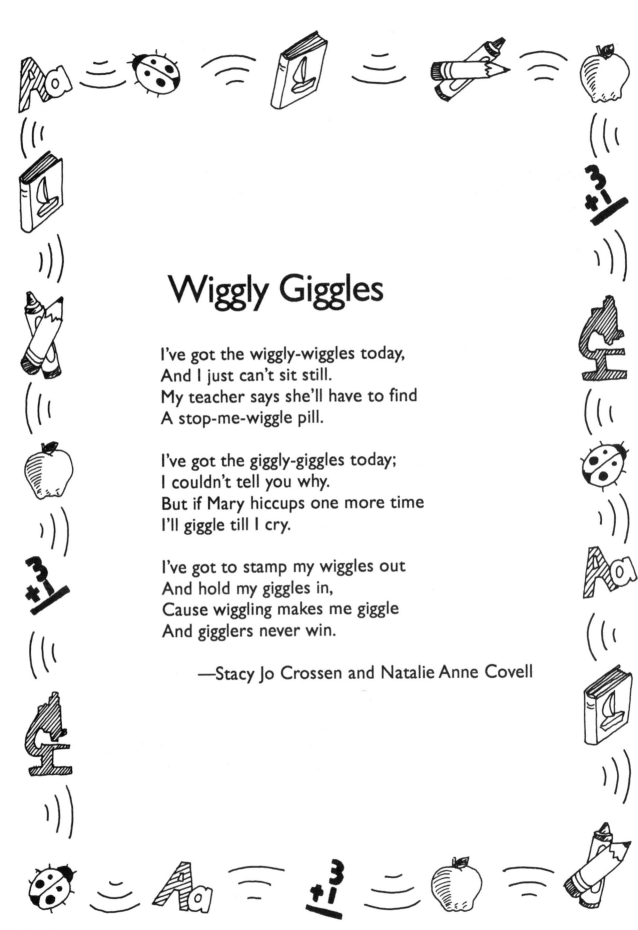

Pathways to Poetry: Poetry Fun for Grades 1-3 © 1994 Fearon Teacher Aids

Language Arts

Building Words
A Class Giggle Book
Writing Jokes for a Giggle
   Box
Creating a "Stop the
Giggles" Product
Sharing Stories That Make
   Me Giggle

Math

Cooked Spaghetti Shapes

Social Studies/Science

Research Hiccups and
   Remedies
Feel Your "Funny Bone"

WIGGLY GIGGLES

Stacy Jo Crossen and Natalie
Anne Covell

Art

Anti-Giggle Symbols
Funny Faces
Clown Faces
Squiggle Art

Music

Singing "Hokey Pokey"
Singing "Looby Loo"
Singing "Wiggle the Wool"

Health/Cooking/Physical Education

Anti-Wiggle Pills
Make Me Laugh
Freeze

Wiggly Giggles

The following suggestions can be used with the poem "Wiggly Giggles."
Select the activities that are most appropriate for the needs and age level
of the children in the class.

Introducing the Poem

1. Introduce the poem by leading the class in a game of "Do What I Do."
   First, wiggle your body in two or more ways, asking the class to do the
   same. Choose volunteers to lead the class in other ways of wiggling.
   Then do something unusual and giggle, asking the class to do the same.
   Choose several volunteers to lead the class in a similar activity.

2. Invite the class to share experiences where it has been difficult to sit
   still and someone has told them to stop wiggling. Briefly talk about
   situations in which the children have had the giggles.

3. Tell children the title of the poem. Ask the children why they think the
   poets might like to write a poem called "Wiggly Giggles." Information
   about the poets could not be located for the Poet Bookmark section
   on page 265.

Shared Listening and Reading

1. Read the poem aloud to the class, asking children to listen carefully to
   find out what makes the child in the poem giggle.

2. Display a copy of the poem on a chart or transparency. Read the
   poem one or more times, inviting the children to read with you. After
   reading discuss the following:

   Where was the child in the poem? How do you know?
   What did the teacher want to give him or her? Is there such a
   thing as a "stop-me-wiggle" pill?
   If you were the teacher, what would you do to keep someone from
   wiggling?
   Why was the child in the poem giggling? Would that make you
   giggle?
   What is meant by the words "stamp my wiggles out," "hold my
   giggles in." and "gigglers never win"?

Does wiggling make you giggle? Have you ever giggled until you were crying?

3. Choose volunteers to pantomime the roles of the child, the teacher, and Mary while the other class members read the poem aloud. Repeat the pantomines and reading several times.

Beyond Listening and Reading Activities

Building Words

Have the children look through the poem to find words made from the words *wiggle* and *giggle*. Record the base words on the chalkboard. Write the words the children identify under the appropriate base word, and discuss what letter or letters were added and/ or changed to form the new word. Expand beyond the poem to include other words formed from the words *wiggle* and *giggle*. You may wish to have children contribute oral sentences using some of the words, or have older children write humorous stories using as many different forms of the words *wiggle* and *giggle* as they can incorporate meaningfully.

wiggle	giggle
wiggles	giggles
wiggly	giggly
wiggling	giggling
wiggler	giggler
wiggled	giggled

A Class Giggle Book

Have the children make a class giggle book with each child copying and completing the sentence "I giggle when _____." Have the children illustrate their pages. Bind them into a class book and display the book in a class library.

Writing Jokes for a Giggle Box

Read aloud several jokes or riddles which appeal to children. (See Books for Read Aloud and Independent Reading at the end of this theme.) Provide notecards or slips of paper. Then invite the class, working individually or with a partner, to write jokes they make up or have heard. Write one joke per card. You may wish younger children to locate and copy jokes from easy joke books. Drop the jokes in a decorated box called "The Giggle Box." At appropriate times in the next few days, invite the class to have giggle time by drawing cards from "The Giggle Box" and reading the jokes aloud.

Creating a "Stop-the-Giggles" Product

Display several advertisements for new products from magazines or newspapers. Discuss the content of the advertisements, such as a picture, name, claims made for the product, packaging format, and price. Divide the class into small groups. Then ask each group to create an advertisement for a new product that is guaranteed to "stop-the-giggles." Display the completed advertisements on a wall or bulletin board.

Sharing Stories That Make Me Giggle

Make available a number of humorous books, such as books by Harry Allard about *The Stupids,* books about *Ameila Bedelia* by Peggy Parish, and a range of others. In cooperative groups, have each group select one of the books to read. After all groups have practiced reading their books, plan a sharing time in which each group reads aloud to the class from the book they selected. After all groups have shared their books, take a class vote on the book that was the funniest.

Cooked Spaghetti Shapes

There is no food more wiggly than spaghetti. Cook up a pot of spaghetti and give each child at least 10 strands on a non-absorbent material like wax paper or plastic. Teach shapes using spaghetti, having the children make squares, circles, triangles, rectangles, and so on. After the lesson, children can make their own shapes and figures.

Research Hiccups and Remedies

Explain to the class that hiccups result from the diaphragm moving up and down too fast. Air rushes in and the opening to the trachea (glottis) snaps causing the "hic" sound. It usually happens when you take in either too much food or too much air. Ask the children to share the hiccup remedies they were taught at home. For example: breathing into a paper bag, eating a teaspoon of sugar, and taking a deep breath.

Feel Your "Funny Bone"

Help children find their funny bones (above the elbow on the pinky side of the body). Point out that the funny bone is the end of the humerus, the large bone in the upper arm. The ulnar nerve passes over the humerus bone and that is why it really hurts when you hit your funny bone. Ask children to try to figure out how the term funny bone originated. If necessary, tell them that the term *funny bone* is a play on the word *humerus.*

Anti-Giggle Symbols

On a paper plate, have each child draw a picture of what makes him or her giggle. Then have the children color the rims of the plates red, and draw red lines through the plate making the international symbol for "No." Display on the bulletin board.

Funny Faces

Using cutout features from different faces in a magazine, have the children design the funniest faces they can. These will make a creative bulletin-board display.

Clown Faces

Using face paint, have each child use a mirror and make the funniest clown face he or she can. You may want to have some photos or pictures of clowns to provide make-up ideas. Children can also add costumes, such as wigs made from yarn, hats, large clothing, neckties, big shoes, and so on. Take photos of the children to display on the bulletin board.

Squiggle Art

Duplicate and distribute the reproducible on page 233. Have children create pictures from the squiggles and share them with one another. Encourage children to make squiggles of their own on another sheet of paper if they want to continue the activity.

Singing

Teach the children the song the "Hokey Pokey" from the book *The Fireside Book of Children's Songs*. Use the song to shake the giggles out. The children may also enjoy learning the song "Looby Loo" from the book *Sally Go Round the Sun*. This can be used as an alternative to the "Hokey Pokey." Or, teach the children the song "Wiggle the Wool" from *The Fireside Book of Fun and Game Songs*.

Anti-Wiggle Pills

Each child can "cook" his or her own anti-wiggle pills following this recipe which makes about 2 to 3 balls:

  1 teaspoon peanut butter
  1 teaspoon honey
  2 teaspoons dry milk

Mix the ingredients and roll into 2 to 3 balls. Roll the balls in shredded coconut, chopped nuts, sprinkles, or powdered sugar.

Make Me Laugh

This game requires that the person who is "It" keeps a straight face while all of his or her classmates try to make "It" laugh. This can be done live or on videotape. Time can be kept with a three-minute timer. If "It" can keep a straight face while the rest of the class tries to make him or her laugh, he or she has shaken the wiggly giggles.

Freeze

One person is "It" and stands behind a line with his or her back to the class. The rest of the class attempts to scoot up and tag the person who is "It." "It" can shout "freeze" at any point and turn around to see where everyone is. As soon as "It" is tagged, "It" may chase the person to the line and tag back. The one who tags gets to be "It."

232

Squiggle Art

Name _____

Directions: Create pictures from these wiggly squiggles. In the last box, create a squiggle picture of your own.

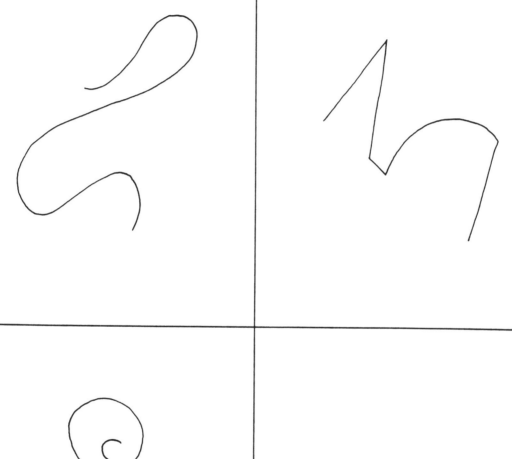

233

Rhinos Purple, Hippos Green

My sister says
I shouldn't color
Rhinos purple,
Hippos green.
She says
I shouldn't be so stupid.
Those are things
She's never seen.
But I don't care
What my sister says.
I don't care
What my sister's seen.
I will color
What I want to —
Rhinos purple
Hippos green.

—Michael Patrick Hearn

Pathways to Poetry: Poetry Fun for Grades 1-3 © 1994 Fearon Teacher Aids

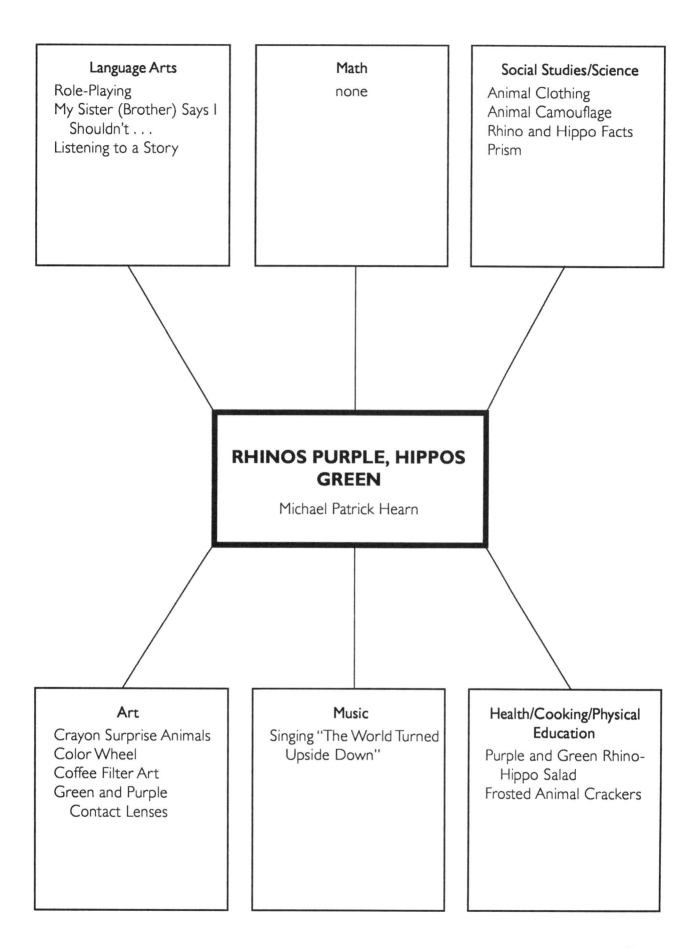

Language Arts

Role-Playing
My Sister (Brother) Says I
   Shouldn't . . .
Listening to a Story

Math

Social Studies/Science

Animal Clothing
Animal Camouflage
Rhino and Hippo Facts
Prism

RHINOS PURPLE, HIPPOS GREEN

Michael Patrick Hearn

Art

Crayon Surprise Animals
Color Wheel
Coffee Filter Art
Green and Purple
   Contact Lenses

Music

Singing "The World Turned
Upside Down"

Health/Cooking/Physical Education

Purple and Green Rhino-
   Hippo Salad
Frosted Animal Crackers

Rhinos Purple, Hippos Green

The following suggestions can be used with the poem "Rhinos Purple, Hippos Green." Select the activities that are most appropriate for the needs and age level of the children in the class.

Introducing the Poem

1. Initiate a discussion about sibling relationships by surveying the class to determine how many have older sisters or brothers. Ask those children who have older brothers or sisters if their siblings sometimes "boss" them around, telling them things they should or shouldn't do. If you have had personal experiences of this nature, share some stories from your life first. Likewise, invite children who have younger brothers or sisters to talk about ways in which they are the ones doing the "bossing" around.

2. Ask whether the children are ever told by older brothers or sisters that a paper or work they brought home from school was dumb or silly. Encourage children to describe situations in which this might have occurred.

3. Tell the class the poem is about something a sister told her younger brother or sister he or she shouldn't do.

4. Share biographical information about the poet, Michael Patrick Hearn. Refer to the Poet Bookmarks section on page 265. The bookmarks can be duplicated for the children or used to share information about each poet while studying his or her poem.

Shared Listening and Reading

1. Read the poem aloud, asking the class to listen carefully to find out what the sister says not to do. Afterwards, encourage children to comment and compare any similar experiences they may have had with art work or other school-related work.

2. Display a copy of the poem on a chart or transparency. Have the class read the poem with you. Talk about whether or not the children think it was nice of the sister to use the word *stupid*. Invite comments about how the child in the poem probably felt, and whether or not he

or she really did care even though he or she said, "I don't care." Re-read the poem one or more times, selecting from among the General Suggestions for Listening to and Reading the Poems on page 6.

3. Call attention to the use of the word *Rhinos* for the word *Rhinoceroses* and the word *Hippos* for the word *Hippopotamuses.* Write the complete words for each animal on the chalkboard, and have the children say the animal names aloud. Invite the class to read the poem again using the words *Rhinoceroses* and *Hippopotamuses* instead *of Rhinos* and *Hippos.* Children may wish to read the poem more than once since it is fun to say the words *Rhinoceroses* and *Hippopotamuses.*

4. Discuss the title of the poem and whether or not it suits the content. Invite the children to suggest one or more alternate titles.

Beyond Listening and Reading Activities

LANGUAGE ARTS

Role-Playing

Invite volunteers to role-play the scene between the sister and the brother or sister, creating the dialogue. Role-play the same scene several times, with different volunteers doing the acting. You may wish to extend the poem by asking other volunteers to create a scene in which the boy or girl responds to what his or her sister said.

Have the class come up with other situations in which the sister says her brother or sister shouldn't do something. List the situations on the chalkboard. Then select different class members to role-play the scene. Follow each role-playing scene with discussion about the behaviors reflected.

My Sister (Brother) Says I Shouldn't . . .

Have each child complete the phrase "My sister (brother) says I shouldn't . . ." (using either *sister* or *brother*) and illustrate it. Bind the completed pages into a class book.

Listening to a Story

Read aloud the book *The Pain and the Great One* by Judy Blume. Discuss the situations described from the view point of the boy and his older sister. Help children conclude that the same actions and behaviors can be viewed differently by different people.

Animal Clothing

Duplicate and distribute the reproducible on page 241. Have children individually or in groups list all the animals they can think of that fall into the categories of spots, stripes, one color, and scales. Have each group share their lists discussing the animals that were included in each category.

Animal Camouflage

Have the children read informational books to find out the actual colors of hippos and rhinos. As a class, make a list of other animals that use camouflage to help them fit into their environment and hide from predators, such as polar bears, green tree frogs, and chameleons.

Rhino and Hippo Facts

Help the children locate the continent of Africa on a globe or a world map. Point out where rhinos and hippos live. Then provide a variety of nonfiction books about rhinos and hippos and challenge the children to research interesting facts. For example, the gestation period for a hippo is 650 days.

Prism

Have the children look through a prism that separates light into its components. Share this information with the class. First discovered by Newton, light is separated because the colors have different wavelengths and the shorter waves can't keep up with the longer ones as the light passes through the prism. While traveling through the air, the colors all combine into white light. For more information, read *The Magic of Color* by Hilda Simon.

Crayon Surprise Animals

Provide pictures and nonfiction books for the children to select a favorite African animal to draw. Have each child reach into a paper bag and randomly select four crayons. These are the colors the children may use to draw and color their animals. Share the completed pictures.

Color Wheel

Duplicate and distribute the reproducible on page 242. Give the children Styrofoam or aluminum trays with compartments filled with primary colors of tempera paint—red, blue, and yellow—plastic containers of water, small paintbrushes, and paper towels for wiping the brushes. Have the children fill in the primary colors on the reproducible color wheel. Then help the children mix the secondary colors on the tray—green, purple, and orange. Older children can mix the adjacent colors to make additional colors—blue-violet, yellow green, and so on.

Coffee Filter Art

Prepare water dyed with primary colors of food coloring. Give each child a cone-shaped coffee filter. Have children fold the filters into fourths and dip them into the colored water. The colors will mix on the filter and make attractive tie-dyed circles to hang up on the walls.

Green and Purple Contact Lenses

Have the children cut out 3-inch diameter circles of green and purple construction paper. Cut out the centers of the circles. Give each child 3-inch circles of green or purple transparency film or plastic wrap. Tape the plastic to the construction-paper circles. Then staple the "contact lenses" to tongue depressors. Invite children to explore what the world looks like through green or purple "contact lenses."

Singing

Teach the children the song "The World Turned Upside Down" from *The Fireside Book of Children's Songs*.

Purple and Green Rhino-Hippo Salad

Have the children bring in purple or green ingredients for a salad, such as purple cabbage, green lettuce, turnips, green beans, purple onions, and so on. Brainstorm purple and green vegetables ahead of time and send a note home to parents, inviting them to send in a small quantity of one of the vegetables on the list. Use Green Goddess dressing or Ranch with green food coloring. Encourage the children to try a small taste of the unusual salad.

239

Frosted Animal Crackers

Bring in animal crackers, white frosting, and food coloring. Have the children help you mix various colors of frosting in margarine containers. After you have mixed the primary and secondary colors, have each child frost three different animals using different colors for each. Then eat!

Animal Clothing

Name _____

Directions: Complete the following chart of animal coverings.

ANIMAL CLOTHING			
STRIPES	SPOTS	SCALES	ONE COLOR
_____	_____	_____	_____
_____	_____	_____	_____
_____	_____	_____	_____
_____	_____	_____	_____
_____	_____	_____	_____
_____	_____	_____	_____
_____	_____	_____	_____
_____	_____	_____	_____
_____	_____	_____	_____
_____	_____	_____	_____
_____	_____	_____	_____
_____	_____	_____	_____
_____	_____	_____	_____
_____	_____	_____	_____
_____	_____	_____	_____

Color Wheel

Name _____

Directions: Follow your teacher's directions.

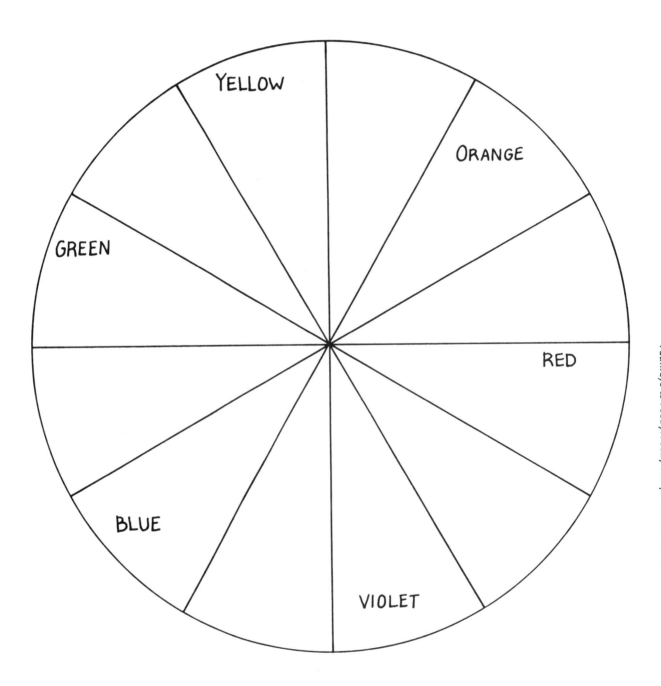

Pathways to Poetry: Poetry Fun for Grades 1-3 © 1994 Fearon Teacher Aids

Laura

Laura's new this year in school
She acts so opposite, it seems like a rule.
If someone says yes, Laura says no.
If someone says high, Laura says low.
If you say bottom, she'll say top.
If you say go, she'll always stop.
If you say short, Laura says tall.
If you say none, she says all.
If you say beginning, Laura says end . . .
But today she asked me to be her friend.
I said maybe
But not quite yes.
Then I said, "Want to take a walk?"
And Laura said, "I guess."

—Jeff Moss

Pathways to Poetry: Poetry Fun for Grades 1-3 © 1994 Fearon Teacher Aids

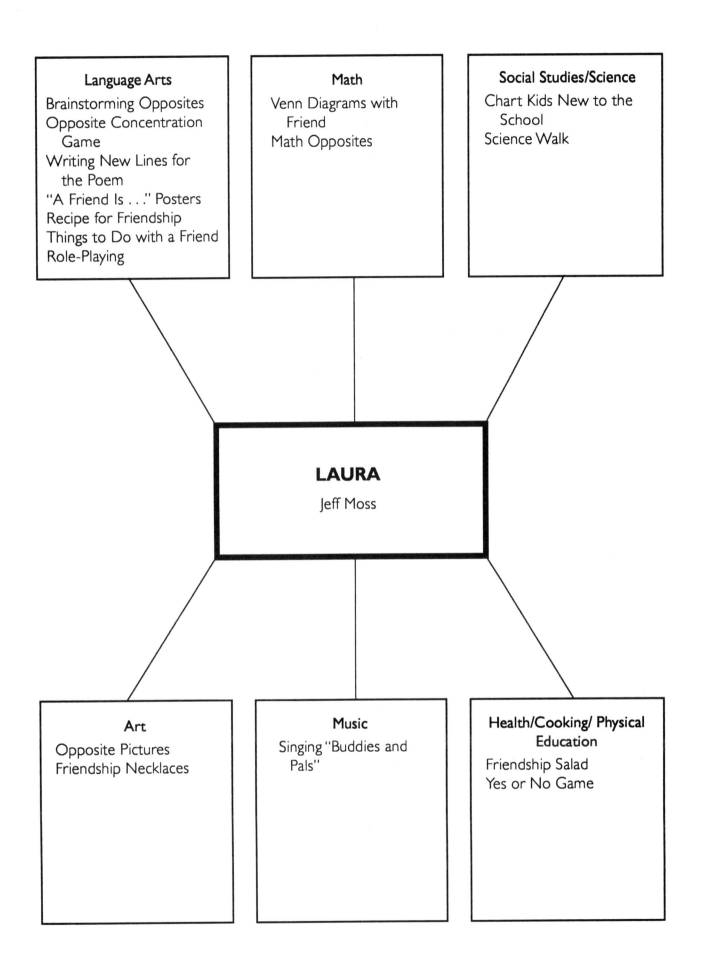

Language Arts

Brainstorming Opposites
Opposite Concentration
    Game
Writing New Lines for
    the Poem
"A Friend Is . . ." Posters
Recipe for Friendship
Things to Do with a Friend
Role-Playing

Math

Venn Diagrams with
    Friend
Math Opposites

Social Studies/Science

Chart Kids New to the
    School
Science Walk

LAURA

Jeff Moss

Art

Opposite Pictures
Friendship Necklaces

Music

Singing "Buddies and
    Pals"

**Health/Cooking/ Physical
Education**

Friendship Salad
Yes or No Game

244

Laura

The following suggestions can be used with the poem "Laura." Select the activities that are most appropriate for the needs and age level of the children in the class.

Introducing the Poem

1. Survey the class to find out how many children have been enrolled in more than one school since kindergarten. Invite those children who have attended more than one school to talk about their experiences. Stimulate the discussion by encouraging children to comment on their feelings about leaving their old school, how they felt about leaving their friends at the old school, and whether it was easy to make friends at the new school. Ask those children who have always attended the same school to tell how they feel about having "new" children in the classroom and the things they may have done to help a new child feel welcome.

2. Tell the children that the poem is about a girl named Laura who is new in school that year. Have the children speculate about what Laura might be like.

3. Share biographical information about the poet, Jeff Moss. Refer to the Poet Bookmarks section on page 265. The bookmarks can be duplicated for the children or used to share information about each poet while studying his or her poem.

Shared Listening and Reading

1. Read the poem to the children. Invite children's comments about Laura's behavior. Have children talk about why Laura might have acted the way she did, why she might have asked someone to be her friend, and how they might have responded had she asked them to be her friend.

2. Display a copy of the poem on a chart or transparency. Invite the children to read the poem with you. Have children note the rhyme pattern, which is rhyming couplets until the last four lines. Then have the children read the poem aloud several times, selecting from among

the General Suggestions for Reading and Listening to the Poems on page 6.

3. Encourage the class to speculate as to whether the "I" who speaks in the poem is a boy or a girl. Help the children to conclude that it could be either a girl or boy.

4. After the children are quite familiar with the words to the poem, select one child to be Laura and say only the words that Laura says. Then select several other children to read the opposite words said by the other children in the poem. Have the remainder of the class serve as the narrators. Underline each speaking part in a different color for easier reading. You may need to point out that the opposite words to be spoken do not appear in quotation marks, and that quotation marks for the speaking parts only appear in the last two lines.

5. Ask the class to substitute a boy's name for the name Laura in the poem. Make the needed substitutions of the name and the pronouns *she* and *her* using sticky notes. Then let the class reread the poem and have different children read the parts as they did when the poem used the name Laura.

Beyond Listening and Reading Activities

LANGUAGE ARTS

Brainstorming Opposites

Within a specified time limit, have cooperative groups brainstorm lists of opposite words other than those used in the poem. (With younger children, you may wish to conduct the brainstorming in a whole-class group and provide the stimulus word for children to come up with the opposite.) In sharing the lists, suggest that the groups have class members guess the opposite word, using a format similar to the poem. For example, "We say up, you say ___," with class members saying "down."

Opposite Concentration Game

Duplicate and distribute the reproducible on page 251. Have children cut out the cards. With a partner, children can play a game of opposite concentration by turning the cards face down. They then try to match two cards that are opposites. The one who makes the opposite match gets to keep the cards and gets a second turn. The player with the most matches is the winner.

Writing New Lines for the Poem

Duplicate and distribute copies of the poem "Laura." Have children cross out the opposite words that appear in lines three through nine of the poem. These words are: yes-no, high-low, bottom-top, go-stop, short-tall, none-all, and beginning-end. Ask children to create new lines for the poem by writing different opposite words above the crossed-out words. As an added challenge for older students, suggest they try to come up with opposites to make rhyming couplets as in the poem. Plan a time for children to share their new versions of the poem.

"A Friend Is . . ." Posters

Encourage the children to discuss friendship. Ask questions, such as "What makes a friend?" "What does it take to be a friend?" "What do you do to show someone you are a friend?" and "What does a friend do to show that he or she is a friend to you?" Then have the class make posters, individually or with a partner, depicting different aspects of friendship. Instruct children to complete the sentence "A friend is . . . ."

Recipe for Friendship

Review with the class what a recipe contains, such as ingredients, quantities, and directions or procedures to follow. Then suggest cooperative groups write a recipe for friendship. Suggest children think of specific things that are important to a good friendship, such as fairness, taking turns, kindness, honesty, and so on. Display the completed recipes on a bulletin board.

Recipe for Friendship

1 cup kindness
1/4 cup fairness
2 tablespoons of smiles
1 teaspoon laughs
Mix together and serve.

Things to Do with a Friend

Have the class make individual lists of things they like to do with friends. (You may wish to suggest a specific number of activities be listed.) Then ask each child to rank the activities on his or her list from the most favorite activity to the least favorite activity. During a sharing time, compare the lists of favorite activities.

Role-Playing

Divide the class into pairs. Have the partners role-play situations involving friendship. For example: A new child enters the class. What will you say to him or her? What can you do to make him or her feel welcome?

Have children work with their partners for a brief time to develop the scene. Then have each pair role-play the scene for the class. As time permits, provide several situations for role-playing.

Venn Diagrams with Friend

Have each pair of children fill in a Venn Diagram, which is a graphic way of showing similarities and differences. The children need to talk to find out what activities they both like. Write these activities in the center of the overlapping circles. The unique activities are written in each child's individual circle.

Math Opposites

Have the children make up a list of math opposites, such as multiply–divide, add–subtract, plus–minus, more than–less than, higher–lower, more–less, bigger–smaller, and so on.

Chart Kids New to the School

Make up a timeline of when children first came in new to the school. You can do this by months or school years. Have each child draw himself or herself on a paper doll pattern. Place the figure on the appropriate month or year on the timeline.

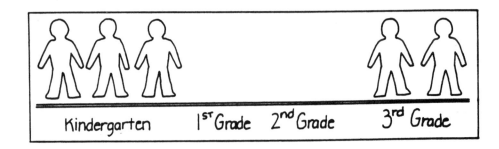

Science Walk

Have children work with a friend on a science walk to collect as many different nature items as they can find. Explain to the children that it is important to not upset the environment as they are collecting objects. Upon returning to the classroom, ask each pair to classify their items by making a circle around similar objects with a piece of yarn, and pasting the objects and yarn to a heavy sheet of cardboard. Display and share the collections.

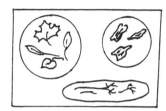

Opposite Pictures

Give each child a black ½ sheet of construction paper and a full sheet of white construction paper. Instruct children to fold the white paper in half. Next, cut out designs from the center of the black paper without cutting through the edge. Lastly, paste the black sheet on one side of the white paper while the cutouts are pasted on the other side of the white paper.

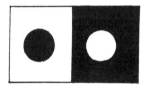

Friendship Necklaces

Give each pair of children one margarine lid and a heart-shaped pattern. Have the children cut out the heart and then divide it in half with a jagged cut. Each child gets a half. Punch holes in the tops of the two heart halves and invite the children to select a color of yarn to attach to the heart halves. Encourage the children to wear their friendship hearts.

Singing

Teach the children the song "Buddies and Pals" from *Tom Glazer's Do Your Ears Hang Low?*

Friendship Salad

Have each child bring in one fruit. Each child can use a plastic knife to cut up the fruit and add it to a huge friendship fruit salad. Add colored miniature marshmallows for fun. The fruit juices make the dressing.

Yes or No Game

Hide an item in a "mystery" box. The children must guess what is in the box, by asking questions that can be answered with "yes" or "no." Encourage the children to zero in on each item by asking general questions first. Give children examples, such as "Is it alive?" "Is it green?" and "Is it hard?" if necessary.

250

Opposite Concentration Game

Directions: Cut out the cards. With a partner, turn the cards face down and play a game of opposite concentration.

up	down	big	little
high	low	hot	cold
happy	sad	in	out
black	white	hard	soft

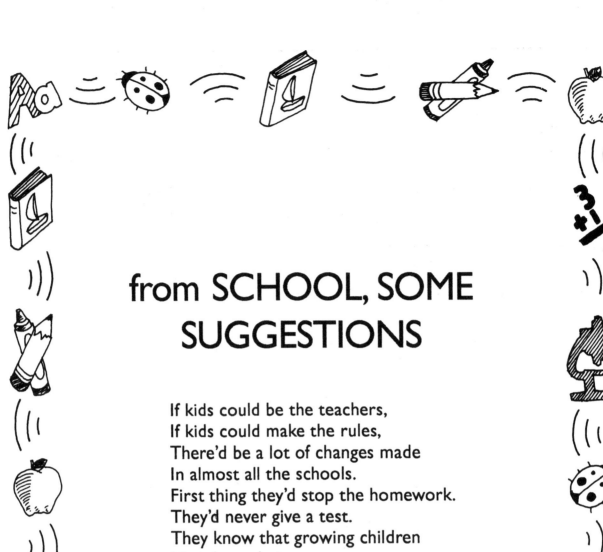

from SCHOOL, SOME SUGGESTIONS

If kids could be the teachers,
If kids could make the rules,
There'd be a lot of changes made
In almost all the schools.
First thing they'd stop the homework.
They'd never give a test.
They know that growing children
Must have their proper rest.
They'd make the lunchtime longer —
Let's say from twelve to two,
So every growing boy or girl
Had time enough to chew!

—Bobbi Katz

Pathways to Poetry: Poetry Fun for Grades 1-3 © 1994 Fearon Teacher Aids

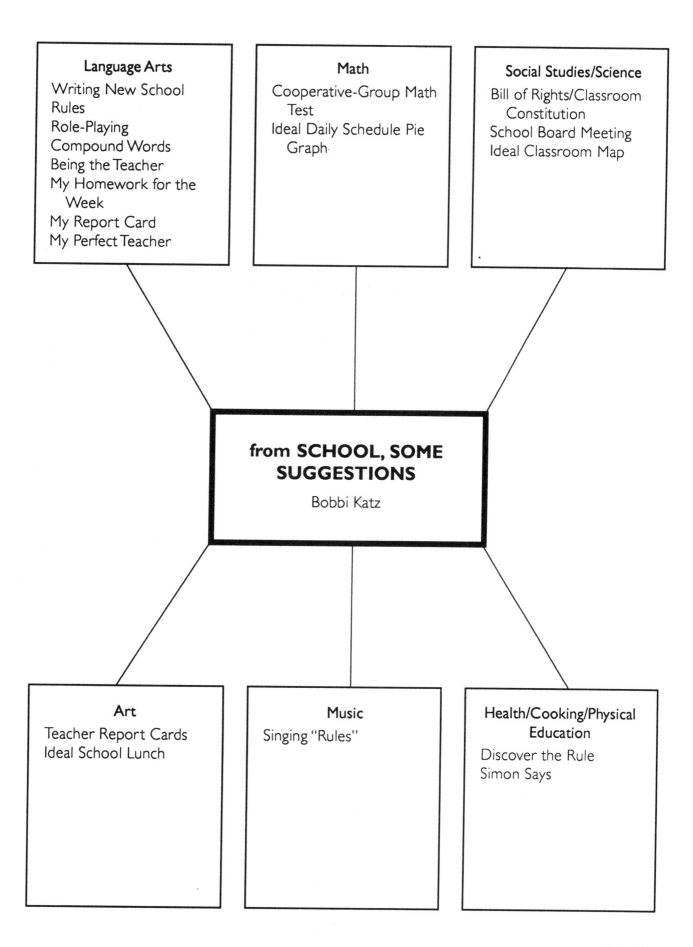

Language Arts

Writing New School Rules
Role-Playing
Compound Words
Being the Teacher
My Homework for the Week
My Report Card
My Perfect Teacher

Math

Cooperative-Group Math Test
Ideal Daily Schedule Pie Graph

Social Studies/Science

Bill of Rights/Classroom Constitution
School Board Meeting
Ideal Classroom Map

from SCHOOL, SOME SUGGESTIONS

Bobbi Katz

Art

Teacher Report Cards
Ideal School Lunch

Music

Singing "Rules"

Health/Cooking/Physical Education

Discover the Rule
Simon Says

from School: Some Suggestions

The following suggestions can be used with the poem "from School: Some Suggestions." Select the activities that are most appropriate for the needs and age level of the children in the class.

Introducing the Poem

1. Ask the children to imagine that they are the teachers. Have each child tell one thing he or she likes about school and would not change. Continue by telling children they can make some changes. Have each child write (or state orally) an ending to the following sentence: "If I were the teacher, I would _____." Give each child an opportunity to share his or her ending.

2. Tell the children the title of the poem. Point out that the poet mentions a number of changes that children might make if they were the teachers. Clarify the meaning of the word suggestions, if necessary.

3. Share biographical information about the poet, Bobbi Katz. Refer to the Poet Bookmarks section on page 265. The bookmarks can be duplicated for the children or used to share information about each poet while studying his or her poem.

Shared Listening and Reading

1. Read the poem aloud to the class. Encourage children to comment about the poem. Read the poem aloud a second time and ask children to compare the changes they suggested with those mentioned in the poem.

2. Display a copy of the poem on a chart or transparency. As you read the poem aloud, invite children to join in the reading. Discuss the reason given for not giving homework and tests. Ask the children what does the idea that growing children need proper rest have to do with homework and tests? Also, discuss the reason given for lengthening the lunch hour. Have children compare the length of their lunch hour with the length suggested in the poem.

3. Have the class reread the poem several times, selecting from among the General Suggestions for Reading and Listening to the Poems on page 6.

Writing New School Rules

Divide the class into cooperative work groups. Distribute a copy of the reproducible on page 259 to each group. Have each group develop a list of school changes they would make if they could make the rules. For each change listed, have the children state a reason why the change should be made. Instruct children not to list changes mentioned in the poem. When the groups are finished, plan a time for all groups to share their lists.

Role-Playing

In advance, write on slips of paper school changes mentioned in the poem and some changes that were mentioned by children in the Writing New School Rules activity. Place the slips of paper in a paper bag. Make role identification names by writing "TEACHER" on two or more tagboard strips and "KID" on two to four strips. (You may also wish to make one saying "PRINCIPAL.") Attach yarn to the tagboard strips for children to wear around their necks.

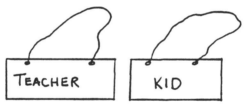

Select volunteers to play the role of the Teachers while others play the Kids role. The Kids draw a slip of paper from the paper bag identifying the change, and then role-play the scene with the Teachers or Principal in which they propose the change. The Kids must come up with reasons for the change, while the Teachers or Principal take the opposing viewpoint with reasons why the change should not be made. Continue the activity with different players and changes.

Compound Words

Draw the children's attention to the compound words *homework* and *lunchroom* used in the poem. Have the children identify the two words which form each compound word and talk about the meaning. Invite children to name other compound words, especially ones associated with school, such as chalkboard, classroom, lunchbox, bookshelf, playground, and schoolyard. List the words on the chalk-board. For one or more of the words, quickly illustrate the two words separately and then the compound word.

Provide drawing paper for each child. Instruct the children to first fold the papers into four parts. Have the children then illustrate four compound words, first showing the two parts of the word then the compound word. The children can select from among those listed on the chalkboard or others they may think of. Have the children write the words by their illustrations.

Being the Teacher

Over a period of several days, select different children to "be the teacher" for supervising or conducting specific tasks. You may wish to have the class compile a list of tasks in which they would like to serve as the teacher, such as taking lunch count, giving instructions for playing a game, explaining homework, or giving a spelling test. Take time periodically to encourage the children to discuss what it was like being the teacher.

My Homework for the Week

Duplicate and distribute the reproducible on page 260. Help the children brainstorm types of homework that they could assign for themselves for each day listed, such as read their library books for 15 minutes, count to one hundred by fives, and other assignments relevant to your curriculum and children. Then have the children write out their own homework assignments for each day. Send the page home on Monday, asking children to return the sheets on Friday with their parent or guardians' signatures. At that time, discuss with children their feelings about assigning their own homework.

My Report Card

Duplicate and distribute the reproducible on page 261. Discuss the grading system. Invite each child to complete his or her own report card and write a comment. You may wish the class to share their report cards by posting them on a bulletin board, or you may prefer to have each child individually discuss his or her report card with you.

My Perfect Teacher

If possible, introduce this activity by reading aloud the book *Miss Nelson Is Missing* by Harry Allard. After discussing the book, engage the class in a discussion about the qualities of teachers they like best, cautioning the children not to name specific teachers they may have had. Provide writing and drawing paper and invite each child to write a description of his or her perfect teacher, and make an illustration of him or her. Suggest children include what he or she would do, say, and be like as a teacher. Have children share their completed work.

Cooperative-Group Math Test

Divide the class into pairs. Have children write math problems or examples for a test on a sticky note with their names written under the example. Collect all of the sticky notes, arrange the notes on a page and duplicate the test for each child in the class. After everyone has taken the test, the papers are passed around so that each pair marks the example or problem they wrote.

Ideal Daily Schedule Pie Graph

Introduce the concept of a pie graph and draw a large size pie on the chalkboard. Show the children what their six-hour day looks like on a pie graph. Then hand out actual paper pie plates, have the children divide the pie plates into six sections, and then draw in each section how they would like to spend that time.

Bill of Rights/Classroom Constitution

Read to the class, *Shh! We're Writing the Constitution* by Jean Fritz. Tell the children that our country's laws are found in the Constitution. All the other laws that states, cities, and even schools make have to agree with the Constitution. Tell the children about some of the rights that the Constitution guarantees to citizens—freedom of speech, freedom of religion, freedom of the press, freedom to assemble, the right to vote, and so on. Have the children develop a "Children's Bill of Rights" for the classroom. Have all the children sign it and then post it in a conspicuous place where it can be referred to often.

School Board Meeting

Either attend a school board meeting with the class or invite a school board member to describe how school rules are made. The children can make their school rule suggestions to the school board member and learn that the Constitution guarantees the right to petition to make changes in a peaceful way.

Ideal Classroom Map

Ask the children to brainstorm all the things they would like to see added to the classroom environment if they had their way. After the list is on the chalkboard, ask the children to include all of their individual preferences on one giant map of the classroom.

Teacher Report Cards

Discuss what the children think teachers should be graded on in report cards. Have the children work in groups to design and fill out a teacher report card. Make available paper, crayons, scissors, and paste. Have each group share the report cards.

Ideal School Lunch

Have children cut pictures from magazines of food items that would make an ideal school lunch. Have the children make a collage of food pictures on a large paper plate. Have each child share his or her ideal lunch plate with the class.

Singing

Teach the children the song "Rules" from *The Fireside Book of Fun and Game Songs.*

Discover the Rule

Everyone sits in a circle and the person chosen as "It" leaves the room. The children decide on a "rule" to be followed when answering questions when "It" returns to the room. The rule could be, for example, yawning before answering a question, answers must begin with a certain letter of the alphabet, answers have to be one syllable, the answer must contain a color, and so on. The person who is "It" begins to ask questions of individuals and the person who answers must adhere to the rule. When "It" guesses the rule, a new person is "It" and a new rule is chosen.

Simon Says

Everyone must follow the rules and wait until the leader says, "Simon Says" before asking the children to follow his or her verbal directions. This is a familiar game that children of this age still enjoy.

Writing New School Rules

Name: _____

Directions: Write a list of school changes. For each change, state a reason why the change should be made.

Rule 1: _____

_____

Reason: _____

_____

Rule 2: _____

_____

Reason: _____

_____

Rule 3: _____

_____

Reason: _____

_____

Rule 4: _____

_____

Reason: _____

_____

Homework for the Week

Name: _____

Directions: Write your homework assignments each day.

Dear Parent(s) or Guardian:
We are reading poems about school. One of the poems is named "from School: Some Suggestions," and it tells of changes children might make in school if they were the teachers. Your child has developed his or her own homework assignments for this week. Please initial each day when your child completes the homework and send this form back to school on Friday.

Monday _____

_____

_____

_____

Tuesday _____

_____

_____

_____

Wednesday _____

_____

_____

_____

Thursday _____

_____

_____

_____

Pathways to Poetry: Poetry Fun for Grades 1–3 © 1994 Fearon Teacher Aids

My Report Card

Directions: Complete your own report card and write comments.

Report Card

School _____

Student _____ Grade _____

Marking Code			
+ Outstanding ✓ Average - Needs to improve			
Reading		Science	
Writing		Social Studies	
Spelling		Art	
Handwriting		Music	
Mathematics		Physical Education	

COMMENTS: _____

_____

_____

_____

_____

_____

Pathways to Poetry: Poetry Fun for Grades 1–3 © 1994 Fearon Teacher Aids

Suggested Books

Themed Poetry Books

Best Friends. Lee Bennett Hopkins. New York, NY: Harper & Row, 1986.

Don't Read This Book, Whatever You Do: More Poems About School. Kalli Dakos. New York, NY: Four Winds Press, 1993.

If You're Not Here, Please Raise Your Hand : Poems About School. Kalli Dakos. New York, NY: Four Winds Press, 1990.

Today We Are Brother and Sister. Arnold Adoff. New York, NY: Lothrop, Lee & Shepard, 1981.

Books for Read-Aloud and Independent Reading

Amelia Bedelia. Peggy Parish. New York, NY: Scholastic, 1970. Amelia, the lovable maid, takes directions "literally," creating all kinds of havoc and hilarious situations. Numerous other titles are in the *Amelia Bedelia* series.

The Art Lesson. Tomie dePaola. New York, NY: G. P. Putnam's Sons, 1989. Young Tommy, who loves drawing pictures at home, is frustrated and dismayed when he starts school and discovers that he must follow rules in the art lesson rather than having the freedom to imagine and create.

Arthur's Teacher Trouble. Marc Brown. Boston, MA: Little, Brown and Co., 1986. Arthur, a third grader, complains about the strictness of his teacher, and the homework given on the first day of school. He dutifully studies the list of words for the spellathon, and to his amazement, he is chosen to participate.

Bennett Cerf's Book of Animal Riddles. Bennett Cerf. New York, NY: Random House, 1959. A well-known favorite book of animal jokes.

B-e-s-t Friends. Patricia Reilly Giff. New York, NY: Dell, 1988. One of *The New Kids at the Polk Street School* series. Stacy learns to appreciate the new girl at school, Annie—even though her clothes are strange, she whistles, and her grandfather eats tomatoes and potatoes for breakfast.

Best Friends. Steven Kellogg. New York, NY: Dial Books, 1986. Kathy and Louise Jenkins are best friends and do everything together. But when Louise goes away for the summer, Kathy misses her. Kathy is both lonely and even angry that Louise is having a good time.

Can You Match This? Jokes about Unlikely Pairs. Rick Walton and Ann Walton. Minneapolis, MN: Lerner, 1990. This is a collection of jokes beginning with the lead-in "What do you get when . . . ?"

Clowning Around!: Jokes About the Circus. Rick Walton and Ann Walton. Minneapolis, MN: Lerner, 1990. A collection of 57 questions and answers about the circus.

The Day the Teacher Went Bananas. James Howe. New York, NY: E. P. Dutton, 1984. The new teacher was the best ever, teaching the class in exciting ways. The kids are sad when they find out he must return to the zoo.

Frog and Toad Are Friends. Arnold Lobel. New York, NY: Harper & Row, 1970. Five delightful stories about Frog and Toad, the two good friends who always help each other out.

It Happens to Everyone. Bernice Myers. New York, NY: Lothrop, Lee & Shepard, 1990. Michael is nervous about the first day of school, and so is his new teacher, Mrs. Daniels.

The Magic of Color. Hilda Simon. New York, NY: Lothrop, Lee & Shepard, 1981. In this informational book, basic questions, such as "What is color?" "What are the primary and complimentary colors?" and "What are optical illusions?" are explained and illustrated in colorful detailed drawings.

Miss Nelson Is Missing. Harry Allard. New York, NY: Scholastic, 1978. Kind, beautiful Miss Nelson cannot control her class. However, when she is suddenly absent, the weird-looking, strict Miss Viola Swamp is the substitute and the class begins to appreciate Miss Nelson.

Never Spit on Your Shoes. Denys Cazet. New York, NY: Orchard Books, 1990. Arnie, a puppy, tells his mother of hardships of his first day of first grade, including sitting at a desk, helping make class rules, and mistaking the girls' bathroom for the boys' bathroom. Detailed illustrations reveal the bedlam not included in his report.

The Pain and the Great One. Judy Blume. Scarsdale, NY: Bradbury Press, 1974. A six-year old boy (The Pain) and his eight-year old sister (The Great One) tell all about each other, each viewing the other as a trouble-maker and best-loved in the family.

Rosie and Michael. Judith Viorst. New York, NY: Atheneum, 1985. What makes a friendship special? Rosie and Michael's special friendship is explained in this book.

Shh! We're Writing the Constitution. Jean Fritz. New York, NY: G.P. Putnam's Sons, 1987. How the Constitution came to be written and ratified is described. The full text of the document drawn up by the Constitutional Convention of 1787 is included.

The Show-and-Tell War and Other Stories about Adam Joshua. Janice Lee Smith. New York, NY: HarperCollins, 1989. Returning to school in September produces anxiety for Joshua. He has to deal with Elliott Banks, and he worries that his little sister and dog will forget him while he's away.

The Stupids Step Out. Harry Allard. New York, NY: Houghton Mifflin, 1977. The Stanley Q. Stupid family engage in behaviors which are both silly and in many instances stupid. Several other titles about the Stupids are available.

The Teacher from the Black Lagoon. Mike Thaler. New York, NY: Scholastic, 1989. On the first day of school, a child "daydreams" that his teacher, Mrs. Green, does horrendous things to the class and has a frightening monster appearance. He awakens to discover the real Mrs. Green, and rushes to hug her.

This Is The Way We Go To School: A Book About Children Around the World. Edith Baer. New York, NY: Scholastic, 1990. Limited text written in rhyme and illustrations provide clues as to school children's nationalities as they use many different modes of transportation in getting to school.

Today Was a Terrible Day. Patricia Reilly Giff. New York, NY: Viking Press, 1980. Ronald Morgan, who is learning to read, has a day of humorous mishaps in Miss Tyler's second grade class, but soon discovers that he can read.

Tyrannosaurus Wrecks: A Book of Dinosaur Riddles. Noelle Sterne. New York, NY: Harper & Row, 1979. An illustrated collection of riddles pertaining to dinosaurs.

Will I Have a Friend? Miriam Cohen. New York, NY: MacMillan, 1967. Jim is anxious about his first day of school and wonders whether he will have a friend. His anxieties are forgotten by the end of the day when he makes a new friend, Paul.

Bookmarks

Poet Bookmarks

Poet: Lois Lenski
Author of: Snack

Early Years: She was born in Springfield, Ohio on October 14, 1893, and died September 11, 1974 in Tarpon Springs, Florida. As a child, she learned to be a good cook. When she was only six, she began to sew for her dolls. She became interested in art when she was in third grade.

Besides Writing Poetry: She was both an artist and a writer. In addition to illustrating all of her own books, she illustrated 57 books by others.

Writings: She is widely know for her regional books. *Strawberry Girl* won the Newbery Medal Award in 1956. Her other writings include:
> *Lois Lenski's Big Book of Mr. Small*
> *The Little Auto*
> *City Poems*

Tidbits: As she began her career, she carried a sketchbook with her and made drawings of everything she observed. Then she started carrying a notebook to also write notes about her observations.

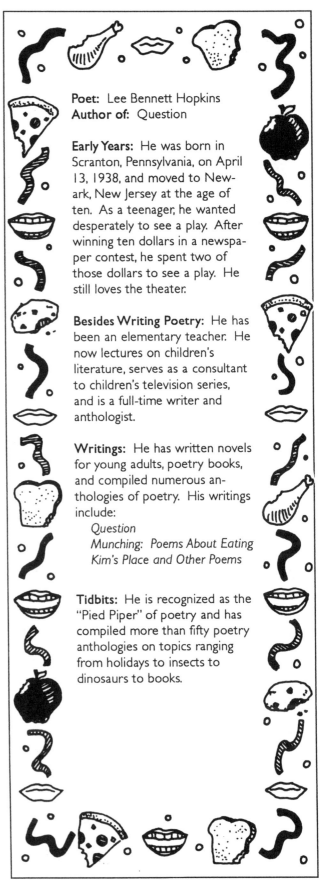

Poet: Lee Bennett Hopkins
Author of: Question

Early Years: He was born in Scranton, Pennsylvania, on April 13, 1938, and moved to Newark, New Jersey at the age of ten. As a teenager, he wanted desperately to see a play. After winning ten dollars in a newspaper contest, he spent two of those dollars to see a play. He still loves the theater.

Besides Writing Poetry: He has been an elementary teacher. He now lectures on children's literature, serves as a consultant to children's television series, and is a full-time writer and anthologist.

Writings: He has written novels for young adults, poetry books, and compiled numerous anthologies of poetry. His writings include:
> *Question*
> *Munching: Poems About Eating*
> *Kim's Place and Other Poems*

Tidbits: He is recognized as the "Pied Piper" of poetry and has compiled more than fifty poetry anthologies on topics ranging from holidays to insects to dinosaurs to books.

Pathways to Poetry: Poetry Fun for Grades 1-3 © 1994 Fearon Teacher Aids

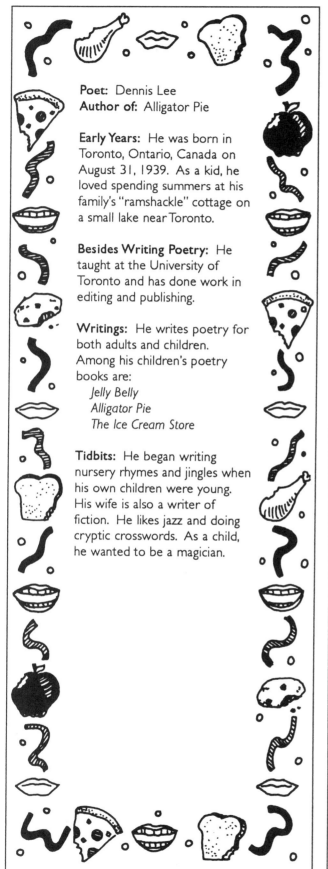

Poet: Dennis Lee
Author of: Alligator Pie

Early Years: He was born in Toronto, Ontario, Canada on August 31, 1939. As a kid, he loved spending summers at his family's "ramshackle" cottage on a small lake near Toronto.

Besides Writing Poetry: He taught at the University of Toronto and has done work in editing and publishing.

Writings: He writes poetry for both adults and children. Among his children's poetry books are:
Jelly Belly
Alligator Pie
The Ice Cream Store

Tidbits: He began writing nursery rhymes and jingles when his own children were young. His wife is also a writer of fiction. He likes jazz and doing cryptic crosswords. As a child, he wanted to be a magician.

Poet: Eve Merriam
Author of: How do you make a pizza grow?

Early Years: She was born in Germantown, Pennsylvania, on July 19, 1916. She lived in a suburb surrounded by woods and as a child came to appreciate nature. Her parents emigrated from Russia and owned a chain of women's dress shops.

Besides Writing Poetry: She worked as a sales clerk in a department store and as a fashion copywriter. She has been a poetry and fiction writer for adults and children. She has had her work produced as plays on-and off-Broadway.

Writings: Her poetry books for children include:
A Word or Two With You
Blackberry Ink
A Sky Full of Poems

Tidbits: She loves to travel and to browse in libraries and second-hand book stores. She enjoys bike riding, swimming, and walking.

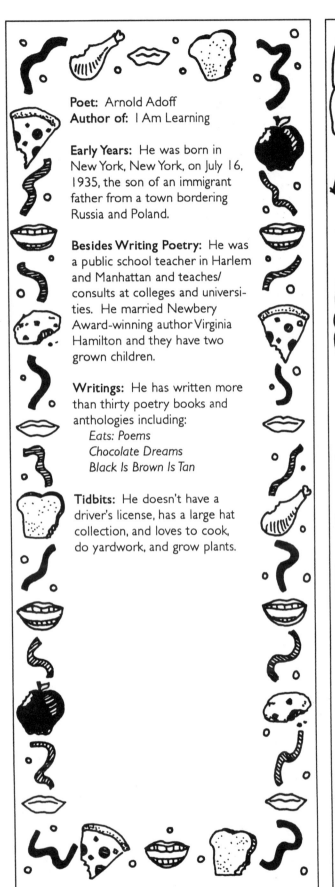

Poet: Arnold Adoff
Author of: I Am Learning

Early Years: He was born in New York, New York, on July 16, 1935, the son of an immigrant father from a town bordering Russia and Poland.

Besides Writing Poetry: He was a public school teacher in Harlem and Manhattan and teaches/consults at colleges and universities. He married Newbery Award-winning author Virginia Hamilton and they have two grown children.

Writings: He has written more than thirty poetry books and anthologies including:
> *Eats: Poems*
> *Chocolate Dreams*
> *Black Is Brown Is Tan*

Tidbits: He doesn't have a driver's license, has a large hat collection, and loves to cook, do yardwork, and grow plants.

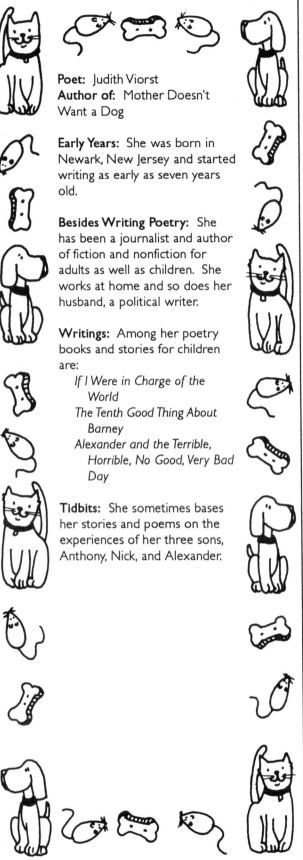

Poet: Judith Viorst
Author of: Mother Doesn't Want a Dog

Early Years: She was born in Newark, New Jersey and started writing as early as seven years old.

Besides Writing Poetry: She has been a journalist and author of fiction and nonfiction for adults as well as children. She works at home and so does her husband, a political writer.

Writings: Among her poetry books and stories for children are:
> *If I Were in Charge of the World*
> *The Tenth Good Thing About Barney*
> *Alexander and the Terrible, Horrible, No Good, Very Bad Day*

Tidbits: She sometimes bases her stories and poems on the experiences of her three sons, Anthony, Nick, and Alexander.

Pathways to Poetry: Poetry Fun for Grades 1-3 © 1994 Fearon Teacher Aids

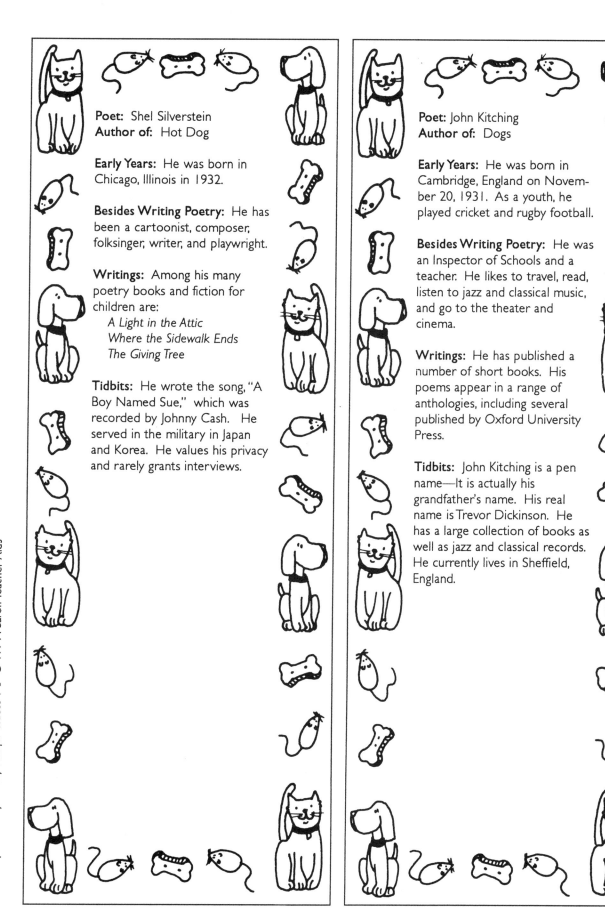

Poet: Shel Silverstein
Author of: Hot Dog

Early Years: He was born in Chicago, Illinois in 1932.

Besides Writing Poetry: He has been a cartoonist, composer, folksinger, writer, and playwright.

Writings: Among his many poetry books and fiction for children are:
> A Light in the Attic
> Where the Sidewalk Ends
> The Giving Tree

Tidbits: He wrote the song, "A Boy Named Sue," which was recorded by Johnny Cash. He served in the military in Japan and Korea. He values his privacy and rarely grants interviews.

Poet: John Kitching
Author of: Dogs

Early Years: He was born in Cambridge, England on November 20, 1931. As a youth, he played cricket and rugby football.

Besides Writing Poetry: He was an Inspector of Schools and a teacher. He likes to travel, read, listen to jazz and classical music, and go to the theater and cinema.

Writings: He has published a number of short books. His poems appear in a range of anthologies, including several published by Oxford University Press.

Tidbits: John Kitching is a pen name—It is actually his grandfather's name. His real name is Trevor Dickinson. He has a large collection of books as well as jazz and classical records. He currently lives in Sheffield, England.

Pathways to Poetry: Poetry Fun for Grades 1-3 © 1994 Fearon Teacher Aids

Poet: Eleanor Farjeon
Author of: Cats

Early Years: She was born in London, England on February 13, 1881, and died in 1965. Her father, a well-known writer, didn't believe in formal schooling. He told the governess not to teach Eleanor anything she didn't want to know. Eleanor began to write verses and stories at age seven.

Besides Writing Poetry: She was a writer for her entire lifetime. She also wrote topical and nonsense verse for the London Daily Herald as well as writing for periodicals.

Writings: She wrote children's fantasies, verses, and plays, including:
  The Little Bookroom
  Over the Garden Wall
  The Children's Bells, a Selection of Poems

Tidbits: Even with bad eyesight, she read constantly from the more than 8,000 books in her Father's library. She went to the theater frequently, even as a child.

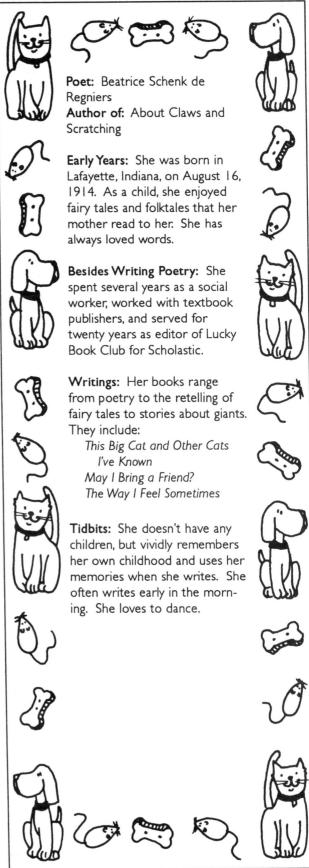

Poet: Beatrice Schenk de Regniers
Author of: About Claws and Scratching

Early Years: She was born in Lafayette, Indiana, on August 16, 1914. As a child, she enjoyed fairy tales and folktales that her mother read to her. She has always loved words.

Besides Writing Poetry: She spent several years as a social worker, worked with textbook publishers, and served for twenty years as editor of Lucky Book Club for Scholastic.

Writings: Her books range from poetry to the retelling of fairy tales to stories about giants. They include:
  This Big Cat and Other Cats I've Known
  May I Bring a Friend?
  The Way I Feel Sometimes

Tidbits: She doesn't have any children, but vividly remembers her own childhood and uses her memories when she writes. She often writes early in the morning. She loves to dance.

Pathways to Poetry: Poetry Fun for Grades 1–3 © 1994 Fearon Teacher Aids

Poet: Richard J. Margolis
Author of: Two Wheels

Early Years: He was born in St. Paul, Minnesota, on June 30, 1929, and died in 1991.

Besides Writing Poetry: He held various positions, including editor and publisher, editorial director for a newspaper, and consultant to many private and government agencies.

Writings: His published books of stories, fables, and poems include:
Secrets of a Small Brother
Wish Again, Big Bear
The Upside-Down King

Tidbits: His writing ideas usually occurred to him early in the morning. He wrote mostly about friendship.

Poet: Charlotte Zolotow
Author of: Nobody Loves Me

Early Years: She was born in Norfolk, Virginia, on June 26, 1915. At the age of three, she said that she was going to be an author and illustrate her own books.

Besides Writing Poetry: She spent many years as an editor in a children's book department, and has lectured at universities and conferences. She has written many picture books for young children.

Writings: Her extensive list of books includes:
William's Doll
The Hating Book
Some Things Go Together

Tidbits: Many of her books have been made into films and filmstrips. She has also won many awards for her writing and editing.

Poet: Lois Simmie
Author of: Mean

Early Years: She was born in 1932 in Edam, Saskatchewan, Canada.

Besides Writing Poetry: She has been a writer in residence, and was writing adult novels and short stories before she began writing for children. One of her short stories, "Red Shoes," was made into a feature film in 1986.

Writings: Her published titles include:
  Auntie's Knitting a Baby
  An Armadillo Is not a Pillow
  What Holds Up the Moon

Tidbits: The idea for the book *Auntie's Knitting a Baby* came about when she visited an aunt who was knitting a baby bonnet.

Poet: Samuel Exler
Author of: A Magic Chant

Early Years: He was born in Brooklyn, New York in 1922, the son of immigrants from Austria and Hungary. As a young child, he loved to read fairy tales and funny poems.

Besides Writing Poetry: After graduating from Brooklyn College, he went into the infantry and was stationed in Europe during World War II. His work experiences have ranged from working in a hospital kitchen to advertising copywriter to being a psychotherapist. He has two grown daughters.

Writings: Most of his poems are written for adults, and appear in magazines, such as *New York Quarterly, Poetry East,* and *Plainsong.* He has published one book of poetry for adults.

Tidbits: Today he lives in Woodstock, New York.

Pathways to Poetry: Poetry Fun for Grades 1-3 © 1994 Fearon Teacher Aids

Poet: Jack Prelutsky
Author of: I'm Tired of Being Little

Early Years: He was born in Brooklyn, New York, on September 8, 1940. He studied voice at the High School of Music and Art in New York City.

Besides Writing Poetry: He has worked as a cab driver, busboy, photographer, potter, folksinger, opera singer, and furniture mover.

Writings: He has written many volumes of poetry including:
New Kid on the Block
Rainy Day Saturday
Something Big Has Been Here

Tidbits: He likes to ride bikes, play racquetball, cook, and listen to classical music. He collects frog knickknacks. He has a collection of almost 2,000 volumes of children's poetry.

Poet: Nancy White Carlstrom
Author of: Birthday, Birthday, Birthday

Early Years: She was born in Washington, Pennsylvania, on August 4, 1948. While in high school, she worked in the children's department of a local library, and began to think about writing children's books.

Besides Writing Poetry: She taught in the elementary grades and she owned a children's bookstore in Seattle. She now devotes full time to mothering her two sons, Jesse and Joshua, and writing. She currently lives in Alaska and is writing about the unique changes of the seasons.

Writings: Her books include:
Jesse Bear, What Will You Wear?
Wild Wild Sunflower Child Anna
Graham Cracker Animals
1-2-3

Tidbits: Often, she thinks of the titles for her books first, and then develops the words. She sometimes calls her first son, Jesse, Jesse Bear.

Pathways to Poetry: Poetry Fun for Grades 1-3 © 1994 Fearon Teacher Aids

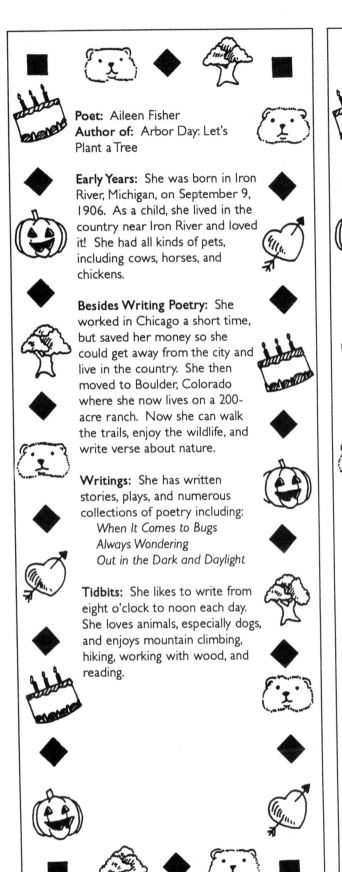

Poet: Aileen Fisher
Author of: Arbor Day: Let's Plant a Tree

Early Years: She was born in Iron River, Michigan, on September 9, 1906. As a child, she lived in the country near Iron River and loved it! She had all kinds of pets, including cows, horses, and chickens.

Besides Writing Poetry: She worked in Chicago a short time, but saved her money so she could get away from the city and live in the country. She then moved to Boulder, Colorado where she now lives on a 200-acre ranch. Now she can walk the trails, enjoy the wildlife, and write verse about nature.

Writings: She has written stories, plays, and numerous collections of poetry including:
  When It Comes to Bugs
  Always Wondering
  Out in the Dark and Daylight

Tidbits: She likes to write from eight o'clock to noon each day. She loves animals, especially dogs, and enjoys mountain climbing, hiking, working with wood, and reading.

Poet: Lilian Moore
Author of: Ground Hog Day

Early Years: She was born in New York, New York, on March 17, 1909, St. Patrick's Day. She loved going to a neighborhood library in the Bronx and coming back with an armful of books—reading all the way home.

Besides Writing Poetry: She was a teacher in New York City, working with children who could not read. For many years she was editor of Arrow Book Club at Scholastic. Since childhood, she has always thought of herself as a writer.

Writings: Her extensive publications of stories and poems include:
  See My Lovely Poison Ivy and Other Poems
  About Witches, Ghosts, and Things
  Something New Begins

Tidbits: She enjoys chamber music and gardening. She has always liked growing things, and even had a window box when she lived in New York City. She now lives on a farm.

Pathways to Poetry: Poetry Fun for Grades 1-3 © 1994 Fearon Teacher Aids

Poet: Aileen Fisher
Author of: October Fun

Early Years: She was born in Iron River, Michigan, on September 9, 1906. As a child, she lived in the country near Iron River and loved it! She had all kinds of pets, including cows, horses, and chickens.

Besides Writing Poetry: She worked in Chicago a short time, but saved her money so she could get away from the city and live in the country. She then moved to Boulder, Colorado where she now lives on a 200-acre ranch. Now she can walk the trails, enjoy the wildlife, and write verse about nature.

Writings: She has written stories, plays, and numerous collections of poetry including:
When It Comes to Bugs
Always Wondering
Out in the Dark and Daylight

Tidbits: She likes to write from eight o'clock to noon each day. She loves animals, especially dogs, and enjoys mountain climbing, hiking, working with wood, and reading.

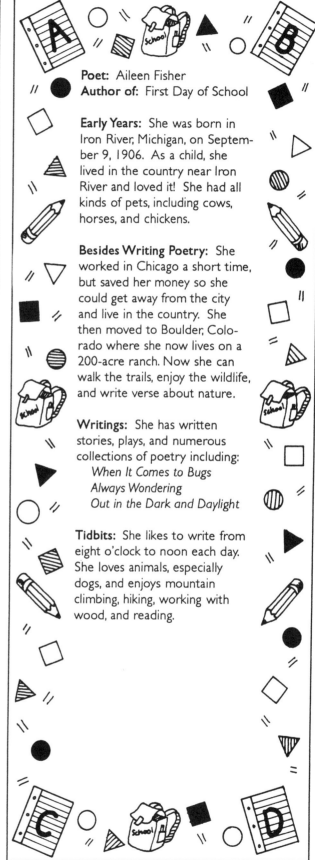

Poet: Aileen Fisher
Author of: First Day of School

Early Years: She was born in Iron River, Michigan, on September 9, 1906. As a child, she lived in the country near Iron River and loved it! She had all kinds of pets, including cows, horses, and chickens.

Besides Writing Poetry: She worked in Chicago a short time, but saved her money so she could get away from the city and live in the country. She then moved to Boulder, Colorado where she now lives on a 200-acre ranch. Now she can walk the trails, enjoy the wildlife, and write verse about nature.

Writings: She has written stories, plays, and numerous collections of poetry including:
When It Comes to Bugs
Always Wondering
Out in the Dark and Daylight

Tidbits: She likes to write from eight o'clock to noon each day. She loves animals, especially dogs, and enjoys mountain climbing, hiking, working with wood, and reading.

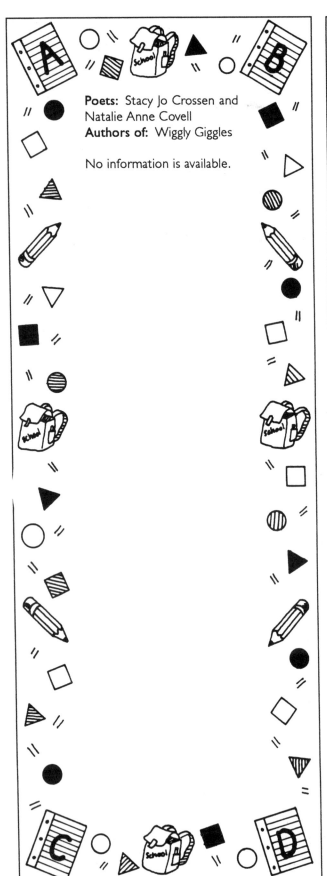

Poets: Stacy Jo Crossen and Natalie Anne Covell
Authors of: Wiggly Giggles

No information is available.

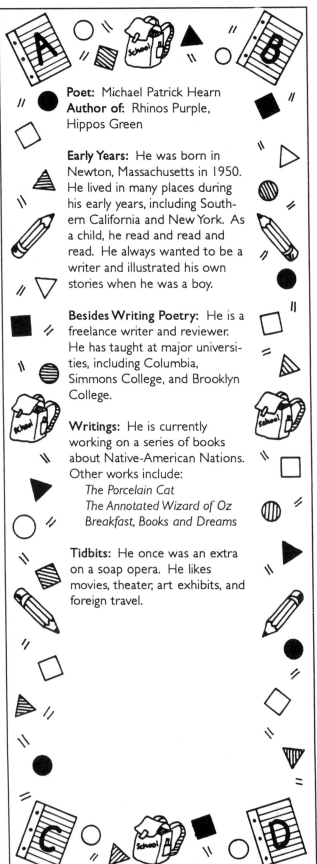

Poet: Michael Patrick Hearn
Author of: Rhinos Purple, Hippos Green

Early Years: He was born in Newton, Massachusetts in 1950. He lived in many places during his early years, including Southern California and New York. As a child, he read and read and read. He always wanted to be a writer and illustrated his own stories when he was a boy.

Besides Writing Poetry: He is a freelance writer and reviewer. He has taught at major universities, including Columbia, Simmons College, and Brooklyn College.

Writings: He is currently working on a series of books about Native-American Nations. Other works include:
The Porcelain Cat
The Annotated Wizard of Oz
Breakfast, Books and Dreams

Tidbits: He once was an extra on a soap opera. He likes movies, theater, art exhibits, and foreign travel.

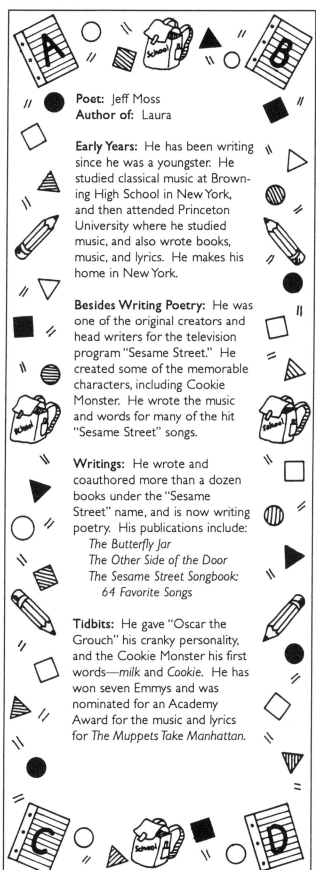

Poet: Jeff Moss
Author of: Laura

Early Years: He has been writing since he was a youngster. He studied classical music at Browning High School in New York, and then attended Princeton University where he studied music, and also wrote books, music, and lyrics. He makes his home in New York.

Besides Writing Poetry: He was one of the original creators and head writers for the television program "Sesame Street." He created some of the memorable characters, including Cookie Monster. He wrote the music and words for many of the hit "Sesame Street" songs.

Writings: He wrote and coauthored more than a dozen books under the "Sesame Street" name, and is now writing poetry. His publications include:
The Butterfly Jar
The Other Side of the Door
The Sesame Street Songbook:
  64 Favorite Songs

Tidbits: He gave "Oscar the Grouch" his cranky personality, and the Cookie Monster his first words—*milk* and *Cookie*. He has won seven Emmys and was nominated for an Academy Award for the music and lyrics for *The Muppets Take Manhattan*.

Poet: Bobbi Katz
Author of: from School, Some Suggestions

Early Years: She was born in Newburgh, New York on May 2, 1933.

Besides Writing Poetry: She has been a fashion editor and social worker. Currently, she is an editor of books for young readers at Random House.

Writings: She has contributed poetry to numerous anthologies and magazines. Her published books include:
Upside-Down and Inside-Out
Snow Bunny
Ghosts and Goosebumps

Tidbits: She had a weekly radio program for many years. She can read and speak French, Spanish, and Hebrew.

Author Bookmarks

Name: Phylliss J. Adams

Early Years: She was born in Denver, Missouri, on December 5, 1931. She attended a "one-room" country school and graduated from high school at the age of 15. Her advanced degrees are from the University of Denver, with post-doctoral work at the University of Colorado.

Besides Writing About Poetry: She taught elementary grades in Missouri, Iowa, and Colorado. She has been a professor at several universities, and was named Professor Emeritus at California State University, San Bernardino. She is a frequent speaker at reading conferences in the United States as well as internationally. She is a past-president of the International Reading Association.

Writings: In addition to articles in professional journals, she was a member of the author team for two elementary reading textbook series. She has co-authored 32 children's books including:
Brad's New Tooth
The Day the Dark Clouds Came
Shadow Magic

Tidbits: She loves to travel and has visited more than 90 countries. In her travels, she collects children's books published in the native language(s) of the various countries. She also collects elementary school reading texts which were published prior to the year of her birth.

Name: Ellen L. Kronowitz

Early Years: She was born in Brooklyn, New York on July 15, 1945. The desks in the public school she attended were nailed to the floor—and inkwells were really filled with ink! Her favorite book was *Mr. Popper's Penguins*. All of her advanced degrees are from Teachers College, Columbia University.

Besides Writing About Poetry: She has been an elementary school teacher in New York and currently is a professor at California State University, San Bernardino. She teaches social studies methods and supervises student teachers. She served for six years as her university's liaison to the Hillside-University Demonstration School.

Writings: In addition to articles and conference presentations, she has written two texts to help beginning teachers through their first year of teaching. The titles are:
Beyond Student Teaching
Right Foot Forward

Tidbits: She has four cats and owns a horse named Cindy. She enjoys gardening, water aerobics, reading, movies, and traveling to far-off places.

Pathways to Poetry: Poetry Fun for Grades 1-3 © 1994 Fearon Teacher Aids

Credits

Laura from *The Butterfly Jar* by Jeff Moss. Copyright © 1989 by Jeff Moss. Used by permission of Bantam Books, a division of bantam Doubleday Dell Publishing Group, Inc.

Hot Dog from *A Light in the Attic* by Shel Silverstein. Copyright © 1981 by Evil Eye Music, Inc. Selection reprinted by permission of HarperCollins Publishers.

October Fun from *In the Dark and Daylight* by Aileen Fisher. Text copyright © 1980 by Aileen Fisher. Selection reprinted by permission of HarperCollins Publishers.

First Day of School, text only, from *Always Wondering* by Aileen Fisher. Copyright © 1991 by Aileen Fisher. Selection reprinted by permission of HarperCollins Publishers.

Alligator Pie by Dennis Lee. Copyright © 1983 Dennis Lee. Reprinted by permission of Sterling Lord Associates (Canada) Ltd.

Birthday, Birthday, Birthday reprinted with permission of Macmillan Publishing from *Graham Cracker Animals 1-2-3* by Nancy White Carlstrom. Copyright © 1989 by Nancy White Carlstrom.

Two Wheels reprinted with permission of Macmillan Publishing from *Secrets of a Small Brother* by Richard J. Margolis. Copyright © 1984 by Richard J. Margolis.

Ground Hog Day from *Think of Shadows* by Lilian Moore. Copyright © 1975, 1980 by Lilian Moore. Reprinted by permission of Marian Reiner for the author.

How do you make a pizza grow? from *Blackberry Ink* by Eve Merriam. Copyright © 1985 by Eve Merriam. Reprinted by permission of Marian Reiner.

About Claws and Scratching from *This Big Cat and Other Cats I've Known* by Beatrice Schenk de Regniers. Copyright © 1958, 1985, 1986 by Beatrice Schenk de Regniers. Reprinted by permission of Marian Reiner for the author.

References

Comprehensive Poetry Anthologies

And the Green Grass Grew All Around: Folk Poetry from Everyone. Alvin Schwartz. New York, NY: HarperCollins, 1992.

The Butterfly Jar. Jeff Moss. New York, NY: Bantam Books, 1989.

A Cup of Sunshine. Jill Bennett. San Diego, CA: Harcourt Brace Jovanovich, 1991.

Kid's Pick The Funniest Poems. Bruce Lansky. New York, NY: Simon & Schuster, 1991.

Knock At a Star. X. J. Kennedy and Dorothy M. Kennedy. Boston, MA: Little, Brown & Co., 1982.

A Light in the Attic. Shel Silverstein. New York, NY: Harper & Row, 1981.

Make a Joyful Sound: Poems for Children by African American Poets. Deborah Slier Shine. New York, NY: Checkerboard Press, 1991.

The New Kid on the Block. Jack Prelutsky. New York, NY: Greenwillow, 1984.

The Other Side of the Door. Jeff Moss. New York, NY: Bantam Books, 1991.

Piping Down the Valleys Wild. Nancy Larrick. New York, NY: Dial, 1982.

Poetry Place Anthology. Rosemary Alexander et. al. Jefferson City, MO: Scholastic, 1990.

The Random House Book of Poetry. Jack Prelutsky. New York, NY: Random House, 1983.

Read-aloud Rhymes For the Very Young. Jack Prelutsky. New York, NY: Alfred A. Knopf, 1986.

Sing a Song of Popcorn. Beatrice Schenk de Regniers et. al. New York, NY: Scholastic, 1988.

Something Big Has Been Here. Jack Prelutsky. New York, NY: Greenwillow, 1990.

Sunflakes: Poems for Children. Lilian Moore. New York, NY: Clarion, 1992.

Talking Like the Rain. X. J. Kennedy and Dorothy M. Kennedy. Boston, MA: Little, Brown & Co, 1992.

Tomie dePaola's Book of Poems. Tomie dePaola. New York, NY: G. P. Putnam's Sons, 1989.

Where the Sidewalk Ends. Shel Silverstein. New York, NY: Harper & Row, 1974.

Music Books

The Fireside Book of Children's Songs. Marie Winn. New York, NY: Simon & Schuster, 1966.

The Fireside Book of Fun and Game Songs. Marie Winn. New York, NY: Simon & Schuster, 1974.

The Fireside Song Book of Birds and Beasts. Jane Yolen. New York, NY: Simon & Schuster, 1972.

The Holiday Song Book. Robert Quackenbush. New York, NY: Lothrop, Lee & Shepard, 1977.

An Illustrated Treasury of Songs. National Gallery of Art, Washington, D.C. New York, NY: Rizolli International Publications, 1991.

1002 The Complete Children's Song Book. Carl Anderson. San Francisco, CA: Shattinger-International Music Corp., 1986.

Sally Go Round the Sun. Edith Fowke. New York, NY: Doubleday & Company, Inc., 1971.

The Sesame Street Song Book. Joe Raposo and Jeffrey Moss. New York, NY: Simon & Schuster, 1971.

Sharon, Lois & Bram's Mother Goose. Sharon, Lois, and Bram. Boston, MA: Atlantic Monthly Press, 1985.

Singing Bee! Jane Hart. New York, NY: Lothrop, Lee & Shepard, 1982.

Tom Glazer's Do Your Ears Hang Low? Tom Glazer. Garden City, NY: Doubleday & Company, Inc., 1980.

Notes

Notes